LIFE
and
MEDICINE

Every Patient
Teaches a Lesson

Yongxin Li, M.D., Ph.D.

Copyright

LIFE AND MEDICINE

Every Patient Teaches a Lesson

ISBN-13: 978-0692545539

ISBN-10: 0692545530

First Paperback Edition: October 2015

This book is dedicated to:

My wife, Zhou (Jo), who makes my life complete;
My children, Jason and Megan, who are my hope;
Dad, Shanquan, who gave me courage;
Mom, Yueyou, who taught me to smile;
Aunty, Qianru, who showed me how to love;
Aunty, Shan, and Uncle, Hai, who always supported me.

Table of Contents

Introduction

我有三宝持而保之：一曰慈，二曰俭，三曰不敢为天下先。
(I have just three things to teach: compassion, simplicity, and humility. These three are your greatest treasures.)

—老子 (Lao Tzu, 571 B.C., Chinese Philosopher)

Every patient you see is a lesson in much more than the malady from which he suffers.

—William Osler (1849-1919, Canadian Physician and Professor of Medicine)

The Platinum Rule of Medicine: "Treat every patient like you'd want a member of your family treated!"

—Dr. Edward C. Rosenow III (Professor of Medicine at the Mayo Clinic Medical School)

... The only way to be truly satisfied is to do what you believe is great work. And the only way to do great work is to love what you do.

—Steve Jobs (1955 – 2011, American Entrepreneur and Inventor)

For the past year, I have read dozens of doctors' memoirs, which have inspired me to write my own. So far, I have not found any stories similar to mine. I had a dream to write a book when I was at college. Until recently, I have been too busy to write anything down. This memoir consists of different stories about my family and my patients. The stories about my patients illustrate what I learned from them about "life and medicine" during the first 15 years of my internal medicine practice. Each patient teaches me at least one lesson.

Many years ago, I learned the art of living, the Five F's (**Family, Friends, Fun/Fellowship, Forgive, Forget**..........**Work)**, from a book by Dr. Edward C. Rosenow III called *The Art of Living and the Art of Medicine*.[1] I have been using the above philosophy to prioritize my life through my daily activities. After years of caring for patients, I have established my own way of living and practicing medicine, the Five S's: **Smile, Simplicity, Sympathy/empathy, Serenity,** and **Service**. In this memoir, I will describe how I have been trying to apply these five principles in the care of patients.

Smile conveys kindness, which is almost certainly the most important virtue in life. Although Mom has never read me a bedtime story, her smile has affected me and will stay with me all my life. Everyone has his or her bad days. One has to be happy to make someone else happy. I smile a lot, hoping that my patients will leave the clinic with a smile too. No one can make everyone happy. Nevertheless, smiling is the starting point of expressing warmth and compassion and communicating with patients effectively. A good physician-patient relationship relies on trust and communication. As people say, the best way to be happy is to make others happy.

Some of my patients' daughters would occasionally tell me, "Mama was complaining about everything at home, but she actually came home happy after seeing you. And you didn't give her any new medicine."

Frequently, my medicine is just a smile and listening. In fact, elderly patients tend to leave the clinic with fewer pills and, hopefully, with a smile too. I don't mind spending more time talking with my patients during office visits as long as they smile.

Simplicity, by my own definition, means making things balance without overdoing anything. The proverb says you do not need more than enough of anything. I have learned that moderation is the key to everything in life and medicine. One should never do anything excessively. Too much exercise may hurt your joints and even your heart, and excess eating can cause many diseases, including obesity and diabetes. Eating right and exercising judiciously will make you live better and longer.

More is not always better in medicine. People frequently end up in the emergency department because they take too much medicine, not because they run out of medicine. In spite of consuming over 80 percent of the world's legally produced opioids, American people may not receive the world's best non-cancer chronic pain management, and there are thousands of overdose deaths from prescription painkillers each year.[2, 3]

All medications have benefits and side effects. You always have some discomfort somewhere in the body, but you do not have to take medicine for each and every ailment in order to stay happy and healthy. It has been proven that the more medications patients take, the less favorable clinical outcomes they will achieve. Sometimes doing nothing at all is just the best thing to do in life and medicine.

Sympathy/empathy not only makes me care about how my patients are feeling about their diseases and personal issues, but it also helps me understand and share their experiences and emotions. Everyone has his or her hardships. Being sick affects people mentally, physically, and financially. I learned that a patient kept being admitted for heart failure because he could not afford the copayment for his diuretics. Another patient had numerous asthma attacks, for she could not pay $300 to her landlord to move out of the dirty old apartment.

Unless they have both Medicare and Medicaid, many patients need to pay high copayments for brand-name medications, tests, procedures, and imaging studies. Without health insurance, paying medical bills is just a nightmare. Confucius (551-479 B.C., Chinese philosopher) once said, *"What you do not wish for yourself, do not do to others."* I consider it unethical to order unnecessary tests, perform unnecessary procedures, prescribe unnecessary medications, or schedule unnecessary office

11

visits for personal gain. This type of "medical care" is harmful to both patients and society.

Serenity is peace of mind. Take it easy and be patient. Don't take yourself too seriously. Nobody is perfect, and nothing is perfect. There is no emergency for most things in life. I don't answer my phone or text while driving a car. When stressed out or frustrated, I take a step back and get a deep breath. Why can't I deal with this problem if I have done more difficult jobs in the past? There is always a way out.

I remember a patient who complained of being depressed and nervous and having difficulty sleeping. He wanted some pills to make him feel better. When he finished his story, I found that the cause of all his problems was his dislike of his supervisor.

"Why are you still working since you retired from New York years ago?" I asked.

"I just got the job a few months ago because I was too bored to stay at home all the time," he replied.

"So, you're doing your job, not to pay your bills, but to pass the time. Is that correct?"

"That's correct."

"Let's look at it this way: Why don't you fire your boss and go home to relax? You can get another job when you feel better after a break."

"You're exactly right," he smiled.

"Do you still need a pill?"

"Not anymore," he laughed. "Your advice is the pill."

The reality is that many patients have already received prescriptions for depression, anxiety, and insomnia before they finish telling their stories. It is true that a lot of people have to work to make ends meet. I felt very sad when one of my patients said to me, "I wouldn't need all these mental drugs and painkillers if you could pay my bills for me, Doc." But still, I do not think that taking more pills is the solution to these issues.

Feeling good or bad depends on how you look at things. Your attitude determines your happiness in life. Optimistic people are healthier. The less you worry and the fewer pills you take, the more smiles you have.

Service implies adherence to the Platinum Rule of Medicine: *Treat every patient like you'd want a member of your family treated.* When

12

taking care of patients, there is nothing more gratifying than hearing these words:

"I feel safe/I think I'm going to get well as soon as you enter the room."

"I know Mom will be okay when you are on call tonight."

"You've saved my life, Doctor Li!"

One's ability is limited no matter how hard one works or how well one is educated or how smart one is. I have been trying my best to take care of my patients. Every doctor makes mistakes, and so do I. I am deeply grateful that my patients and their families forgive my mistakes. Nobody can know everything in medicine. Even though I keep learning and improving, I still make mistakes in both life and medicine time after time. William Osler (1849-1919, Canadian physician and professor of medicine) stated, *"The good physician treats the disease; the great physician treats the patient who has the disease."* In the beginning, I treated the disease only. Now, I hope to reach my goal: becoming a doctor who treats the patient with the disease.

As stated above, the art of living is the Five F's: **Family, Friends, Fun/Fellowship, Forgive,** and **Forget.......... Work**. It says that **work** or **service** is the last priority. According to the Platinum Rule of Medicine, you need to treat your patients like your family members. Thus, a doctor's job – caring for patients as family members – has become the first priority of life. Life is so contradictory and beautiful. I feel privileged to be able to serve patients and contribute to their well-being. Since I love what I do, I should go all out to do great work.

I planned to write this memoir for myself and my family only; in other words, the intended readers were supposed to be my family and me. Nonetheless, if you want to read about the current state of American medicine, the life and times of a Chinese doctor, and some views and opinions on health-related issues, I am sure you will find something here that interests you. Whether you are a medical student or just interested in medicine, you can get some ideas about how one doctor learns and grows. I think that my memoir is unique in these ways:

1. As an immigrant physician, I received medical school education in China while I completed graduate medical education (residency

training) in the United States. So I view American medicine from a different perspective. I believe that this is the first English medical memoir ever written mainly about American health care by a Chinese immigrant physician who received medical school education outside of the U.S., according to my search on Amazon and Google (please correct me if I am wrong).

2. I have never been a board member, a chief of staff, a department chair, an executive at a hospital, or a medical director of a nursing home and hospice company. I do not know the inside details of health care administration and management. I provide an outsider's view of the medical care delivery system.

3. Most memoirs by doctors (on the market) talk about events in the emergency department, operating room, academic medical centers, huge city hospitals, or house calls in rural areas. My memoir shows the typical experience of a primary care doctor at a small community level.

4. Many of the stories described in my book are not like the heroic events found in most doctors' memoirs. I describe some real events seen in American private practices that have to do with both patients and doctors.

5. I traveled to China almost yearly during these 15 years. Jo, my wife, communicates daily with our family and friends in China through the phone, FaceTime, WeChat, e-mail, etc. My stories about seeing doctors in China provide readers with some information about China's health care.

6. Many books on the shelf by prominent doctors give general, broad pictures of the American health system, but I provide minor events to help people grasp the subtleties of the system. In pathological terms, I use a microscopic description while others use a gross description. Thus, this memoir has more stories than other memoirs do, and some of the stories are short in length. However, each of these distinctive stories will elucidate something about health care and related issues.

7. Most authors write their patients' stories chronologically while I try to group stories with similar subjects into one chapter. Each of my stories can stand on its own. Readers can choose a story from any point in the memoir and can understand the whole context or situation. I hope readers will get something out of one of my stories.

The patients' names and other characteristics have been altered to protect their privacy. Some patients of mine have read their own stories in the book and made comments. However, I don't have contact information to reach other patients or their families. If some patients happen to recognize their stories in the book, I am sure they will like them. After all, these patients are my teachers, so they will enjoy reading their student's writing. Some stories may also involve doctors. Once again, no real names are mentioned here, and identifying characteristics have been changed. Nobody is perfect. My memoir demonstrates that doctors are no exception.

The conversations and settings in the book may not be 100 percent accurate because most of the events happened many years ago and were written just by memory. While writing this memoir, I did not have the privilege to review any medical records, since I had already relocated to another town. The cases presented in this book are used to describe my personal experience with patients, and I tried to give the general case overview while omitting the exact clinical details. The laboratory results and other clinical parameters are the actual values coming from my case index cards.

The medicine in this book can be viewed as common medical knowledge, yet it should not be used as a real diagnostic or treatment guide. The major sources of the medical information in this book are Wikipedia.org, Medscape.com, and Mayoclinic.org. All the statistics have their references. Any reader who wants to know more about the diseases in this book can visit these websites and refer to those references.

Chapter 1: Father depicts my father's life and my early years, the epitome of Chinese society from the 1950s to the 1990s.

Chapter 2: Beginning demonstrates how I learned about medicine and the health system during the first few years of my practice.

Chapter 3: Faith explores the issues related to religion arising from my practice.

Chapter 4: Wife tells stories about my wife and the American wives of my patients

Chapter 5: Diabetes illustrates how I treated patients with diabetes.

Chapter 6: Seeing Doctors in China portrays healthcare in China from my viewpoint.

Chapter 7: End of Life addresses end of life care.

Chapter 8: Fight for Life describes exceptional patients and how I felt when seeing them.

Chapter 9: Medicine as Art and Business reveals the business aspect of medicine and explains how I learned good bedside manners.

Chapter 10: Overdone deals with overtreatment issues.

Chapter 11: Unsatisfactory Medicine expresses my opinions about some of the health care issues in the U.S.

I enjoyed the writing process, which has caused me to think more deeply about "life and medicine" and made me become a better person. During the early stage of my memoir writing, my stories were filled with complaints and fault-finding. As I revised the draft, my language became more neutral and objective. And I have become happier too.

"Are you this happy all the time, Doc?" a new patient asked me recently.

"I try to be," I replied with a big smile. A lot of studies have shown that writing can help people cope with their problems and make them happier.[4] However, sometimes when writing my memoir, I could not help but be emotional about things that were unfair and irrational. Nowadays, I look at things differently. It is likely that I will change more – hopefully for the better – when I write my new memoir in the future.

1. Father

My father gave me the greatest gift anyone could give another person, he believed in me.

Jim Valvano (1946-1993, American Coach)

It was my father who persuaded me to apply for medical school. Thus, I am lucky to be able to practice medicine in this great country, the United States of America.

Dad and Me

It has been 18 years since my dad passed away. But his smiling face frequently appears in my dreams. Truly, Dad continues to look over me even though I cannot see or talk with him anymore. I have become as bald as him in recent years. One of Dad's former students said to me a few years ago, "You look exactly like your father, Uncle Li." She is absolutely right. Dad smiled a lot, and so do I. Dad liked buying books and loved reading, and so do I. Dad liked English, and so do I. Dad liked a simple life... and so do I. His spirit will always be with me, his grandchildren, and the generations to come.

My dad, Shanquan, was born in Guangzhou (广州, also known as Canton), China in 1929. Dad was a smart kid and well-liked by his teachers. He performed a lot of chemical experiments at home during his high school years. One of the rooms in the house became a chemistry laboratory. He was popular and had numerous friends.

He majored in chemistry at Lingnan University, which was a private college. The college tuition was so expensive that my grandparents could barely afford it. My aunt, Dad's sister, did not have a chance to pursue her college education because my grandparents could not support two students. In China back then, it was common that families had a priority to assist their sons. My aunt still complained about this gender discrimination years later. Eventually, my aunt was able to enter a medical school after she worked for the new government for five years. There were no private colleges by then. All the colleges and universities were run by the government and free for students.

The new Chinese government came to power in 1949, after Dad had been at college for about one year. Dad was eager to work for the new government like most young people at the time, thinking that the new government would bring prosperity to China and that they could help the government speed up the process. He quit his college study and started to work for the new government. My grandmother was very disappointed in Dad's decision, for she wanted her son to be a scientist or an engineer. She did not like the government job, which was historically considered dangerous in China. My grandmother told Dad to leave mainland China for Hong Kong (still a British colony), but Dad did not follow her advice.

Dad became a government official and lived comfortably with a good salary. He married my mother in 1954. My family was enjoying a good life as my parents had good jobs with decent incomes. Even grandparents were working then. When I was born in 1955, they hired a wet nurse to breastfeed and take care of me. I have a rare first name in Chinese, Xin (昕), which is almost never used in everyday conversation and even in writing. "Xin" means "dawn" in Chinese, and it is infrequently used in names. I remember that nurses or pharmacists often pronounced my name wrong when I saw doctors at a clinic or a hospital. Some school teachers had difficulty saying it. When I grew up, I asked Dad why he chose this unusual name for me.

"After you were born, I asked your granduncle to help me choose a name for you," Dad replied. "He looked up this word in a dictionary." I have learned that unpopular names make people have fewer friends and fewer opportunities.

Good times did not last long. Soon, what my grandmother was afraid of started to take place. The new Chinese government launched political movements endlessly. During the **Hundred Flowers Movement** in 1956, **Mao Zedong**, the president of the People's Republic of China, began to encourage criticism of the government. Dad was the head of the publicity division in a local government. He gave speeches at many conferences to urge people to criticize and advise the government. Finally, Mao Zedong could not tolerate the criticism anymore. The critics were pounced on in the following **Anti-Rightist Movement**. (For more details on this topic, see *Wikipedia: Anti-Rightist Movement.*)

The **Anti-Rightist Movement** was initiated by Mao Zedong. Any intellectuals whom Mao Zedong considered disloyal or disobedient were labeled as "**rightists**." These rightists were politically persecuted, demoted, and sent to labor camps or jails. It was not surprising that Dad was branded as a "rightist" and sent to a labor camp at the age of 29. He was one of the half million intellectuals who were disgraced and lost their jobs in Mao's campaign from 1957 to 1959.

Although there were no physicians in my extended family for many generations (my aunt entered a medical school to study public health), it seems that I had an early relationship with health care system during my childhood. I remember that I entered a hospital kindergarten around four years of age. This kindergarten accepted mostly the children of healthcare personnel working at that hospital. One relative of my family worked as a chef in the kindergarten kitchen. This hospital kindergarten was considered as one of the best in the district. All the teachers had a teaching diploma, which was not common in China more than half a century ago. I was blessed to attend this excellent kindergarten through my family connection.

One time, kids needed to tell stories about their families in class. All other kids were excited to talk about their doctor or nurse parents. I just heard that Dad had gone to a farm, yet I did not know what kind of job he had at that time. I was four years old then when Dad was sent to the labor camp. Although I was too young to know the political issues, I felt uncomfortable telling my classmates that my father worked on a farm, and my mother worked at a department store.

"What does your father do there?" one of the classmates asked.

"I don't know," I replied uneasily.

Whenever someone asked me what my father did for a living, I always felt embarrassed and hurt until Dad resumed his job in 1978.

Dad became defiant and wanted to leave the labor camp. In order to obtain a sick leave certificate, he had to figure out how to pretend to be sick. He had a lot of chemistry knowledge and learned how to generate abnormal blood test results after reading many biochemistry books. He told me that he could make his blood samples turn black and get the lab report indicating he had liver failure. I do not recall the details of how he did that. I regret that I did not ask him more about it while he was still alive. Dad left the labor camp on sick leave. He was proud to tell me that he had shown several of his friends how to do the same trick to leave the labor camp.

After he had left the labor camp around 1961, Dad did not have any income at all. He started to make a living by painting plastic utensils like buckets, bowls, and vases. With a background of chemistry training, Dad was good at preparing appropriate dyes and solvents. In those days, so few people possessed these skills that Dad was able to obtain good long-term contracts. He could make a decent income through this kind of "neighborhood industry". Of course, he did not have health insurance. Back then, the medical cost was so low that it was not a big issue.

I entered an elementary school in 1962. The school was located a few blocks away from home. All the students in my class lived on the same street. I had been selected to attend a language boarding school, where young kids were trained to be expert interpreters or diplomats. Dad did not allow me to go, for he was afraid of losing me. I still think that Dad made the wrong decision about it.

However, Dad had made the right decision about my health. Since I was thin and weak, Dad said to me, "You won't achieve anything if you aren't healthy." Dad could swim well. Nevertheless, he did not think he was good enough to teach me. Dad asked his cousin, Uncle B, to teach me how to swim. Uncle B used to be an athlete, and he was also a "rightist", who had just come home from a labor camp. Owing to Uncle B's excellent instruction, I picked up swimming quickly. I had become much stronger after swimming daily for two years. Uncle B taught swimming lessons to many children in our extended family. All the children loved Uncle B. He was funny, and he knew a lot of interesting stories.

For unknown reasons, I fell behind in school during that period. I had difficulty understanding what teachers taught in the classroom, and I was not able to finish my homework on my own. Thus, I often needed to seek assistance from my classmates. Dad was teaching a relative's son math, and said to me one day, "Don't waste your time playing all day. Look at my student who comes here twice a week to learn math and physics. Yet you don't learn anything while there is a teacher at home."

Dad asked Uncle B to help me with math. Uncle B taught me math several times as he lived in our home after he escaped from the labor camp. Although I do not learn a new subject quickly, I am good at it after I have learned it. I accidentally overheard Uncle B tell my father that I was not a good learner. That hurt me a lot but stimulated me to make greater efforts. I tried to solve math problems on my own. I thought about math day and night for one week. All of a sudden, I was able to solve every math problem that I could not understand before. I have not needed any help with math from that moment on.

Dad did all the painting work in our house, which sometimes looked like a small factory or warehouse. I helped him process and clean plastic utensils after he drew pictures on them. Dad had learned how to draw from a professional painter during his childhood. "I don't consider myself a professional artist," Dad said to me. "But I can make a living as a painting craftsman." I worked one to two hours almost every day when I was 8-11 years old. Nowadays, this kind of work would possibly be called "child labor." I do not regret that I did it. And I think I have become a better person through working during my childhood.

It is estimated that 30 million Chinese people died of famine in 1959-1961 as a consequence of the wrong economic policy of the government. Dad would have died of hunger and torture if he had not escaped from the labor camp. My family led a reasonably normal life from 1962 to 1966. During this period, China's economy improved gradually after the government adopted a better economic policy. (For more details on this topic, see *Wikipedia: Great Chinese Famine*.)

Then again, Mao Zedong launched another political movement when the Chinese economy revived. The **Cultural Revolution** broke out in 1966 after Dad had worked at home for a few years. This radical sociopolitical movement gave rise to political zealotry, violence, military rule, purges, social chaos, and economic disaster. Dad was publicly denounced many times in a large school playground, where he fell and fractured his ankle. He was hospitalized for three months and evaded further humiliation. A black poster board with Dad's name on it was hung on the front door of our house. (For more details on this topic, see *Wikipedia: Cultural Revolution*.)

Dad liked to read and bought numerous books. His bedroom was packed with books from the floor to the ceiling. Many of Dad's friends came and borrowed books. Dad kept a logbook that recorded who borrowed his books. However, on three separate occasions, **Red Guards** entered our home to confiscate any books and items they considered to be "bourgeois." Dad felt very sad that he lost the majority of his books. The **Red Guards** were made up of politically active students who carried out attacks on culture (books, arts, temples, etc.), intellectuals, and disfavored people during the Cultural Revolution in 1966 and 1967.

Not long afterward, Dad was sent to a rural area, where he stayed and did farm work for about a year. When he returned home, he started to make a living by painting Mao's badges in the house. During this crazy period, Mao's badges were regarded as necessities of life. People had to wear them when they went to work or school. Of course, I did a lot of work painting badges as well when I was 13-15 years old. When another political movement was launched by the government, Dad was forced to leave the city and move to a remote village all over again. This time, he left home with my grandfather, who had been accused of embezzlement.

My grandfather suffered a stroke and became paralyzed within two years. As a result of this illness, both Dad and my grandfather returned home for good. However, Dad remained unemployed because nobody would hire a "rightist". He could not find any painting work either. Dad spent his time teaching English to the children of relatives and friends for free. He continued to be a volunteer English teacher until the last few years of his life. Dad had a lot of students, and many of them got good jobs after learning English from him.

Dad taught me some English lessons and laid a good foundation for me. Soon after that, he said to me, "You're so good at self-learning that I don't need to teach you anymore. You can learn English on your own from now on." Since then, I started to learn English by myself and continue to do so even now.

I entered middle school in 1968 when the Cultural Revolution slowed down a little. What teachers taught at the school was too simple for me. I had learned all the high school math and college calculus by myself. In one semester, I got perfect test scores in math, chemistry, and physics. Initially, I was not good at English and needed assistance from one of my classmates to prepare for English exams. I had become the best English student in the class soon after Dad taught me English pronunciation and basic grammar.

I graduated from high school in 1972 and did not have a chance to go to college, for most colleges and universities were closed during the 10-year Cultural Revolution. According to the government's policy, if a family had more than one child, one of them would be assigned to work in the countryside. Nobody wanted to go to the countryside because of the poor living conditions. Since I was the only child of the family, I was lucky to be able to stay in the city. I was assigned to work at a printing factory with a minimum wage. We lived a decent life as my mother worked, and I had a job.

Finally, the Cultural Revolution ended in 1976 when Mao Zedong died. Only one month after Mao's death, the **Gang of Four,** a political faction consisting of four radical officials including Mao Zedong's last wife **Jiang Qing**, was deposed, marking the end of a turbulent political era in China. I recall that the government organized street parades to celebrate the downfall of the Gang of Four. The printing factory where I worked held a dinner party that every employee attended to cheer for the coming of a new era. (For more details on this topic, see *Wikipedia: Gang of Four.*)

The moderate officials including **Deng Xiaoping** came into power and adopted the "open door" policy in China. Things were getting better and better. Dad got a teaching job at a nursing school in 1978, and he resumed his position as head of the publicity section in the district government in 1979.

The government resumed the college entrance examination in 1977, and I registered for the examination. Back then, the examinees needed to choose which colleges and majors they wanted before the exam. My original choices were mathematics, computer science, and chemistry at various universities. Dad thought that I should have chosen more practical fields. He went to the printing factory to see me and persuade me to change my decision. I followed his instructions to change my college choices to engineer institutes and a medical school. And I remember how joyful Dad was when I received the admission notice from the medical school.

I was working the evening shift in the printing factory when the factory manager delivered the admission letter to me. I stopped working right away and headed for home. Dad knew that I had gotten excellent scores on the entrance examination. Dad and I had been waiting for this moment for almost a month, for other examinees had already received their admission letters.

"You must have good news since you came home so early today," he said to me when I entered the house at 6:30 p.m. I usually got home at 1:30 a.m. after working the evening shift.

"Yes, I got accepted to a medical school," I smiled.

"I'm too excited to finish my meal!" he smiled while having supper at home.

Dad enjoyed the simple life and did not seek luxury. He spent most of his leisure time reading books or teaching English or playing Chinese Chess and **Mahjong**. **Mahjong** is a Chinese game played by four people with 144 domino-like tiles marked in suits. Dad, an excellent Chinese Chess player, read a lot of books about chess, attended many amateur chess tournaments, and won several amateur titles. He taught me some basic chess skills, and I used them to win against many of my co-workers when I was working at the printing factory. Dad also taught me to play Mahjong. I learned how to play, but I did not like it.

Although he had some power and many connections, Dad did not take bribes. Furthermore, he even declined to accept a house that the government gave to him for almost free (at about 10 percent of the market price). He said that he was comfortable living in our own house and did not want the government to spend more money on him.

Refusing to accept a "free" house from the government was virtually unimaginable! The house is worth at least half a million U.S. dollars today. I am proud to say that Dad was conceivably the only one government official to perform a "noble" deed like this in China. Sometimes, Mom complains to me, "Your dad was so stupid that he refused to take the house the government gave to him. If he had taken it, you would have a better place to live when you're in China."

"You don't need to worry about me," I said to Mom. "Dad left me a much more valuable thing... a good brain (a virtue of curiosity and simplicity). I'm a physician in America and can afford to buy my own houses."

"I know that," Mom said with a cheerful smile.

Throughout the next 10 years, there were no more political movements launched by the government. Dad worked hard for the government, attending conferences, giving speeches, and traveling frequently. He was not involved in the **Tiananmen Square incident of 1989**, which was triggered by college students, not by the government.

During my medical school years, Dad came to visit me and played table tennis with me many times. He was in his early 50s and healthy at the time. It was rare that a father came to school and played with his son. Some of my classmates were amazed by that.

Dad introduced his high school classmate, Dr. Zhao, to me while I was a medical student. Dr. Zhao was a well-known dermatologist, who had published several dermatology books. Dr. Zhao let me translate some dermatology articles from English to Chinese, which were published in a medical journal. This made me very happy because I could see my works printed on paper for the first time. Dr. Zhao also took care of me when I was burnt by acid during a chemical experiment. I have lost contact with Dr. Zhao, but I always remember how he helped me through the difficult time.

When I was in the last year of medical school, Dad persuaded me to do research instead of clinical work at the hospital. Being a professor doing research at a university or research institute was considered the most prestigious in China 30 years ago. So I enrolled in the master's program in pathophysiology at Jinan University in 1983. I hoped that Dad would be satisfied with my obedience. When I applied to Ph.D.programs in the U.S., my father tried his best to ask his friends and relatives to provide financial support documents for my visa to go to the U.S. In the end, I received a full scholarship from a US University, and I arrived in the U.S. in August 1986.

Dad was a heavy smoker and suffered from emphysema. He retired at 60 years of age and enjoyed a simple and relaxing life until his final year when he was diagnosed with liver cancer. Dad and Mom traveled to the U.S. and visited me in Virginia in 1991 when I was working on my Ph.D. dissertation at the University of Virginia. My parents lived with us for a month. In addition, they traveled to New York, where my classmate, Dr. Henry Chen, was very kind to make arrangements for them to tour New York City and take a bus tour to Niagara Falls and Atlantic City. They even spent several nights at Dr. Henry Chen's apartment. I will never forget Henry's kindness to my family.

After my parents had come back from New York, I took them to see Washington D.C. on a weekend. Dad told me that the U.S. trip was the best trip of his life. During this period, I was busy finishing my Ph.D. thesis and under a lot of stress. I still regret that I did not spend more time with him while he was in the U.S.

Dad always loved me and did his best to help me all his life. I will do the same for my children. I wish I could see Dad or hear his voice again, just one more time. Tearfully, I wrote this chapter on Father's Day in 2014. I wish that Dad could read my memoir, and I could show off to him my 30 English dictionaries and thousands of books on my iPad. Dad, I miss you! I am sure you are watching me writing in English about you.

Dad's Illness

I always think about Dad whenever I see patients, especially when I am providing palliative treatment for terminally ill patients. As described in **Chapter 7**, **End of Life**: **"Die in Your Hand,"** Mrs. Peterson chose to leave this world the way she liked and departed peacefully with dignity by the aid of modern and humane medicine in the U.S. Not everybody can be this lucky in other countries, e.g. in China.

In the spring of 1995, my heart sank when I opened Dad's letter and learned that he was diagnosed with liver cancer. Two months earlier while being hospitalized for chronic lung disease, Dad was found to have liver masses with significantly elevated levels of alpha-fetoprotein, indicating a diagnosis of liver cancer.

Primary liver cancer is the second most common cancer in China. Each year, approximately 360,000 people in China are diagnosed with liver cancer, and most of them will die from it.[1] The majority of the liver cancer deaths (more than 80 percent) were linked to hepatitis B virus, hepatitis C virus, aflatoxins (potent fungal toxins found in many crops including maize and peanut), alcohol drinking, and tobacco smoking.[2] Dad's liver cancer was presumably caused by hepatitis B.

I knew that Dad would not live long, and made arrangements to go back to China to see him in the summer of 1995. It was the first time that I had traveled to China and seen my parents since I left for the U.S. in 1986. I came with my wife, son, and daughter. Dad was very happy to see his grandchildren for the first time. He organized a party for our homecoming. More than one hundred people attended the party. However, I had to return to the U.S. after staying with Dad in China for three weeks.

Having seen many doctors for his cancer, Dad made up his mind not to pursue aggressive intervention since surgery could not remove his tumor. He suffered from severe emphysema, which did not make him a good candidate for radiation or chemotherapy either. I still think that he made the right decision. In fact, he might have died much sooner and suffered more if he had chosen to go through aggressive treatments. He lived a decent life for more than one year after the diagnosis. It has been proven in the U.S. that patients with terminal illnesses will live longer with a better quality of life if they choose to receive palliative and hospice services instead of aggressive interventions.

After Dad had decided not to have aggressive treatments, he maintained most of his usual activities (reading, chatting, and playing chess or Mahjong). He was comfortable and lived out his remaining days with dignity until the last three months of his life. I called him every other day to find out how he was doing. During this time, I was in my first year of residency training in internal medicine in the U.S. Dad started to lose more weight and suffered fullness of the abdomen due to ascites, but he was without any significant pain. He did not need any pain treatment until the last three weeks of his life. When I noticed that my father was not doing well, I traveled back to China to see him in the summer of 1996, just six weeks before he died.

Since Dad gave up conventional treatments (like most people with incurable diseases), he naturally went to see a traditional Chinese medicine doctor. This doctor, recommended by one of my father's friends, had cured a few patients with liver cancer anecdotally. Dad had been seeing him for four months. After returning to China, I found that Dad had become very emaciated, with a distended abdomen due to ascites. I accompanied him to see the doctor and filled the prescriptions for him. This doctor worked at the Provincial Hospital of Chinese Traditional Medicine, which was supposed to be the best traditional medicine hospital in the province (state).

While waiting with Dad in the waiting room, I read the advertisement about this well-known liver expert in the hallway. This doctor could treat all kinds of liver diseases, including liver cancer and viral hepatitis B. He described diseases using modern medical terms and used modern blood tests. However, he used herbal medicine to treat his patients. According to my estimation, this doctor saw about 30 patients per evening, and it took about two and a half hours to finish his job. In China, it was not unusual for a doctor to be surrounded by 10 to 15 patients and family members. Everyone watched the doctor see other patients without privacy. After waiting about an hour, it was Dad's turn to see the doctor.

"What's wrong?" the doctor asked, looking at Dad's record booklet. He raised his head to get a quick half-second look at my father's face and then put his fingers on my father's left wrist to check his pulse for two seconds.

"I feel fullness in my stomach," Dad said weakly.

"Fullness...um." The doctor started to write his prescription without looking up again or touching Dad's abdomen. The doctor placed a piece of carbon paper between his prescription and the medical record booklet. That way, a copy of the prescription would be imprinted on the record booklet when he finished his writing. Back then, the hospital kept only inpatient medical records in the hospital, while patients carried their outpatient record booklets with them. The doctor handed the prescription to Dad emotionlessly and without any eye contact. The whole course of that visit lasted less than three minutes and cost three dollars. The office note for that day consisted of:

Liver cancer.

The fullness of abdomen.

Next visit: one week.

The prescription: XXX.

I took the prescription to the hospital pharmacy and waited about 30-40 minutes to get the medicine. It cost about 15-20 dollars, and it consisted of a large bag of herbs and a tiny packet of pills (including a diuretic called furosemide, a common Western medication). People earned about $10 per day 20 years ago. The medical cost was reasonable. Apparently, this herbal medicine doctor understood that his herbs needed help from Western medicine. The Western medication, furosemide, costing only 50 cents, did work effectively for Dad's ascites. The big bag of herbs was basically used as decoration or a placebo, and it was obviously a financial tool with which the hospital could make money. The government regulates the price of Western medicine, but not the price of herbal medicine. So even nowadays, no matter what kind of doctor you see in China, you will probably come out of the hospital or clinic with bags or boxes of herbal medicine, along with small packets of Western medicine.

I accompanied Dad to see this doctor twice, but then Dad became too weak to go anymore. Dad wanted to continue to take this doctor's medication. I just took his record booklet to the pharmacy and told the pharmacist to fill the prescription in the booklet. Twenty years ago, you could fill a prescription in your record booklet without seeing or calling a doctor for authorization.

During the first 10 days of my stay in China, Dad could walk a few blocks with me to a nearby restaurant early in the morning. We had breakfast together and chatted. Then his condition worsened gradually, and he was not able to walk that distance anymore. As a result of the worsening ascites, he had more difficulty breathing and more discomfort from the distention of his abdomen. Walking around the house became more difficult, and he ate less and less. His mental status remained stable, and he spent most of his time reading his books while lying in bed. Our home did not have air conditioning, just like most households in China during that time, and people often used electric fans to cool their houses. It was so hot in the summer that Dad sweated heavily and looked uncomfortable. I sensed that my father was near the end of his life, and he would be better off staying in the hospital and receiving some comfort treatment.

It was difficult to get a patient admitted to a hospital in China during those days as the municipal hospitals were full all the time. You needed personal connections for hospital admissions. Fortuitously, I graduated from a medical school located in the same city and had many connections. Dr. Zhiqiang Wei was not only my medical school classmate, but he was also a surgeon specializing in hepatobiliary diseases who worked at a municipal hospital nearby. He helped arrange Dad's admission to the hospital. Back then, most of the hospital rooms had no air conditioning and were non-private. It was common for four to eight patients to share a room. There were only two rooms in that surgical ward that had air conditioning. Dad was lucky to live in a semi-private room with air conditioning. Twenty years ago, hospitals provided such inadequate nursing services that patients had to hire private medical aids to do all the chores, including toileting, bathing, feeding, and taking patients for tests. Thus, I hired a 24-hour medical care aid for Dad.

On the second day of admission, a nurse entered the room to notify us of an ultrasound imaging study that was scheduled for Dad in the morning. She said that I needed to take him to the ultrasound laboratory immediately. This event had happened before the hospital started to hire transporters to take patients for imaging studies or procedures. After arriving at the radiology department, I found out that there were already at least 10 patients ahead of my father waiting outside the ultrasound laboratory. I put in his test slip, and we waited outside.

The waiting area was a balcony on the building, exposed to the sun without any shade. I felt awful when I saw Dad sweating profusely while sitting uncomfortably in the wheelchair with his distended abdomen. We waited outside under the sun for about two hours. When Dad was finally called in, he looked like he was about to pass out with his labored breathing. He got into the exam room just at the right time. He appeared alive again as soon as he was pushed into the ultrasound laboratory. The cool air coming from the air conditioning inside had rescued him physically.

However, Dad was tortured mentally inside the exam room. Dad was intelligent, with one year of college education, and he knew the severity of his disease. Nonetheless, nobody had told him frankly how bad it actually was. During the ultrasound exam, the doctor was teaching her students. Without asking for approval, the doctor spoke loudly to her students while pointing at Dad's ultrasound images on the screen of the machine, "Look here... multiple liver cancer masses, metastasized to bile ducts, a large amount of ascites. It's a terminal disease." I noticed that Dad's face became gloomy at that time. He furrowed his brow and looked down to the ground quietly while he was listening to the doctor's brutal teachings. Dad absorbed the news in silence and did not ask me to tell him more about his liver cancer.

Dr. Wei did not think he had much to offer after he reviewed Dad's dismal ultrasound images. He recommended that my Dad undergo intrahepatic chemotherapy if he could tolerate it. He said he could give Dad some nutrient/energy treatments to make him stronger. It was common practice in China for patients to receive this kind of nutrition treatment. I needed to walk to the pharmacy and pick up the albumin bottles myself. I had a choice to buy either the albumin made in China or the one imported from the U.S. The price of American albumin was five times higher. Without any hesitation, I chose to use the American albumin.

Dad developed significant shortness of breath while receiving IV "energy" fluid, which contained vitamins, amino acids, and albumin. There was no IV pump, and the IV rate was adjusted by counting drops per minute. I talked to a nurse about Dad's condition. She said that all the doctors left for their lunch break and that she would send one for me. More than 20-30 minutes passed, yet nobody came to check on Dad. Nobody had cell phones back then. I had to go out of the hospital to find a paid phone to call Dr. Wei, who was at home, to inform him of Dad's condition. Dr. Wei called the nursing station to stop the IV fluid treatment and give IV diuretics. Dad felt more comfortable and returned to his baseline conditions gradually.

From that point on, Dad told me that he did not want to have any more treatments, and he just wanted to be made comfortable. As Dad was a clever man with a clear mind, he knew that he was terminally ill. Although I had not completed my internal medicine residency training in the U.S. at the time, I had learned about palliative care and was involved in palliative treatments for several VA patients, who also happened to die from liver diseases. Palliative care was unthinkable in China back then. It is not a common practice even now. I talked to Dr. Wei about the option of palliative treatment for Dad. I told him how palliative care was provided in the U.S. and asked if he could use a similar regimen. He was a little puzzled, but he agreed to help me. He told me that he needed to get approval if he used more morphine than usual and that he would try his best to do what I wanted for my father. He did me a very great favor, and I was grateful to him. I will always remember how Dr. Wei helped me care for Dad in those difficult circumstances. Thanks to my connections and the medical knowledge I had learned in the U.S., my father could at least partially receive palliative care, a treatment that was little known in China 20 years ago.

Forty years ago, my grandfather suffered a bad stroke and was confined to bed for five years. He stayed in a dark room, and he never came out of the room during the last three years of his life. Like most Chinese people, we could not afford a wheelchair. Other family members and I helped my grandfather with grooming, toileting, eating, and so on. However, nobody helped my grandfather sit up in his chair daily or took him out of his dark room. I should have done much more for my grandfather. When I visit China now, I see many stroke victims sitting in their wheelchairs outside their homes, in the park, or on the streets. I imagine that people suffering from strokes also receive much better care than they did in the past.

My grandfather did reasonably well and never became sick until the last three days of his life when he reached 70 years of age. He became agitated, confused, unresponsive, and then comatose on the last day. My grandfather kept yelling and struggling all day without any treatment. There were no hospice or palliative services in China four decades ago. Elderly people often died at home in that way. My grandfather suffered a lot during his last few days.

Dad told all the grandchildren to enter my grandfather's room to have a final look at my grandfather. I will never forget my grandfather's agonal breathing. After my grandfather took his last deep breath and stopped breathing, Dad walked up to close my grandfather's eyelids. I admired my Dad for being so calm at the time.

My uncle, Hai, also died of liver cancer just a few years earlier in the 1990s. He was a retired military general and enjoyed the high level of medical care in China. Nevertheless, his son (my cousin) told me that my uncle died miserably without any comfort treatment in the hospital. According to him, my uncle became confused and fought violently during the last two weeks of his life. He had to be restrained to the bed rail. He writhed and screamed for three days until he died.

I stayed four weeks with Dad and then had to leave and return to the U.S., for I could not predict how long Dad would live. And I had a maximum of four weeks' vacation time while I was still in residency training. If I had stayed longer, I would have lost my residency position, which was extremely difficult to obtain. I felt bad that I could not stay with Dad during the most difficult time of his life – the end of his life. Dad said, "Don't worry about me. I can handle things myself. Go back to America to finish your study." I was the only son without brothers and sisters. Two months earlier, Dad had actually told me not to come back to see him before I booked the plane ticket.

Now, I was leaving. I understood that Dad was near the end of his life, and I could not come back to see him again. It was not like nowadays when people can see each other at different ends of the earth through Skype or FaceTime. In the end, I did not have the courage to tell my father candidly that his cancer was incurable and that he was dying. I still wonder if I would do the same now, after becoming a seasoned physician with more life experiences.

"I hope you can get better. I've told Dr. Wei to take good care of you while I'm not here," I said to Dad, holding my tears in.

"Do you think I can get better?" Dad asked softly.

"I hope so," I was.

"Oh." Dad did not want to say more. I knew Dad understood everything. He had considerable knowledge of medicine. I remembered him telling me many stories about doctors and medical conditions. He also had many friends who were doctors. He had seen my uncle die from liver cancer, as well as my uncle's brother and mother. Several of my father's friends also died from liver cancer. Liver cancer is so common and dreadful in China that it is called the "king of cancer."

"Take care, Dad. Goodbye." I dared not to look at him anymore and left the room quickly. I ran outside to cry, and I am weeping now as I write this section of my memoir.

Dad lived for two more weeks after I returned to the United States. I called him every day. Initially, Dad could talk on the phone for 10 to 15 minutes. As time passed, he did not want to talk for so long. I could hear him struggling to breathe. I sensed his mental frustration and physical misery. However, I could not see or touch him again. Dad's mind remained clear until the last two days. Dad said to me over the phone,

"Son, just make me comfortable. My stomach is too full." I called Dr. Wei and asked him if he could perform one more paracentesis (removal of ascitic fluid from the abdominal cavity) on my father. Dr. Wei carried out the paracentesis the next morning, informing me that he could only drain out a small amount of bloody fluid. The distention of my father's abdomen was due to cancerous growths and extensions.

During the last phone conversation, Dad groaned with pain, "Son, just let me go…let me go." Dad hung up the phone. Those were the last words I would ever hear from Dad because he did not answer the phone when I called him again. I have not heard his voice since then. I wept and called Dr. Wei.

"My father sounds miserable," I said. "He told me to let him go. Could you please give my father more morphine shots to comfort him?"

"I understand what you mean," Dr. Wei replied. "I will make your father comfortable."

"Thank you very much for all that you have done for my father."

"Don't worry. I will do my best."

As his disease progressed, and the comfort treatment was administered, Dad became more at ease and slept more. He finally sank into a coma during the last two days of his life. Dad passed away peacefully at the age of 67. I feel sorrowful that I could not hold Dad's hand when he passed away. And I regret that I had not talked with him more while he was still alive.

Thanks to Dad's encouragement, I was able to work as a physician. It is the life I love. I am grateful to the United States of America for giving me the opportunity to study the best medicine in the world. Some of my father's sufferings were alleviated by using my medical knowledge acquired in the United States. I wish that people in China could receive better care near the end of life, so that they could leave this world peacefully with dignity.

2. Beginning

千里之行始于足下。
(A journey of a thousand miles must begin with the first step.)

—老子 (Lao Tzu, 571 B.C., Chinese Philosopher)

The value of experience is not in seeing much, but in seeing wisely. Medicine is learned by the bedside and not in the classroom.

—Williams Osler (1849-1919, Canadian Physician and Professor of Medicine)

During the third year of my internal medicine training in a northern state, I asked Jo (my wife), "Where should I practice medicine after I finish my residency?"

"To the south!" Jo replied. "I'd like to live in a warm and sunny area."

We had lived in the north for more than eight years and did not like cold weather and snow. After I had decided to go to work in the south, one of the attending physicians asked me, "Why do you want to go down south? Do you have a visa problem?"

"I'm a U.S. citizen, and I can work wherever I want in America. But my wife prefers a warmer climate." (If they are not U.S. permanent residents or citizens, international medical graduates that wish to practice medicine in the U.S. after residency training must work in rural areas in need of doctors, like the south.)

"Be careful down there."

"I will."

Just as planned, I accepted the job offer from a multiple specialty clinic (also a diabetes treatment facility) in a southern state. I have always been curious and interested in learning new things. I chose this clinic because I thought I could learn more by working with and covering for specialists. And I did.

Learning

This southern state is hot and humid. We can see deer, rabbits, and even foxes around our house. Birds chirping and singing outside our window wake us up early in the morning. Occasionally, we hear woodpeckers drumming and see turtles walking around in the backyard. Mosquitoes are busy biting us whenever we step out of the house. But still, we like to walk the trail through the woods behind our house, enjoying the smell of pine trees and the sound of cicadas.

After we settled down here, our children, Jason and Megan, entered a school that was only a two-minute walk from our house. My wife, Jo, took them to school in the morning and picked them up from school in the afternoon. As our children grew up, they started walking themselves and eventually rode their bikes to school. Finally, they drove to the school after they had learned how to drive a car.

As most internists do, I saw patients in the clinic, made rounds at the hospital, and visited nursing home patients on weekends. During the first year of my practice, I was involved in many endocrinology consults in the clinic, for one of the two endocrinologists left the practice and the other endocrinologist, Dr. Vaughan, was too busy to finish all the consults timely. My work was similar to that of an endocrinology fellow. I saw the referred patients first, and then I presented the cases to Dr. Vaughan, who entered the room to talk with the patients again. I stopped doing consults after one year when a new endocrinologist joined our practice. During that period, I had learned a lot about endocrinology.

Mom had returned to China after she stayed with us about one year. In the summer of 1999, we went back to China and brought Mom to America again as she already obtained her permanent residence status. After Mom had arrived, we traveled frequently and went to the beach a few times per year. In the winter of 1999, we drove to Atlanta and visited the CNN headquarters, Olympic Park, and the Coca-Cola Museum in downtown Atlanta. We met our friend, Linda, and her daughter, Vickie,

41

there. They had lived in the U.S. for eight years. Linda was about 43 years old then, and she worked at a store. Vickie was studying at a pharmacy school. We had not seen them for 15 years. After we had come back home, Mom kept saying to us, "How come Linda has changed so much that I can't recognize her at all?"

Thinking about what Mom said about Linda, I had the same feeling about her and thought that Linda looked strange. She used to be slim with a heart-shaped face. Now she had a chubby face with a big jaw, a big nose, big hands, and thickened lips. She, only 43 years old, had already suffered diabetes and bad knees for years. She walked with a lumbering gait like an old woman. Linda's face reminded me of some of the figures found in endocrinology atlases. I said to Mom and Jo, "Linda seems to have a medical disorder I've seen in books before. Let me think. It looks like acro... yes, acromegaly."

Jo and I turned on the computer and looked up 'acromegaly' on Wikipedia, an online encyclopedia. Linda had almost all the features of this disorder: enlarged hands and feet, enlarged facial structures, muscle weakness, deepened voice, arthritis, and diabetes. I called Vickie, "I think your mother may have acromegaly. Although it's a rare disease, your mom has many symptoms of it." I explained to her what acromegaly was.

Acromegaly is a serious medical disorder caused by excessive production of growth hormone (GH). The most common cause of acromegaly is a tumor (adenoma) within the anterior pituitary gland, located in the middle of the head. Acromegaly is a rare disease. Only three to four out of a million people are diagnosed yearly. Acromegaly develops slowly and gradually, so many people do not notice the changes in their physical appearance. Frequently, a primary care doctor may not recognize the features of acromegaly. A family member or friend tends to point out the changes first, after having not seen the person for a long time. The average time from the onset of symptoms to the diagnosis is 12 years. Patients are diagnosed with acromegaly commonly at 40-45 years of age.

Excessive growth hormone stimulates overproduction of another hormone: insulin-like growth factor-1 (IGF-1). IGF-1 causes excessive growth of soft tissue, cartilage, and bone in the face, hands, and feet. Heart disorders (cardiomyopathy, valve problems, arrhythmia, and heart failure), high blood pressure and diabetes mellitus, arthritis, sleep apnea, etc. are more common in patients with acromegaly. When acromegaly is suspected, the first step is to measure the blood level of IGF-1, which can be withdrawn at any time of day. If the elevation of IGF-1 is confirmed, the next step is to do an MRI (magnetic resonance imaging) of the head to determine whether an adenoma exists in the pituitary. The treatment of acromegaly includes surgery, medication, and radiation. Most patients can be treated successfully.

"Really?" Vickie sounded surprised.

"You can read about acromegaly on Wiki. You should take your mother to see her family doctor and ask him to check the blood level of IGF-1."

"It sounds right. My mom has headaches and poor vision too. I'm going to take Mom to see her doctor next month. Thank you very much."

"Uncle Li, you are exactly right," Vickie called me two months later. "I took Mom to see her family doctor, who ordered a test for IGF-1. The IGF level was significantly elevated. Mom was referred to see an endocrinologist, who confirmed the diagnosis of acromegaly. Mom was found to have a pituitary tumor on brain MRI. She's going to see a neurosurgeon for surgery next week."

"I'm glad your Mom got the right diagnosis," I said. "I hope she will do well with the surgery. I'm waiting to hear the good news."

Linda successfully underwent brain surgery. Her arthritis and diabetes had improved considerably after surgery. I was happy that I had applied my knowledge of endocrinology to the diagnosis of a rare disease. And I enjoy the experience of solving complicated cases to help patients.

Mrs. Sims's illness is one of the complicated cases that I solved during the first few months after I started my practice. Mrs. Sims was in her early 60s when she came to see me in a wheelchair for the first office visit. She complained of weakness and pain in both hips, which had developed for about nine months. Over those months, she had seen 13 doctors, including many specialists. She was referred to see some specialists at the University Medical Center, the best in the state. But still, she was getting worse every day. One month before the visit, she was so weak that she began to use a wheelchair to move around. She told me some of her stories:

Mrs. Sims saw an orthopedist, who said to her, "Your hip joints look bone-on-bone. You need hip replacement surgery." It was true that she had moderate osteoarthritis in both hips according to the x-ray study. However, osteoarthritis commonly causes pain, not weakness. As a matter of fact, she underwent a right hip replacement surgery 12 years later.

She was diagnosed with a stroke by a neurologist. Yet, the CT (computerized tomography) of her head did not show any evidence of a stroke. She did not even have the typical symptoms and signs of a stroke, e.g., a facial droop, weakness on one side of the body (such as an arm, leg, or both), trouble speaking (slurred speech), or impaired vision.

A psychiatrist thought Mrs. Sims had malingering, which is defined as the act of intentionally feigning or exaggerating physical or psychiatric symptoms for personal gain. Her response was, "I am a registered nurse, and I want to work until I retire at 65. I'm already 61 now. Why would I want to pretend to be sick?"

Since Mrs. Sims had been discharged from the hospital recently, I reviewed her hospital medical records through the clinic computer, which was connected to the hospital. She had early diabetes with an A1C of 6.8% and mild hypertension. She was not on any medications. All her blood tests were normal except a significantly elevated erythrocyte sedimentation rate (Sed rate or **ESR**) of 112 mm/hr (reference values: < 20 mm/hr). The ESR (erythrocyte sedimentation rate) test was performed five months beforehand, but nobody mentioned it in the hospital notes.

The **erythrocyte sedimentation rate (ESR)** is a test that determines how fast red blood cells fall in a test tube in one hour. ESR is affected mainly by fibrinogen, which is elevated during an inflammatory process. The elevated ESR value is seen in some inflammatory disorders such as multiple myeloma, temporal arteritis, polymyalgia rheumatica, systemic lupus erythematosus (SLE), rheumatoid arthritis (RA), inflammatory bowel disease, some chronic infective conditions like tuberculosis and infective endocarditis, and chronic kidney diseases. In many of these disorders, the ESR may be above 100 mm/hr.

Mrs. Sims did not have bowel/lung/heart symptoms or a headache. Her tests for RA and SLE were negative. Her complete blood count and kidney functions were normal. Apparently, Mrs. Sims did not seem to have any of the above disorders with significant elevated ESR, except **polymyalgia rheumatica** (PMR).

Polymyalgia rheumatica is an inflammatory disorder that produces muscle pain and stiffness, usually in the shoulders, neck, upper arms, and hips. It commonly affects people older than 50. Oral corticosteroids are the mainstay of treatment for polymyalgia rheumatica.

"I guess you might be suffering from polymyalgia rheumatica, since you have pain in your neck, shoulders, and hips with significantly elevated ESR," I said to Mrs. Sims after reviewing her medical records and lab results.

"So, what're you going to do about it?" she asked.

"I'm going to start you on prednisone. You should feel better in a few days if my diagnosis is correct. Prednisone can cause high sugar level and other side effects. But I think you'll be fine with prednisone because your diabetes is very mild."

"I'm going to try it as I have seen many doctors without any relief for my pain."

I started her on 20 mg of prednisone per day and planned to see her again in a week.

Mrs. Sims came in for the follow-up visit one week later. She had responded well to the prednisone therapy. She could walk with a cane and be not in her wheelchair anymore.

"Dr. Li, you are the fourteenth doctor I have seen so far for my problem," she said excitedly. "You made the right diagnosis at my first visit. You see, I can walk again."

"I guess I'm just lucky," I smiled. "I'm glad that you've improved so much since the last visit."

Within two months, Mrs. Sims did not need a cane to walk. I gradually tapered the dose of her prednisone while monitoring the Sed rate (ESR), which also dropped close to the normal range within a few months. Since having completed her corticosteroid treatment in nine months, she has never needed it again. After she had retired at 65, she went on two mission trips to Africa. I prescribed her malaria prophylactic antibiotics before she traveled. During office visits, Mrs. Sims was excited to talk about her interesting experiences in Africa. She continues to see me as her primary care doctor at my new office, which is 50 miles away from her home.

Polymyalgia rheumatica is uncommon, but not rare. "In the United States, the average annual incidence of polymyalgia rheumatica (PMR) is 52.5 cases per 100,000 people aged 50 years and older," stated Medscape.com. [1] Why had so many doctors missed her diagnosis for so long? It is likely that I spent a much longer time listening to her, asking her questions, and reviewing her medical records carefully, for I did not have many patients to see during the first three months of my practice. This patient's story illustrates the importance of spending more time and communicating better with the patient. That not only helps reach a correct diagnosis and provide good patient care but also reduce malpractice risk. [2]

Thereafter, I have been trying to devote every minute of an office visit to patient contact, without typing or dictating my notes during or between visits. After an electronic medical record was installed in the clinic, I still tried to spend as little time as possible dealing with the computer. Thus, I could leave more time for conversation with patients during office visits. I usually completed my office notes in the evening or on weekends. The less time I spend talking to the computer, the more I can learn from my patients about life and medicine.

"Good Stuff"

As I walked into the exam room, I noticed Ms. Morris was moaning, vomiting, and pacing the room restlessly. She could not sit down as a result of her pain, anxiety, and agitation.

"Oh, Jesus, help me. Oh, Jesus…me," she was mumbling nervously.

"What's wrong?" I asked.

"I'm sick again."

"Don't worry. I'll take care of you."

The above scene had taken place so many times that I was confident there was nothing seriously wrong with her, and she would recover soon after two or three days of hospital care.

Ms. Morris, in her 40s, was petite and always smiled when she came to the clinic, showing some of her teeth covered with gold. She was not on any psychiatric medication even though she said she had depression in the past. During the first a few years as my patient, she was doing fine without major medical issues.

Then, something strange had happened. Every two or three months, she would develop severe nausea, vomiting, and abdominal pain, and present to the clinic or ER, where she appeared as if she were another person. She told me each time that she fell ill a couple of days after going to a party, bar, restaurant, or somebody's house. Sometimes, she said that she ate some chicken wings at a Chinese restaurant or that someone offered her a drink at a party, making her get sick a few days later. Ms. Morris had to be admitted to the hospital several times per year for more than five years.

Ms. Morris always recovered quickly and fully after two days of IV (intravenous) supportive treatment in the hospital. She did not seem to be a drug seeker, because she never asked for any narcotic pain pills when discharged, even though she required frequent IV morphine injections to control her pain during hospitalization. It occasionally happens that some drug addicts want to be hospitalized to enjoy IV opioids, but they always request prescriptions for oral narcotic painkillers upon discharge.

Ms. Morris's vital signs were normal most of the time except for her fast heart rate, which resolved quickly after pain control treatment. Her laboratory tests showed hypokalemia (low blood potassium level) and dehydration as expected, with normal liver function and pancreatic enzymes. Her urine drug screen was positive for marijuana 20-30 percent of the time at admission. The endoscopies performed by gastroenterologists were non-revealing, and imaging studies including ultrasound, computerized tomography (CT), magnetic resonance imaging (MRI), and nuclear medicine testing were negative. Ms. Morris was referred to the University Medical Center for consultation and came back without a definite diagnosis.

She had had so many admissions requiring IV fluid treatment that her peripheral veins were all damaged. Since the nurses could not get an IV on her, she needed a PICC (peripherally inserted central catheter) line or central venous line for her IV treatment during each hospitalization. PICC line or central venous line placement is costly and time-consuming, and can cause a lot of complications. Thus, she requested the placement of a **port-a-cath**, which was performed by a surgeon.

A **port-a-cath** is a small medical appliance that is installed beneath the skin. A catheter connects the port to a large, deep vein. Drugs or fluids can be injected into the vein through the port, and blood samples can also be drawn from there. The port is usually used by patients with difficulty accessing peripheral veins or patients receiving chemotherapy, and it can stay in the body for years if not infected or malfunctioned.

The negative endoscopy study for Ms. Morris indicated no structural abnormalities of her gastrointestinal (GI) tract. There was nothing wrong with her other organs besides her GI system since she had gone through many imaging studies. Blood tests and stool studies were unrevealing. Even though her urine tests were occasionally positive for marijuana, I remembered that marijuana has been used to reduce nausea and vomiting in chemotherapy for a long time. Ms. Morris recovered completely after each hospitalization, indicating that she suffered some transient and benign disorder that I did not know. I had tried searching through textbooks and the internet many times to figure out what was going on with Ms. Morris. Then, I arrived at the following conclusions: "She is allergic to or intolerant of some food." or "Somebody gave her something bad." or "She just goes crazy periodically."

Initially, when Ms. Morris was hospitalized, I asked the gastroenterology (GI) service for a consultation. After many endoscopies and imaging studies had been performed without any diagnosis, I did not consult them anymore. A GI doctor recommended trials of amitriptyline and other psychiatric medications, but I had already tried several psychiatric medications on Ms. Morris. The psychiatric medications did not prevent or reduce the flare up of her GI symptoms, and they made her feel miserable all the time. I had also told her not to go to any parties or eat out. She always said, "I'm not going anymore." Apparently, she did not follow my instructions. She continued to have episodic attacks of her GI problem, usually after a party or eating out, and went to the emergency room frequently. Sometimes, she showed substantial improvement with the treatments in the ER and was discharged home. When she was too sick to go home, the ER doctor would call me in for an admission.

Ms. Morris continued to be hospitalized every two or three months for her GI problem. Hospitalization did not cost her anything because she was on Medicare and Medicaid. Medicare, which is run by the government, is notoriously well known to check on medical frauds. It even established a department dedicated to investigating and recovering money from doctors, hospitals, and other health facilities. That was what happened to me. The local Medicare office wrote me letters several times stating that Ms. Morris did not meet criteria for hospital admission and that they would refuse to pay the hospital and me. I had to spend a lot of time fighting back by providing explanations about her case. One time, I needed to argue with the medical director of Medicare over the phone. Fortunately, I prevailed each time. After my letters had been reviewed by the medical director and other peer physicians, they accepted my explanation and did not ask the hospital and me to return the payments.

Ms. Morris was on Medicare, which means she was considered disabled, and also on Medicaid, which indicates her income was low. I

49

asked her why she had become disabled. She said one word: depression. However, she was not on any anti-depression drug. It was strange that she had never asked me to fill out any forms to keep her disability status. It is quite common that the Medicare office asks the patient's primary care doctor to re-evaluate a patient's conditions to determine if the patient can maintain disability status.

When patients bring in forms for me to fill out for disability, I usually ask, "Why are you disabled?" or "What reasons do you have for your disability?"

Some patients answer bewilderedly, "I don't know. My previous doctor applied for me sometime in the past."

"Schizophrenia," a patient replied.

"You don't look crazy," I joked.

"You are right. But I can keep my Medicare and Medicaid as long as I am on some kind of mental drug."

When asked the reason for becoming disabled, one of my patients replied bluntly, "Antisocial." It is very ironic that he received financial benefits from the government because he disliked the society and the government. I noticed that patients of this sort usually come from New York, and they are also commonly on 120-180 tablets of opioid painkillers per month plus 90 tablets of alprazolam (an antianxiety agent) per month. Many New Yorkers come back to their southern hometown for retirement (elderly people) or a change in environment (younger people, most of them on disability). These young New Yorkers moving down here maybe belong to their specific group of patients with disabilities. Actually, doctors write more prescriptions for narcotic pain pills in the southern states than in the north, according to a recent CDC (Center for Disease Control, a public health organization located in Atlanta, U.S.A.) report.[1]

I did not believe Ms. Morris's abdomen problem was related to marijuana use until I stumbled upon a case report in one of my medical journals. This case report described two patients suffering cannabinoid (marijuana) hyperemesis syndrome, which is characterized by recurrent nausea, vomiting, and colicky abdominal pain.[2] Apparently, Ms. Morris's presenting features were consistent with this syndrome.

50

Marijuana has been used to reduce nausea and vomiting in chemotherapy for a long time. It is surprisingly intriguing that long-term use of marijuana actually causes nausea and vomiting, instead of being antiemetic. These symptoms can be suppressed briefly by taking a hot shower or bath, and more permanently by abstaining from the use of marijuana.[3] But a hot shower or bath did not help Ms. Morris. After my realization, I told her my suspected diagnosis and urged her to quit marijuana each time I saw her.

"Why do you smoke marijuana?" I asked.

"It's for my arthritis," she smiled. "It is good stuff, and I feel good about it. I like it."

Currently, both medical and recreational marijuana have been legalized in Alaska, Colorado, Oregon, and Washington.[4] However, in all the southern states, marijuana use is still illegal, and police reports about marijuana selling and growing appear in local newspapers or on TV news from time to time. Occasionally, Ms. Morris did not even admit that she took marijuana when her urine turned out to be positive again. She said that the positive urine test was due to somebody smoking the stuff around her.

"Somebody smokes pot/weed/grass around me." This statement is often heard when a patient is found to have a positive urine test for marijuana in the hospital or ER. One of my patients even described in detail how many people were in the car and how he was sitting in the back seat. He said that everybody in the car was smoking pot except for him and that he hated it. On the contrary, patients usually admit using marijuana openly when asked at routine office visits.

"Yes, I do. That's good stuff, man," a patient said, in the same way that Bill Maher, a well-known comedian, talked about marijuana on TV.

"Do you want some, Doc? I can bring you some the next visit for free," the patient continued.

Ms. Morris declined to quit. One day, she walked into the clinic again, anxious and mumbling while walking and turning around painfully in the room. She had lost almost 15 pounds of her body weight within one week after she got sick this time. She could not eat and drink because of severe nausea/vomiting and abdominal pain. She looked tired and depressed. Her skin was shriveled.

Ms. Morris, expecting another hospitalization, said, "I have suffered enough. Believe me, Dr. Li, I'm not going to do this stuff anymore."

True to her word, Ms. Morris kept her promise to stop marijuana use. She has not developed a similar episode since then. Furthermore, her port-a-cath was removed since she had not had any hospital admissions for three years. She continues to do fine at present.

I did not reach the correct diagnosis, for I was sure that her problem might have been just psychiatric as a result of her history of depression. I was also stuck with the concept that marijuana was an effective treatment of nausea and vomiting when it could actually cause nausea and vomiting instead. As I read the book "How Doctors Think" by Dr. Groopman a few years later,[5] I realized that I had made an attribution error in this case: overemphasizing the role of this patient's internal characteristics and failing to evaluate the external factors carefully when assessing her clinical presentations. Ms. Morris's problem started more than 10 years ago, and Google search was still new to me then. Cannabinoid (marijuana) hyperemesis syndrome was first described by Allen et al. in 2004.[6] If I had typed in "effects of marijuana" as the search phrase in Google, I might have found out the cause of her problem much earlier on. And Ms. Morris might have abandoned her "good stuff" sooner.

Many years had passed since Ms. Morris stopped taking her "good stuff". One day, I found a young man, Mr. Martin, lying on the examination table painfully when I entered the exam room. Mr. Martin, in his 20s, came in as a new patient for the first office visit, and he was accompanied by his concerned girlfriend. He was moaning in pain and pressing his hands on the abdomen. Otherwise, he looked healthy, and well developed with a muscular physique.

"How can I help you today?" I asked.

"I've had nausea, vomiting, and abdominal pain for a couple of weeks," he replied unhappily. "I was released from the ER just two days ago. But I still can't eat and drink, and in terrible pain."

"Let me review your record in the hospital first. I'll see what I can do for you."

I pulled up his medical record on the computer, which showed that Mr. Martin had had about 20 ER visits and four hospitalizations for episodic abdominal disorders in the past three years. His lab tests showed only hypokalemia (low potassium level in blood) and dehydration (loss of body fluid). And he had normal endoscopy and imaging studies, and he had seen many specialists. His urine drug screen was always positive for marijuana at each ER visit. This time, Mr. Martin had presented to the ER five times within one month. I saw a familiar painful look in Mr. Martin's eyes that brought me back to Ms. Morris. Mr. Martin's presentation looked exactly like that of Ms. Morris.

"I guess I may have got the right diagnosis for you. Believe it or not, your problem is probably caused by marijuana use," I said to Mr. Martin after examining him. His vital signs (temperature, heart rate, respiration and blood pressure) were normal, and the physical examination was unremarkable.

"Bullsh … All my friends smoke that stuff several times a week, and no one gets sick!" he interrupted me angrily.

"Calm down!" his girlfriend spoke to him. "Listen to Dr. Li."

"But the thing is, everyone is different," I went on. "So, something good for others may be bad for you. I saw a patient more than 10 years ago. She had the same symptoms as yours. Her stomach problem had resolved after she quit smoking marijuana."

"Give me a shot to kill the pain, and I'll leave!" He did not seem to be a drug seeker. Drug addicts always ask for more narcotic pain pills before they leave the office.

"We don't inject IV pain medications in the clinic," I said. "Since you can't take oral medications and haven't eaten for one week, you'd better go to the ER again. There, you can get some IV fluid and pain treatment. I advise you not to smoke marijuana for a few weeks. Then, you'll see if I've got it right or not. You're not going to die from quitting marijuana use. And you can enjoy your life by doing many things other than marijuana, is that right?"

Mr. Martin just lowered his eyes to the floor quietly and said nothing.

"That sounds right," his girlfriend said. "I'll take him to the ER now."

"Medically, it is called cannabinoid (marijuana) hyperemesis syndrome," I spoke to Mr. Martin's girlfriend. "You can look it up on the internet when you have a chance." I wrote down the term on a piece of paper and handed it to her.

"I will," she said. "Thank you very much."

"Come to see me anytime if you have any problems," I said to Mr. Martin. "Otherwise, I'll see you back at the office in a month."

Speechlessly, Mr. Martin left the clinic with his girlfriend. However, Mr. Martin did not come back for a follow-up visit. For a learning purpose, I checked his hospital record and noticed that he had not visited the ER since he saw me 12 months earlier.

Hopefully, his stomach problem has been cured by just giving up the "good stuff," which is not always good for him. As the saying goes, one man's food is another man's poison.

3. Faith

Nothing in life is more wonderful than faith – the one great moving force which we can neither weigh in the balance nor test in the crucible.

—William Osler (1849-1919, Canadian Physician and Professor of Medicine)

未知生，焉知死？
(While you do not know life, how can you know about death?)

—Confucius (551-479 B.C., Chinese Philosopher)

The secret of health for both mind and body is not to mourn for the past, not to worry about the future, or not to anticipate troubles, but to live in the present moment wisely and earnestly.

—Buddha (563-460 B.C., the Founder of Buddhism)

In our old house in China, there was an altar where name boards, pictures of ancestors, and a small porcelain statue of Guanyin (Bodhisattva) were placed. During holidays, food and other sacrifices (roasted pork, cooked chicken, fruits, flowers, etc.) were set up, and joss sticks and candles were burned in front of the altar. Then we would kneel down to worship ancestors according to our position in the family hierarchy. In China, this ceremonial custom or religious ritual allows people to respect and remember our ancestors and traditions.

"Where are we going?" I asked Grandma when she told me that we were going out.

"I'm taking you to a temple," Grandma replied.

"What are we going to do there?"

"We're going to worship the gods in the temple."

"Why do we need to worship the gods?"

"God will bless us. Then you will have a healthy body and bright future."

I remember this conversation taking place when I was around six years old. It was technically my first introduction to religion although I did not quite understand what Grandma said at the time. Grandma went to worship there only once or twice a year. We went to the temple by bus. Inside the temple, there were many large halls that housed not only Buddha statues but also Chinese shen (神, spirit or deity) statues. The temple was crowded with worshipers, who walked through the halls and prayed in front of those statues. One time, Grandma paid a fortune teller to interpret the bamboo slips she picked up in front of the largest Buddha. One of the bamboo slips predicted my cousin would become a teacher, but Grandma said I was too young for the fortune teller to say anything about me.

During those days, people feared to talk about religious issues publicly in China. Most of the temples and churches were even closed in China during the Cultural Revolution from 1966 to 1976. The Cultural Revolution was a radical socio-political movement, which was initiated by Mao Zedong, the former president of China. It gave rise to political zealotry, violence, military rule, purges, social chaos, economic disaster, etc. Some of the temples and churches were converted to factories, schools, or government offices. Thus, I had little knowledge about religions when I was in China. Interestingly, even though I had never entered any church for worship in China, I had worked inside a church for more than five years.

This was the white Catholic Church, which was located on the south bank of the Pearl River. The church had a very high vaulted ceiling and was reconstructed into a two-story printing factory building during the Cultural Revolution. The printing machines were installed on the first floor while the workers did cutting and binding on the second floor. The two towers of the church served as the factory office. They even installed an elevator to transport products or paper rolls between the two floors. I still remember that the second floor was always flooded with sunlight coming in through the huge arched windows.

After graduating from high school, I was assigned to work at this printing factory by the government as most of the universities and colleges were closed during the period. I operated an automatic printing machine on the first floor of the building. After loading paper and inks, I could sit down and watch the machine run itself, enjoying my good time. During the crazy years, there were only loose regulations in the factory. Workers could practice martial arts, play chess or cards, and wander around chatting during working hours without being laid off. I was even named as "Model Worker" owing to my good performance. Playing at work during those years has been one of the unforgettable experiences in my life.

I worked in the church-turned factory from 1972 until I left for medical school in 1978. The printing factory was closed in the 1980s thanks to the new government policy. The church had been renovated and returned to its original shape later. Most of the existing churches had started to open again in China since the 1980s.

Religion presented a culture shock to me when I arrived in the United States 28 years ago. Churches are seen everywhere. For instance, in the county with a population of 100,000, where we live, there are more than 250 churches. Even a few larger new churches are under construction. Religious people are occasionally seen walking from door to door to share the word of God. Physicians here pray first before a medical meeting starts. I was impressed that my daughter was awarded the college diploma with a signed copy of the Bible at the graduation ceremony. Throughout these years, I have learned that religions exert a profound impact on every aspect of life in the U.S.

Blood Transfusion

U sually, the religion that patients practice has little to no impact on their clinical outcome, at least in emergency or critical situations. Nevertheless, medical care associated with blood transfusions is an exception.

At the first office visit, Mr. Fox showed me his Jehovah's Witness wallet card indicating refusal of blood transfusion. One time, he drove 15 miles back to the clinic to leave a videotape about Jehovah's Witnesses for me to watch. The videotape, which was still on the bookshelf in the clinic office, reminded me of his red face whenever I looked at it.

Jehovah's Witnesses is a religious organization that was founded in the 1870s by Charles Taze Russell in Pittsburgh, Pennsylvania, U.S.A. According to its publications, there are around eight million Jehovah's Witness members in the world with over one million Jehovah's Witnesses in the United States. At present, the headquarters of Jehovah's Witnesses (Watchtower Society) is located in Brooklyn, New York. Jehovah's Witnesses' beliefs have originated from their interpretations of the Bible. As stated by their blood doctrines, one should not eat blood, receive a blood transfusion, and donate or store one's own blood for transfusion. They may choose to receive some blood plasma fractions, but not to accept whole blood transfusion or cellular components of blood. The doctrine of refusing blood transfusion has been commonly applied only since 1945. (For more details on this topic, see *Wikipedia: Jehovah's Witnesses*)

Mr. Fox was a 76-year-old, short, red-faced retired mailman. He looked strong even with a protruding belly and walked with fast stride. His diabetes and hypertension were well controlled with only three medications. I don't remember if he had ever complained of anything when he came in for an office visit. "I'm good," he always said with a smile and confidence. He and his wife came to the clinic together all the time. After finishing his visit, he usually stepped out of the room first while his wife remained in the room to continue her visit.

Mr. Fox had been well until one night when he passed bright red blood in the stool. He had come into the emergency department, and his hemoglobin was found to be only 6.5 gram/deciliter (his baseline level was in the range of 14-15 gram/deciliter), indicating he had lost a lot of blood acutely. The coagulation profile (the test for blood clotting capacity) showed normal values with a normal platelet count. Mr. Fox presumably developed an acute lower gastrointestinal bleeding. Blood transfusion treatment was recommended to him in the emergency department. But he declined it because he was a Jehovah's Witness. Mr. Fox was admitted to the hospital for further evaluation and treatment.

"You're having serious bleeding from your bowel. The hemoglobin level is getting lower this morning…it's down to 5.4 gram/deciliter," I said to Mr. Fox when I checked on him in the hospital early in the morning.

Hemoglobin is the protein in red blood cells that carries oxygen from the lungs to the rest of the body through the blood system. Ninety percent of the protein in red blood cells is made up of hemoglobin. Hemoglobin concentration measurement is one of the most commonly performed blood tests, usually as part of a complete blood count, which determines if anemia, a deficiency in the number of red blood cells or their hemoglobin content, exists. Anemia may be caused by blood loss, decreased red blood cell production, or increased red blood cell breakdown. Common causes of blood loss include trauma and gastrointestinal bleeding. Normal levels of hemoglobin (from Wikipedia) are: Men: 13.8 to 18.0 gram/deciliter (138 to 180 gram/liter, or 8.56 to 11.17 mmol/liter) Women: 12.1 to 15.1 gram/deciliter (121 to 151 gram/liter, or 7.51 to 9.37 mmol/liter).

"I know I'm bleeding. But I'm doing okay now," Mr. Fox replied.

"In my opinion, the best treatment for your bleeding is blood transfusion," I continued.

"I am a Jehovah's Witness and do not accept blood transfusions. Do you remember I showed you my blood refusal card at the clinic?"

"Yes, I do remember. Most of the patients with bowel bleeding survive after blood transfusions. You may lose your life if you don't accept a blood transfusion."

"I would rather die than receive a blood transfusion," he said resolutely.

Mr. Fox presumably developed bleeding from diverticula, which is one of the most common causes of gastrointestinal bleeding in elderly people.

The formation of bowel pouches, diverticula, is described as **diverticulosis**, usually within the large intestine or colon, and occasionally in the small intestine. The diverticular disease usually affects the left side of the colon (the sigmoid colon, 95 percent) in the west, while it commonly involves the right side in Asian and African countries. Most people with colonic diverticulosis do not have symptoms. However, the diverticula may bleed, leading to anemia, and it may become infected, resulting in diverticulitis. The majority of the patients suffering diverticular bleeding survive with blood transfusion and other supportive treatments.

His usual red face had turned to a pale one. He looked weak but calm and confident. His vital signs (temperature, heart rate, respiration and blood pressure) were normal at that time, and he was mentally clear. His wife, Mrs. Fox, was sitting at the bedside, and she was a Jehovah's Witness too.

"What do you think about his decision?" I asked Mrs. Fox.

"If it is what he wants, I support it," she said softly.

I discussed with Mr. and Mrs. Fox again about his code status. Mr. Fox had a DNR (do-not-resuscitate) order, which was signed in the emergency department. They firmly maintained their decision on DNR.

Here I was facing a challenging ethical dilemma: respect for patient autonomy versus beneficence. American College of Physicians Ethics Manual stated, "*Beneficence is the duty to promote good and act in the best interest of the patient and the health of society, while respect for patient autonomy is the duty to protect and foster a patient's free, uncoerced choices."*[1] Patient autonomy is defined as *the right of patients to make decisions about their medical care without their healthcare provider trying to influence the decision.*

I had admitted and treated many elderly people with gastrointestinal bleeding in the past. Almost all of them had survived after appropriate treatments including blood transfusion. Mr. Fox was healthy without serious comorbid medical disorders before the admission. Mr. Fox had normal vital signs and maintained his usual mental status. He could communicate well and understood the severity of his disease, along with the available treatments for his condition and the medical consequences of his choice. Therefore, he was considered competent to make his own decision, which was also supported by his family. Furthermore, Mr. Fox expressed his decision about the refusal of blood transfusion before he got sick.

It was sad to see that Mr. Fox might die because he rejected a blood transfusion, which was a safe, common procedure. About five million people need a blood transfusion in the United States each year. Although a blood transfusion can be a life-saving procedure, it is not without risks. Blood transfusions can cause transfusion reactions, non-infectious problems, and rarely, infections. Most blood transfusions go smoothly, but occasionally mild problems can arise. Serious complications seldom develop. However, individuals have rights to make decisions regarding their own medical care, and physicians have the duty to honor their decisions.

After Mr. Fox was admitted, gastroenterology and surgery services were consulted, but they could not have anything to offer because of his refusal of receiving a blood transfusion. I explained to Mr. Fox's whole family what treatment plan I had for his condition without blood transfusion. They did not object to my therapy regimen, neither did they request a transfer to another hospital. I guessed that they had already consulted their Jehovah's Witness congregation. Quite a few fellow Jehovah's Witnesses came to visit him daily.

Mr. Fox stayed in the hospital, receiving IV fluid, IV iron, and subcutaneous injection of erythropoietin and oxygen therapy. IV fluid supplemented his body fluid; IV iron replenished his iron store in the body, and injection of erythropoietin, a hormone, stimulated production of red blood cells and hemoglobin in the bone marrow. These are the standard treatments for severe anemia without blood transfusion. However, the therapy with erythropoietin would take four to six days to show the onset of action, according to UpToDate.com (a medical website).

When I made rounds, Mr. Fox was alert and awake even though looking weak, most of the time sitting in the middle of the room, surrounded by his family members including many children and grandchildren. I repeated the same question about the blood transfusion every day, but he maintained his decision: no blood transfusion. In addition, I talked with their children about Mr. Fox's conditions. They stated that they understood the situation and respected their father's decision. As his hemoglobin dropped lower and lower daily, Mr. Fox appeared weaker and weaker. Yet, he always looked calm and confident.

"How are you doing today?" I asked.

"I'm doing fine. I haven't seen any blood in my stool for two days."

"Your blood count has gone down to 4.5 gram today. I'm very concerned. Do you have shortness of breath or chest pain?" I said to him on the third day of the admission.

"I'm breathing well without pain. And I think I can make it," he said confidently.

Mr. Fox's hemoglobin level reduced to 4.1 g/dL the next morning while his vital signs were stable with a blood pressure of 100/66 mm Hg and normal oxygen saturation. That was the second time within two months I had seen someone's hemoglobin drop so low. I admitted a 92-year-old woman to the same ward just two months ago for severe anemia due to bowel bleeding. She was also a Jehovah's Witness and objected to a blood transfusion. Her daughter and son-in-law, the main care providers, were both Jehovah's witnesses who supported their mother's decision. The similar treatments including fluid, iron and erythropoietin had been given to her. Still, she became lethargic, then unresponsive, and finally comatose three days after she was admitted. Her final hemoglobin was 3.9 g/dL, and she died peacefully on the eighth day of hospitalization. Mr. Fox's hemoglobin level of 4.1 g/dL had approximated her final hemoglobin level.

I visited Mr. Fox at noon, whose face was white as a sheet. Mr. Fox was sitting in the middle of the room, surrounded by several his children. I told him and his family about the blood result and poor outcomes. They said they continued to support Mr. Fox's decision. Mr. Fox appeared weak, but he was alert and able to answer questions appropriately.

"Are you okay?" I said. "Your blood count is still going down today. The treatment you are getting takes a few more days to take effect. I am afraid that you may die in the meanwhile."

"I'm good. Don't worry," he said.

"Do you keep your decision not to accept blood transfusions?" I asked.

"I'm not going to change my decision," he said firmly with a little smile. "No blood transfusion."

He was sitting upright calmly and breathing oxygen through a nasal cannula comfortably, looking very confident and showing no signs of a bad omen. However, Mr. Fox was at a very high risk of dying from blood loss.

If declining blood transfusion, about 34.4 percent of patients with a postoperative hemoglobin level of 4.1 to 5.0 g/dL would die within 30 days of the surgery, according to a study.[2] The patients included in this study population were 57 years old on average. Mr. Fox was 76 years old and had an even higher risk of dying from low blood level.

When walking out of his room, I thought that Mr. Fox looked stronger than the 92-year-old lady and that Mr. Fox might be able to survive. However, when I was seeing patients in the clinic, a nurse called at around three o'clock in the afternoon, "Mr. Fox collapsed all of a sudden while sitting in the chair quietly and talking with his children. He died right away. Dr. Mason from your group happened to be on the floor and checked on him. Mr. Fox was pronounced dead." Mr. Fox was not given CPR (cardiopulmonary resuscitation) because he had a DNR order. His vital signs and oxygen saturation were normal, and he maintained a stable mental status just three hours ago. He would have been transferred to the ICU if he had showed any signs of pending collapse. Without any struggle, he passed away instantly. I hoped that he had gone to the eternity he had been longing for.

"I have been a Jehovah's Witness for more than 30 years. Do you know that I am the one who converted my husband to a Jehovah's Witness 10 years ago?" Mrs. Fox said to me with a smirk during an office visit after her husband died. I have not figured out if the smirk on her face expressed some kind of remorse or proudness or satisfaction.

"How about your children? Are they Jehovah's Witnesses too?"

"None of them."

"Why?"

"I don't know."

"Are you still a Jehovah's Witness?"

"Sure, I am. I won't change in my life."

Jehovah's Witnesses have better clinical outcomes in non-emergent settings. Two of my Jehovah's Witness patients chose to receive erythropoietin treatment to increase blood count and stored their own blood for future use before elective orthopedic surgeries. Both survived their surgeries without transfusion of other people's blood. Another patient of mine did well with an elective heart bypass surgery without blood transfusion.

Some of them may lose their chance to receive life-saving surgeries if they refuse a blood transfusion. I remember how Mr. Oscar's life had been cut short because he declined to take blood. Mr. Oscar was an ESRD (end stage renal disease) patient on hemodialysis who was admitted with new onset of heart failure. Cardiology service was consulted, and his cardiologist ordered echocardiography, which revealed severe aortic stenosis. Mr. Oscar was transferred to a nearby tertiary medical center for possible surgical intervention. He had moderate anemia, a common finding in hemodialysis patients, but his low hemoglobin level was not accepted by the surgical service for an open heart surgery. Being a Jehovah's Witness, Mr. Oscar refused blood transfusion before, during and after surgery. Therefore, he did not undergo the heart surgery and was discharged back to our hospital. He was supposed to continue erythropoietin treatment until his hemoglobin level rose to the acceptable level, and he could be sent back to the tertiary medical center for the aortic surgery. I saw him during his hemodialysis on the weekend when I was on call for the nephrology group. He was stable over the weekend, but he suffered a cardiac arrest in a few days and died after unsuccessful cardiopulmonary resuscitation.

There are many Jehovah's Witnesses around this area. I usually discussed with all my Jehovah's Witness patients about blood transfusion and documented their wishes in the chart at the first office visit as new patients. I talked about the blood issue with them periodically to make sure that they did not have a change in their decision. They always liked to talk with me about their faith. They had even brought me many booklets, videotapes, and discs.

"Could you show which scripture of the Bible tells you not to take blood transfusion?" I asked curiously sometimes.

"It is here," some patients can point out the statement while some have no clue.

"The Bible (NLT, Deuteronomy 12:23) states: *But never consume the blood, for the blood is the life, and you must not consume the lifeblood with the meat,*" I argued sometimes. "It talks about animal blood, not human blood."

"Blood is blood, no matter what you say," they said.

"The Bible does not mention blood transfusion, which is the modern medicine that didn't exist two thousand years ago," I continued.

"We just follow God's word," they replied.

"Okay, okay," I said. "It's your faith… nobody can change but you. Let me know if you change your decision about blood transfusion, so I can document it in your chart."

"We won't change. Would you like to attend our meetings?" they asked.

"Let me think about it at this time," I said. "I want to go to heaven after I die. But only 144,000 Jehovah's Witness people can go to heaven, is that right?"

"You are right. How did you know that?"

"I learned it from the books you gave me."

"We're glad you've read them."

66

"Are you one of those 144,000 people?"

"No. We want to stay on earth."

"How can I become one of them that can go to heaven?"

"Only God can decide."

"Oh, I have to wait for God's decision," I said.

"We are nice people too," they continued. "We Jehovah's Witnesses don't divorce, don't do drugs, and don't smoke."

"I see that," I said while thinking about all my Jehovah's Witness patients.

It is true that Mr. Fox was a nice man without a history of smoking and had been married to his wife for 50 years. His avoidable death did not seem to cause much harm to other people since his family had supported him all along. He had never been hospitalized before the only and last admission. His four-day hospital stay had used much less medical resources than many other patients, for he was DNR without ICU service. I admire him for the bravery of sacrificing his life for his faith. But I am still wondering how Mr. Fox managed to know that God wanted him to choose death instead of life.

Occasionally, Jehovah's Witnesses may be willing to accept blood transfusions when they understand that death is likely without transfusion in critical situations. One night when I was on call for the nephrology group, I received a call around 2 a.m. from the emergency room at the small hospital in a neighboring town. The ER doctor told me that Mrs. Evans presented to the ER with weakness and altered mental status. Mrs. Evans, in her 60s, was an ESRD (end-stage renal disease) patient of our clinic. The ER doctor requested transfer of Mrs. Evans to our hospital since she was due for hemodialysis in that morning. It was very common that ESRD patients were transferred to our hospital from there because the small hospital did not offer hemodialysis service.

When I listened to the ER doctor's report, I noticed that Mrs. Evans had a low hemoglobin level of 5.7 g/dL and low blood pressure. I always accepted the transfer of ESRD patients without hesitation unless our hospital was full. However, this time I was concerned something bad might happen during the transportation due to her severe anemia and other underlying diseases. Thus, I told the ER doctor that Mrs. Evans should receive one or two units of blood before being transported to our hospital. The ER doctor said, "No problem. We'll do it".

It took about an hour to transport ESRD patients from the small hospital to our hospital. A nurse at our hospital called me to inform that Mrs. Evans had arrived at the floor around 6 a.m. I drove to the hospital right away. When examining Mrs. Evans, I found that she was very pale, hypotensive, and too lethargic to answer my questions. I rushed back to the nursing station and ordered IV fluid and oxygen, and I told the nurse to perform stat blood count, check oxygen saturation, and watch Mrs. Evans closely. After quickly reviewing her medical record, I realized that she did not receive a blood transfusion at the small hospital. I called back to the ER of the small hospital to ask why they did not transfuse Mrs. Evans there. The ER nurse there told me that Mrs. Evans refused a blood transfusion because she was a Jehovah's Witness. In the meantime, the result of the stat hemoglobin came back: it was 5.0 g/dL.

Transfusion of packed red blood cells is usually recommended when a patient's hemoglobin level drops below 10 g/dL. Although recent evidence has shown that lowering the transfusion criterion down to 7-8 g/dL produces better patient outcomes, blood transfusion should also be considered according to a patient's underlying medical disorders and present symptoms. Usually, ESRD patients have chronic anemia, and they can tolerate lower levels of hemoglobin. However, Mrs. Evans was symptomatic and unstable with other comorbid diseases including heart disease and stroke. With a hemoglobin level of 5.0 g/dL (her baseline was 10.5 g/dL), Mrs. Evans was at an extremely high risk of dying without blood transfusion.

Now, Mrs. Evans was not mentally sound to make her decision. I needed to obtain consent from the next of kin before ordering a blood transfusion, even in emergency situations. Hence, I called her husband to ask about his decision,

"Is this Mr. Evans?" I asked.

"Yes, speaking," Mr. Evans replied.

"I'm Dr. Li on call for the nephrology group. I need to talk to you about your wife's condition."

"Okay, please."

"Your wife was transferred here early this morning because of severe anemia, low blood count, possibly due to bleeding from her bowel. She refused a blood transfusion last night at that hospital before being transported to here. Today, her blood count is even lower, and she is getting sicker. Now, she can barely open her eyes and is too weak to speak. I think your wife is probably going to die if she does not get a blood transfusion right now."

"Ah? She is going to die without blood transfusion?"

"Yes, you're right. Let me say again. If your wife does not receive a blood transfusion, she will probably die soon no matter what we do. The blood transfusion is the only option for your wife to survive. Now she is too weak to make her decision. You have to make the decision for her."

"What can I do now?"

"I want to know if you would give permission for your wife to receive a blood transfusion."

"I don't want her to die. It's okay to give her blood then."

"You said it is okay to give your wife a blood transfusion. Is that right?"

"Yes, that's right. Please give her blood."

I repeated my questions one more time to make sure Mr. Evans did not change his mind. He offered the same answer. Afterward, I immediately wrote the order: type and match two units of packed red blood cells, and transfuse both units of blood during hemodialysis.

Whole blood is no longer transfused nowadays. After the whole blood is collected, it will be split into components of the blood, such as red blood cells, white blood cells, plasma, clotting factors, and platelets, which are commonly used in modern medicine. Before a blood transfusion is given, typing and matching tests must be performed to ensure that donor and recipient blood are compatible with one another.

Mrs. Evans received two units of packed red blood cells during hemodialysis and survived. She was stable enough to be discharged home one week later. Since she was not my patient, I did not know how she coped with her religious situation after that transfusion.

However, I still remember the disappointment expressed by one of my fellow residents during our internal medicine training 20 years ago when he found out the hospital cafeteria had always used some kind of animal fat to cook scrambled eggs. He had eaten the scrambled eggs almost every day for more than one year.

"John, I just found out they use animal fat to cook scrambled eggs and other hot food," he said disappointedly. "I almost threw up when I heard that. That kind of fat is not allowed in my religion."

"Are you okay since you have sinned so long?" I asked him curiously.

"I think I am okay as I did it without knowing it," he said with a bitter smile. "I just won't eat that kind of food from now on. I'll ask the chef first before I get any food in the cafeteria."

"How do you know the chef tells you the truth?"

"I'm alright as long as I don't eat it knowingly."

I believe that Mrs. Evans would be surely forgiven, for she was too sick to perceive the blood transfusion process in the critical circumstance. The decision about blood transfusion was made by her husband, not by her. And she had received the blood unknowingly. God is always forgiving.

Tithe

Church-goers tend to be healthier and live longer believably through spiritual serenity and fellowship according to some studies.[1] However, there are times when mishaps happen in the church. Quite a few patients of mine developed severe hypoglycemia (low sugar level) as the Sunday sermons ran late, and they ended up in the emergency department. A patient of mine stumbled and sprained her ankle on the doorstep of the church, and her left index finger was crushed by the church door on another occasion. Another patient told me that he suffered two episodes of seizure while attending worship services.

"Why are you looking so depressed?" I asked one of my patients.

"Because some of the church members annoy me all the time. You've got to prescribe some pills for me."

"The church is supposed to make you happy. Why don't you go to another church since there are so many around here?"

"Go to another church?" She was perplexed.

"Why not? There, you can make new friends, enjoy a different environment, and learn something new from another pastor."

"That's a good advice!"

"Do you still need pills to solve your church problems?"

"Not anymore," she smiled.

During an office visit, I said to Mr. Thomas, "What's going on? Both your blood pressure and sugar are out of whack." Mr. Thomas was 68 years old and a very nice man with soft speech. He suffered diabetes, hypertension, and other medical disorders.

"I just can't afford to fill all the medications," he said.

"I seldom prescribe expensive brand-name drugs. All your medications are generic and on the formulary. You need to pay only $5-10 for each one."

"Do you know that I live on social security income only?"

"Now, I know. But a lot of elderly people in this state are in the same financial situation as you. If you don't mind, please tell me how you spend your money."

"Okay. I pay xxx for my apartment, xxx for food, and xxx for other things."

"You still have $100-200 left every month for your medication according to my calculation. You need about $50-80 each month to fill your prescriptions."

"I forgot to tell you... I need to pay almost $100 per month as tithe to my church. Recently, my church had a fund-raising for the new building. I have promised $1,000, and I need to pay it on a monthly payment of $100. How can I have money left for my medications?"

"I suggest you should buy your medicine first before you pay your tithe."

"But the pastors remind us of paying 10 percent of our income as tithe every Sunday."

"I guess I can help you out on this issue. Please read this statement of the New Testament: *Whatever you give is acceptable if you give it eagerly. And give according to what you have, not what you don't have.* Here, Jesus did not mention 10 percent." I showed him the scripture (2 Corinthians 8:12) in one of the Bibles (NLT, New Living Translation) at BibleGateway.com on the computer screen.

"I didn't know that before."

"You'd better fill your prescriptions first after getting your social security check and pay your tithe cheerfully later," I advised him. "I don't think God will be happy if you pay too much tithe and get sick without medication." The scripture (2 Corinthians 8:13) states, *"Of course, I don't mean your giving should make life easy for others and hard for yourselves."*

"Well, I'm going to do what you've said."

"Hey, please make sure not to tell your pastor about what I told you," I smiled.

"No, I won't. It's a secret, isn't it?" he laughed.

Since then, Mr. Thomas had surely followed my instruction. He brought his medication bottles to the clinic at each visit, showing me that he did fill his prescriptions monthly. He remained healthy and cheerful for years.

When I made rounds in the nursing home on one Sunday, I came to see Mr. Tyson, who was a 73-year-old patient on hemodialysis and unresponsive most of the time. He was sleeping with continuous feeding through a gastric feeding tube while his wife Mrs. Tyson was sitting at his bedside.

"Did you go to church today, ma'am?" I asked Mrs. Tyson by courtesy, who was my patient too.

"I can't afford it," she replied.

"How come?"

"The church asks for 10 percent of our income as tithe."

"Did the pastor tell you what scripture says that?"

"He may have told it. But I don't remember."

"In my memory, the New Testament says: give what you can afford and give it cheerfully."

"Really? You know, Mr. Tyson had given much more than 10 percent of his income to the church before he got sick. So, we don't have any savings at all. Now, he is lying in the nursing home, and his pastor doesn't even come here to see him."

"I think you should attend church to meet with other people sometimes. You sit here all day every day and look so depressed."

"I'm worrying about my husband."

"Sitting here all day isn't going to help him. The nursing home staff takes care of your husband here. Interacting with each other in the church is good for your health. But please remember: pay cheerfully."

"I think I should go next week. Thank you very much."

Reading can broaden one's knowledge and give one pleasure, and occasionally it can help others save money and stay healthy.

There are more than 250 churches in the county where I practiced. Some pastor patients of mine own two or three churches. I asked them sometimes, "Do you ask people to pay 10 percent of their income as tithe? Some low-income people can't afford this 10 percent, you know."

"I know some churches do this kind of thing. But my church doesn't do that." They all answered like that. Nevertheless, when I addressed this question to many of my patients, most of them stated that their pastors remind them of paying 10 percent of their income as tithe almost every Sunday. A patient told me that her church requested an even higher percentage of income as tithe.

"Does your church report to you how much money is collected and how the money is spent each year?" I asked occasionally.

"No," most of them replied.

"They did in the past. But not anymore," some said.

"If you pay more tithes, can you go to heaven earlier?" I asked.

"No. I don't want to go there too soon."

"Will you get a better position in heaven if you pay more money?"

"I don't think so. And everybody should be the same in heaven."

"Just make sure to pay your tithe happily," I said, hoping that they will do what I told them to do and that they understand heaven is open to everyone as long as they pay their tithes joyfully. Although going to church or other religious facilities may have some positive effects on well-being, religion is only something in life, but not everything. There are many ways of making life full of happiness.

Afterlife

This is undoubtedly the most sensitive and important subject in religions. I have learned a lot about this issue from the contact with my patients. I first saw Ms. Saint six years ago when her niece brought her in for an office visit. Her niece had been my patient for many years.

"This is my aunt, Dr. Li," her niece said. "She has just come down from New York to live with me."

"Are you 97 years old?" I was surprised while reviewing Ms. Saint's medical record.

"Yes, I am," Ms. Saint replied with a smile.

Ms. Saint was of medium height and slim build with clear mind and speech. Even though she did not drive a car, she walked steadily without a cane. I found out that her major medical disorder was high blood pressure, and she was taking six medications. In my opinion, most of them were unnecessary. After I had adjusted her medications, her blood pressure was well controlled, and she needed to take only one pill per day.

Her niece was her care provider and accompanied her to the clinic for each office visit. At every office visit, Ms. Saint always reminded me to give her some samples of blood pressure pills. I asked her what she did with her time at home every day. She said she spent most of her time reading. Most of my patients are elderly people. I routinely talk to them and their families about end-of-life care whenever I find an appropriate opportunity to do so.

"You are the oldest patient with clear mind and speech whom I can talk with," I said to Ms. Saint one day. "I have patients who are older than you, but all of them are either demented or very sick."

"I suppose I'm very lucky," she said.

"And you live a long life and speak intelligibly and seem to have a lot of wisdom. I'd like to ask you some questions about life and death. Is that okay?"

"Yes, that's okay."

"You are very healthy at 97. But you're going to die someday, aren't you?"

"Yes, I know that," she said with a relaxed smile.

"Where do you go after you die?"

"To heaven, I guess."

"What can you do up there?"

"Probably nothing."

"Why?"

"Only your soul can go to heaven since your body is dead and stays on earth," she smiled. "What can you do without a body?"

Her niece, sitting beside her, was dumbfounded when hearing what her aunt said. I'm entirely surprised at her answer too. She was the only patient of mine who described life and death this way. When asked similar questions, most patients would say, "In heaven, we'll be happy all the time without any pain. We sit next to Jesus (or God). But we are not ready to go there yet." Some say, "We won't go to heaven. We stay on earth after death. Jesus will come down to resurrect us someday in the future."

"So," I asked, "you mean only your spirit can persist while your physical body will disappear after you die. And you can't do much up there. Is that right?"

"Yeah, you've got it," Ms. Saint laughed.

Then I discussed with her about end-of-life care. She firmly expressed her decision to have DNR (do not resuscitate) and no artificial feeding. I documented Ms. Saint's decision in the chart and spoke to her niece sitting beside Ms. Saint, "You've heard what your aunt wants at the end of her life, haven't you?"

"Yes, I've heard that. It's so amazing!" her niece shook her head.

"You are the only care provider for her, and she does not have children. I hope you will respect her wishes in the future."

"Yes, I will."

"Do you go to church?" I turned to Ms. Saint.

"No. I read my own books and magazines at home," Ms. Saint said.

"Oh, you told me that you read a lot of books. Could you show me one of them at the next visit?"

"Sure."

At the next visit, she brought with her one copy of an old magazine, which was published more than half a century ago and contained articles related to metaphysics, the branch of philosophy that deals with the basic causes and nature of things.

"No wonder you talk like a philosopher," I said to her after leafing through her magazine.

"Do you think so?" she laughed like a child.

"Maybe more than a philosopher. God bless you," I laughed too.

"God bless you."

It's really a joyful moment to talk about life and death with this sweet elderly lady with wisdom and humor. Ms. Saint explained life and death simply by using a few words that everybody can understand and remember: soul, body, spirit and physical. We have both body and soul while alive on earth. Only our spirits remain after we die. Hopefully, our souls or spirits will go to heaven.

When it comes to the concept of heaven, people have different interpretations of it.

"Dr. Li, this is my son. He is a pastor in New York. He came down to see me," one of my patients proudly introduced her son to me during an office visit.

"It's nice to meet you, pastor," I said to the pastor.

"Nice to meet you too," he said smiling. "Mom has told me a lot of good things about you."

"Thank you very much. Look at your mother. She is so happy, because her good son is with her today."

"Yeah. Actually, I should have come down more often."

"Me too. I travel to China to see my mother only once a year."

"How old is your mom?"

"She is 76 years old and the same age as your mother. So you are a pastor. May I ask you a question?"

"Sure."

"How many heavens are there?" I asked.

"Seven," he replied confidently and quickly without a blink.

"Really? I've asked many people including quite a few pastors about this. You are the only one who provides a clear-cut and quick answer," I smiled.

"Because you are asking the right person," he laughed. So did his mother.

"How did you know there are seven heavens?"

"The scripture says: xxx," he continued.

"Really, I didn't know that. Thank you for your teaching." I don't recall which scripture he talked about as this conversation took place many years ago. And I have not been able to figure it out so far.

"Three heavens," another pastor patient answered when asked the same question. Indeed, not only do people interpret the concept of heaven differently, but they have different ideas about hell.

When I first met Mr. Pascal, a pastor, he was 87 years old and could walk steadily without a cane. He was obese and had had diabetes for 30-40 years. Fortunately, he had not suffered serious complications of diabetes and still preached in a church on Sundays. He looked confused and was slow in speaking with shaky hands during his first visit as a new patient. I suspected that Mr. Pascal most likely had hypoglycemia.

Hypoglycemia is a condition characterized by abnormally low blood glucose (blood sugar) levels, usually less than 70 mg/dl (3.9 mmol/L). Hypoglycemia is usually associated with the treatment of diabetes. Other medical disorders such as cancers can cause low glucose levels in patients without diabetes, but they are rare. Patients with hypoglycemia may experience symptoms such as palpitations, shakiness, anxiety, sweating, hunger, and tingling sensation around the mouth. If glucose levels become so low that the brain cannot obtain enough glucose as energy, patients can develop confusion, abnormal behavior, visual disturbances, and rarely, seizure and loss of consciousness.

I asked a medical assistant to check his sugar level with a glucometer, which turned out to be only 47 mg/dl (2.6 mmol/L). Apparently, Mr. Pascal was having symptomatic hypoglycemia almost certainly due to taking too much insulin. He started to talk fluently like a real pastor after drinking a can of coke with crackers. Symptoms of low sugar usually start to improve within five minutes after patients consume sugar, such as eating candy, drinking fruit juice, or taking glucose tablets to raise blood sugar level. It may take 10–20 minutes for patients to recover fully.

After reviewing his medications, I found out that Mr. Pascal was using a very high dose of insulin, 80 units twice a day. He told me that he had passed out several times during sermons. I advised him to reduce his insulin dosage by 40 % and told him to make sure to eat three meals per day at the same time. Then he was given instructions about the prevention and treatment of hypoglycemia. And he was instructed to check his sugar level before driving as he still drove a car. He was told not to drive his car if the sugar level is below 70 mg /dL (3.9 mmol/L). Since Mr. Pascal had developed severe symptoms of hypoglycemia (loss of consciousness) in the past, a Glucagon injection kit was prescribed for him, and instructions on its use were provided to his family members.

Glucagon, a hormone secreted by the pancreas, can stimulate the production of glucose in the liver and increase the blood glucose level. It is taken not by mouth, but by injection. If patients are suffering such severe effects of hypoglycemia that they are no longer able to take sugar by mouth, they may need an injection of glucagon, which can be given by close friends or relatives. Individuals usually regain consciousness in 5-15 minutes after a glucagon injection.

"My previous doctor had never reduced my insulin dose by so much," Mr. Pascal hesitated to accept my advice.

"You need to understand this concept: low sugar level can harm you right away," I explained. "You may injure yourself or even die from it. You may kill somebody else if you pass out when driving a car. High sugar level usually causes long-term complications of diabetes unless the sugar level is extremely high, let's say, higher than 500 mg/dL (27.8 mmol/dL). Actually, more elderly people end up in the ER or hospital as a consequence of low sugar than high sugar.[1]"

"Nobody has told me this before," Mr. Pascal said.

"This is a matter of common sense: avoid the immediate danger first, and then talk about the future risk later. Is that right?" I said.

"I follow you," he smiled.

When Mr. Pascal came back one week later, he showed me his sugar logbook: sugar levels were in the range of 90-130 mg/dl (5-7.2 mmol/L). His initial A1C was 6.1%, which was too low for him. I further cut down his dose of insulin by 20% more. He had been doing fine without hypoglycemia since then. Also, his A1C was in the range of about 7-8%, which should be appropriate for his condition.

The **A1C** test is a common blood test for diabetes. The A1C value represents one's average blood sugar level for the past two to three months. High A1C level indicates the poor blood sugar control. For most people with diabetes, the common treatment target is an A1C level of 7% or less. But, the A1C targets should be set according to individuals' condition and adjusted accordingly. The lower A1C targets, the higher incidence of hypoglycemia (low sugar level).

"Hell is too crowded now," Mr. Pascal said seriously during an office visit.

"Why?" I asked curiously.

"Because there are so many bad people on earth."

"How do you know hell is too small?"

"I feel that myself."

"So, where are the bad people going when they die?"

"I don't know. That's my question too."

"Can they go to heaven?"

"I don't think so," he said firmly.

"Can you pray to God and ask him to make hell bigger?"

"Probably so," he smiled.

"By the way, how many heavens are there?"

"Maybe one," he was puzzled and replied after some thinking.

"Are you sure?" I said. "Most versions of the Bible except the King James Version state: God created the heavens and the earth. You see 'heavens' has an 's.' It is plural, meaning more than one heaven. Is that right?"

"I've never paid attention to it."

"The newest scientific concept of the universe is called multiverse: more than one universe coexists. Does it mean 'many heavens'? "

"That's a good point," he said sincerely. "I need to talk about it in my next sermon."

I was happy that my "discovery" was noteworthy. I had searched all the English versions of the Bible (more than 50) at BibleGateway.com and found: only the King James Version (KJV) and a few others state "heaven" in the singular form in Genesis 1.

As most of my patients say, we have not finished enjoying all the good things on earth and are not ready to go to heaven yet. However, everyone will die eventually, and that is the fairest thing in the world. Since we have not known everything in life, how can we know for sure things after life? When our time comes, that is God's intention.

If people believe God is always merciful and fair, then there is no need to worry about how many heavens there are, which heaven is superior, how good the heaven is, or even how bad hell is. The Bible (Matthew 25:41) tells us that hell was not designed for human beings.[2] There should be no torture of humans in hell since a civilized society does not permit it. Thus, what matters is how we live on earth, not where we go when we leave this world.

We had better live in the moment despite what someone said hundreds or thousands of years ago. That way, we will stay healthy and peaceful, enjoying every moment of our lives on earth.

4. Wife

Always being there was the essential secret for a wife.

—Elizabeth von Arnim (1866 – 1941, Australian-Born British Novelist)

My wife, Jo, was my medical school classmate. We started to date at medical school more than three decades ago. During the last summer of medical school, we traveled together to Beijing, Shanghai, and Suzhou by train. When we stopped by each city, we stayed at hotels or in relatives' homes. Back then, we needed to carry a document issued by the medical school (stating the purpose and duration of the trip) in order to buy train tickets or check into hotels. Only married couples with marriage certificates in hand could live in the same room at a hotel. Since we had not married yet, we had to live in separate rooms when we stayed in hotels. Jo and I got married as soon as we graduated from medical school in 1982.

We moved to the U.S. to study and work in 1986. Good time always flies. Finally, we settled down in a small southern town after I finished my residency training in 1998. I worked as an internal medicine physician at a private clinic and earned a much better income than I did as a resident in training. After I had worked at my new job for two years, I became comfortable with my practice. Mom was staying with us during this time. We traveled a lot and went to the beach frequently. In December 2000, our whole family took a trip to Disney in Florida and had a great time there. Everybody was happy with the new life. But as the saying goes, great joy leads to sadness.

My Lucky Wife

"Ouch! I feel a lump in my breast!" Jo shouted one evening in December 2000 when we came back from the Disney trip.

"Really? Let me feel it," I said. I felt a vague tender lump in her left breast. When it comes to breast problems, I was not so concerned about them then. As early as 1997, Jo found a nodule in her right breast and went to a family doctor, who ordered a mammogram and lumpectomy. She was relieved to find that the breast nodule turned out to be a benign tumor (fibroadenoma). Since the spring of 2000, Jo started to experience breast fullness and tenderness from time to time. Nowadays, screening mammography is still controversial for women in their 40s. We did not take it lightly even though Jo was only 41 years old. A screening mammogram performed in October 2000 did not show any suspicious areas according to the radiologist's report.

"Be relaxed. You had a normal mammogram just two months ago. And breast cancer usually isn't painful. You're going to be okay."

"What're we going to do now?"

"We're going to schedule a diagnostic mammogram focusing on that spot."

A Chinese proverb says, "Human fortunes are as unpredictable as the weather." The diagnostic mammogram detected a suspicious nodule. Right away, Jo went to see the surgeon, Dr. Kramer, who recommended either an observation for six months or a lumpectomy. Jo chose to proceed with the lumpectomy, which was performed within one week.

The next day, after Jo underwent the surgery, I walked to the pathology department of the hospital to check on the pathological diagnosis of the breast biopsy. When I entered the pathology department, the pathologist spoke to me, "I'm sorry to tell you that your wife's breast tissue is positive for infiltrating ductal carcinoma."

"Really?!" I did not expect this bad news. Yet, it was not a complete surprise to me, since Dr. Kramer had called me after the lumpectomy to inform me that the breast tissue did not look good. I did not tell Jo what Dr. Kramer was so concerned about. My whole body was hot, and my head was overwhelmed with thoughts about the bad news.

"Could we look at the slides together?" I said to the pathologist. I was skilled in reading pathology slides thanks to my two years of residency training in pathology.

"Sure," he replied.

I sat down at a microscope with the pathologist. This microscope was equipped with multiple eyepieces so that several people could examine the same slide at the same time together. It brought me back to the time when I was receiving pathology residency training many years ago. During the pathology training, when we talked about a "good" case or an "interesting slide" at pathology meetings, it usually meant a "bad" diagnosis for a patient.

I started to shake while looking at my wife's breast tissue under the microscope even though I appeared to be calm outside. Although I had diagnosed breast cancer countless times under the supervision of attending pathologists, I never expected that I would examine my wife's biopsy slides. And it's malignant! It's cancer! Not till that day did I truly experience the shock when receiving a cancer diagnosis. The cancer diagnosis would change the life course of a patient and exert a great impact on her or his family.

"Any other alternative diagnoses?" I desperately asked as I looked at the devil cancer cells under the microscope. Now, the sheets of infiltrating cancer cells appeared to be packs of ravening wolves, and the enlarged nuclei with dark nucleoli looked like the hungry eyes of the wolves.

"I don't think so. The diagnosis is obvious," he said while showing me the sheets of cancer cells. "We can send the slides to wherever you want for a second opinion."

"Thank you very much for showing me the slides," I said sadly. "I'll let you know as soon as possible when I figure out where to send the slides."

After leaving the pathology department at the very end of the hospital building, I walked slowly through the long hallway to the wards to finish my noon rounds. I usually walked briskly in the hospital and ran up the stairs without taking an elevator. That day I took the elevator to the different floors and shuffled into the patient rooms. But still, I managed to maintain my usual smile when talking with the nurses and my patients.

Having finished rounding on my patients, I sat down at the nursing station to dictate my hospital notes. I was so nervous that I could not concentrate on the dictation and had to repeat my dictation many times with my slurred voice. I pressed the wrong buttons on the dictation phone several times with my trembling hands.

Jo knew I would go to the pathology department to get the results at noon. She was too anxious to wait for my phone call. It was around one o'clock in the afternoon when Jo paged me and asked me what the diagnosis was.

"The news is not good," I said sorrowfully. I had delivered bad news to patients numerous times. It was the first time I had to deliver bad news to my own family.

"I figured you must have had bad news. I know you would have called me already if you had good news." She started to cry.

"I'm coming home right now," I said and headed for home.

Jo was still weeping when I got home. "Look at the kids… they're so young," she said. "They are going to lose their mother soon. I won't be able to watch them grow up." Jason and Megan were nine and seven years old, respectively, during that time.

"Don't be so pessimistic," I said. "We've caught it early, and you're going to be cured."

Later that day, Jo and I thought about where to seek a second opinion to confirm the cancer diagnosis, and we decided to consult Dr. Jianhua Luo (our medical school classmate), who is a pathology professor at the University of Pittsburgh School of Medicine. The next day, I went to the pathology department and asked the secretary to send the slides to the University of Pittsburgh. Dr. Luo called us within a week and stated that the diagnosis was correct after the slides were examined by Dr. Luo himself and the department chair. We deeply appreciate Dr. Lou's invaluable help.

There was no more suspension. The cancer was real. It's dreadful! We were talking a major life-changing event here. Soon, our family life would be occupied by seeing specialists, undergoing surgeries, receiving chemotherapy, taking medications, having tests and follow-up visits, etc. I reduced my office hours to six hours and would take a three-hour noon break (from 11 a.m. to 2 p.m.) every day. Thus, I had enough time to help Jo go through the fight against her cancer while I could keep my job.

No matter how bad the news was, we had to accept the diagnosis of breast cancer and needed to take action. We went to see the surgeon, Dr. Kramer, for his advice. Dr. Kramer said that the next step would be to perform another wider lumpectomy or mastectomy, since the cancer cells had reached the margins of the dissected breast tissue. However, Jo would need to receive radiation therapy after surgery if she chose a lumpectomy. So she chose to have a mastectomy, which was done within a week. When the surgery was over, Jo stayed in the hospital for two days. Jo's brother, Willie, traveled from California to our town to help us out during the surgery period. Willie has always been a great brother, for he also took care of me when I was wounded in a car accident in 1989.

I went to the pathology lab to watch the pathologist perform a gross dissection of my wife's breast tissue after the mastectomy. I smelled the familiar odor of formalin evaporated from the specimens. During my pathology residency, I had dissected many breast tissues removed during surgery.

"They look clean," the pathologist said while dissecting the breast tissue and lymph nodes on the cutting board inside a fume hood.

We prayed that the lymph nodes would be negative for cancer. Then again, it was just more bad news. I went to the pathology department at noon the next day and read the slides with the pathologist, who showed me the lymph nodes with metastatic cancer cells. Three of the lymph nodes were positive for metastatic cancer, indicating the cancer had spread at least locally. It meant that Jo had to undergo chemotherapy because of the spreading cancer.

On my way home I was wondering *why bad things happen to good people*. Jo was so young, still three months shy of her 42nd birthday. She was hearty, witty, always ready to help others, and maybe too candid sometimes. With no family history of breast cancer, she ate healthy food, took no medication, and even practiced some Qi-gong (a Chinese system of postures, exercises, breathing techniques, and meditations). Why her? My father lost his battle with liver cancer just a few years ago at the age of 67. I feared that I might lose my wife to cancer too. As people say, "Life is fair, because it's unfair to everyone."

After I had got home, I searched the internet to learn about the latest recommendations for breast cancer chemotherapy, primarily those published by MD Anderson Cancer Center, Sloan-Kettering Cancer Center, and NIH. NIH (National Institutes of Health) had just published the new guideline for breast cancer therapy two months earlier.[1]

Afterward, Jo and I went to see the oncologist, Dr. Hall, in town. He was a very friendly doctor, who discussed in detail with us about the chemo regimen, and it was consistent with what I had learned online and from the new NIH guideline. We agreed with him to do the regimen.

Jo went for a whole body scan to investigate if breast cancer had spread to other areas of the body. Fortunately, the scan turned out to be negative. Before the chemotherapy started, Jo was referred to see a cardiologist and underwent echocardiography to evaluate her heart's function and structure because the chemotherapy could cause damage to her heart. Then, Jo underwent another surgery for the placement of a perfusion port (port-a-cath).

A **port-a-cath** is a small medical appliance that is installed beneath the skin. A catheter connects the port to a large, deep vein. Drugs or fluids can be injected into the vein through the port, and blood samples can also be drawn from there. The port is usually used by patients with difficulty accessing peripheral veins or patients receiving chemotherapy, and it can stay in the body for years if not infected or malfunctioned.

Finally, she went to a big city nearby to buy a wig, for her hair would fall out during chemotherapy. Jo needed to receive four cycles of chemo; each one was separated by three weeks. The modern chemotherapy is better tolerated by patients with cancer, and they can just receive chemo at a doctor's office most of the time. Janie, our cousin, traveled from England to help her out. Then Jo's sister, Wendy, came from California to care for Jo after Janie went back to England. We'll never forget their help and kindness.

"The chemo feels like nothing," Jo said. She felt pretty normal after the first cycle of chemo, with all her hair and a good appetite. But before long, Jo started to develop fatigue, nausea, vomiting, and a poor appetite after the second cycle of chemo. She lost all her hair and had to wear her wig when going out. After the third cycle, the real misery came. She developed severe nausea, vomiting, fatigue, and a low white cell count. Sometimes, she was too weak to say anything and too nauseated to eat anything.

"I don't want to do it anymore," she said weakly.

"Just one more cycle," I said. "I hope you can finish it. The final decision is yours. You still have a few more days to reconsider. Just relax this time."

"Okay, okay. I'll try," she said.

As the white cell count had dropped significantly between the third and fourth cycles, Jo needed to take antibiotics to prevent infections. She also received Neupogen injections to stimulate white cell production. Finally, she bravely underwent the last cycle of chemo and recovered uneventfully. Of course, it took months for Jo's hair to grow back again.

One day, Jo was wearing her wig when she walked to the school to pick up our kids. One of our friends did not know about my wife's chemo and asked, "Where did you get your hair done? It looks so wonderful."

"It's a wig! I just finished my chemo for breast cancer," Jo said.

"I'm sorry to hear that. But it really looks good."

As a matter of fact, Jo felt uncomfortable and hot when wearing her wig, and it also irritated her scalp. Fortunately, Jo had regrown most of her hair six months after the chemo and did not need to wear her wig anymore. We traveled to China as usual the next year. Jo developed gross hematuria (the presence of blood in the urine) after she came back from China. It resolved after antibiotic treatment. However, she had another episode of hematuria after the next trip to China. She was concerned and went to see her oncologist, who ordered a CT of her abdomen and pelvis. The CT revealed a uterine mass, which was consistent with a fibroid, a common benign tumor.

Dr. Hall, the oncologist, recommended the removal of her uterus and ovaries for safety. We knew that removal of ovaries had been used to treat metastatic breast cancer for years. Therefore, the hysterectomy and oophorectomy would be a good option to get rid of the unknown uterine tumor and to prevent the breast cancer from spreading. Jo took Dr. Hall's advice to undergo the surgery in 2003. Her sister Wendy flew over again to help her during the surgery period. The surgery went smoothly, and Jo developed only urinary retention, which resolved quickly.

After the chemotherapy, Jo took Tamoxifen (an estrogen antagonist used to treat breast cancer) for three years. Eventually, new aromatase inhibitors (newer medications used in the treatment of breast cancer) came on the market, and Jo switched from Tamoxifen to an aromatase inhibitor. She could not tolerate the first inhibitor because of severe body pain. Then Jo tried another one, which was well tolerated. She completed five years of treatment with an aromatase inhibitor after Tamoxifen.

Jo is very grateful for the excellent cancer treatment, which was available even in a small town in the United States. Jo was able to finish a lumpectomy, mastectomy, and port-a-cath placement surgery in three weeks and then start chemo in the fourth week. She had received the most current chemo regimen at the time, according to the newly published guideline by NIH in November 2000.[1] And she could take the new breast cancer drug, the aromatase inhibitor, which had just hit the shelf.

As expected, the U.S. is ranked number one in the world for breast cancer treatment.[2] Our local hospital has a policy that all newly diagnosed breast cancer patients can be seen by a surgeon within two weeks. When reflecting about her breast cancer ordeal, Jo owes her health to timely surgeries, the latest chemo regimen, the newest oral drug, strong support from family members, and the excellent services provided by her doctors, nurses, and other healthcare personnel.

Jo feels lucky to be alive and healthy. She is determined to enjoy every moment of her life: Nobody knows what will happen next.

Everything happens for a reason even though the reason is often unknown. I guess this is destiny.

One day while sitting and chatting with Jo in the bedroom, I accidentally looked at the framed art print (*A woman sleeping in a red chair* by Pablo Picasso) on the wall. Suddenly, I was astonished to find out: the woman in the picture had only one breast! Jo bought this picture at a local craft store one year before her diagnosis of breast cancer. Although I had looked at it numerous times, I had never paid attention to this woman's breast until that day. Maybe, *you will never appreciate what you have until you lose it.*

We both exclaimed, "Did we hang the wrong picture?!"

As the cliché goes, "Every cloud has a silver lining." Going through all these events changed my perspective as a doctor. For example, I had no idea how uncomfortable it was for a patient to sit on the edge of the exam table and wait for her or his doctor to come in until I accompanied Jo to her doctor's visits. When sitting on the exam table with her feet dangling and no back support, Jo felt woozy after a long wait, and sometimes she felt chilly and got goose bumps in a skimpy hospital garment. Apparently, a lot of elderly people have difficulty just climbing up onto the exam table, and they may fall off it. (One of my patients even developed cardiac arrest while sitting on the exam table and waiting for her doctor at another clinic.) Ever afterward, I told my medical assistants or nurses to let my patients sit and wait in the chair instead of on the exam table.

The doctors who treated Jo have served as great role models of professionalism for me and inspired me to abide by the Platinum Rule of Medicine: *Treat every patient like you'd want a member of your family treated.*[3]

Wedding Ring

Few people wore wedding rings in China in the early 1980s. Even after living in the U.S. for years, we still do not have a ring. However, being without a wedding ring in the U.S. can lead to some embarrassing moments.

A 65-year-old lady came to see me for an office visit, soon after I began to practice at the new clinic.

"How can I help you? You look really healthy," I asked.

"I just come by for a checkup," she replied. "I accompanied my husband to see Dr. Vaughan that day, and I saw you in the hallway. I know you are the new doctor here. That's the reason I am here today."

As usual, I took her history, performed a physical examination, and reviewed her medications. At the end of the visit, she finally asked, "Are you married?"

"Yes. And I have two children," I replied.

"I thought you were single, as I noticed you did not wear a ring that day. Actually, I wanted to introduce my daughter to you. Anyway, it's nice meeting you."

She has never seen me again since that visit. I realized that she only saw me for the sake of her daughter. Without a ring, I got myself into trouble again.

A female patient patted my hand and said teasingly during an office visit, "Are you married? You don't wear a ring. You know I need a man to take care of me."

"Yes, I'm married, even though I don't have a ring on my finger," I pulled back my hand quickly and pointed to my head while smiling. "My ring is here in my brain, you know. My wife and I got married in China in the 1980s. Back then, not only did people not wear rings, but they might even get into trouble if they did."

"Oh, really?"

"It's true. In addition, a Chinese woman keeps her last name after she gets married. My wife still keeps her family name, Wang."

"This is new to me. I've really learned something today."

"I hope you will find a good man soon."

"I only want you," she laughed.

"Anyway, I'm married. What can I do?" I laughed too.

"Okay, okay. I'll find another man then," she giggled.

In a few years, she came to the clinic as usual. She put out her hand and said happily, "Please look at my ring, Dr. Li."

"You are married now. Congratulations."

She continued to be my patient for more than 12 years until I left town. I remembered that she had worn her ring all the time since then, while I still have not bought my own wedding ring after all these years. Nowadays, all the younger couples have wedding rings in China. I guess I am just too lazy or stubborn to change. Since I have become older with fewer and grayer hairs, I haven't had any of these awkward moments in a long time. Nevertheless, I did learn more and more about American wives. Not only is the ring important, but also the name.

Certainly, people have difficulty pronouncing Chinese names or differentiating between Chinese last names and first names. Yet I did not expect an awkward "name" moment would happen to me this way in the U.S. Since I am a women's rights advocate, I do not like to see a woman lose her identity after she gets married. When my daughter Megan was born, I wanted her to use my wife's last name (Wang) instead of mine (Li). So my daughter is named Megan Wang.

We ran into trouble one time when we traveled to California. When we took Jason and Megan to do rock climbing, we needed to sign a parental consent form before our children could climb the wall.

"Are you Megan's father? She has a different last name…Wang," the attendant asked while looking at my driver's license.

"Yes, she just uses her mother's name," I replied.

"That's weird," she looked at me suspiciously. Eventually, she was okay with the consent and let Megan do rock climbing.

"It's you. I thought I was seeing somebody else," I said to Mrs. Rice when I entered the room. "Did you change your name?"

Mrs. Rice (formerly Mrs. Riley) came in for an office visit. Mrs. Rice was 82 years old with mild diabetes and hypertension. Her late husband, Mr. Riley (also my patient), died five years earlier.

"I got married again recently," Mrs. Rice said. "Now I realize it was a big mistake to change my name. I still haven't finished the name change for my credit card, bank account, driving license, etc."

"In China, people don't change names after getting married," I said playfully. "You should have consulted me before changing your name. Please make sure not to change the name of your house to your new husband's name by accident."

"I should have talked to you about it first," she smiled. "Well, I did take care of my property issues before the marriage."

"That's good for you and your family."

Sometimes, elderly people may disappoint their family members if they do not handle their financial issues properly before marrying again.

Both Mr. and Mrs. Snow, in their 80s, were my patients. Mrs. Snow had died from heart and kidney failure one year earlier. Mr. Snow came to the clinic to see me for a routine follow-up visit two months after Mrs. Snow passed away. Other than having hypertension and requiring some assistance with Viagra (a drug used to treat erectile dysfunction), he was healthy. Nonetheless, I noticed that he had lost 20 pounds over the past four months. I do not like to see weight loss in elderly people.

"How are you doing, Mr. Snow?" I asked. "You are losing weight."

"Maybe I was busy taking care of my wife all that time," he replied. "Actually, I'm feeling better since I lost some weight. I can walk faster than before." He flexed his right elbow to show me his bulging biceps.

"I am always very careful whenever someone loses weight. I know you quit smoking more than 10 years ago. I am still concerned. I'll order a CT scan of your chest to make sure you don't have lung cancer."

"Do I need that? I'm doing fine."

"I think you need that."

"Okay, let's do it then."

Unfortunately, he was found to have a large mass in the lung. He saw the lung doctor within a week and received a bronchoscopy with biopsy, which showed unresectable lung cancer. Then he started to undergo chemotherapy and radiation therapy. In the meantime, he got married while receiving cancer treatment. He continued to ask for prescriptions for Viagra and told me that Viagra did work. He got sicker and sicker during the last few months of his life. He was hospitalized by his oncologists many times. Sometimes, I stopped by his room on the oncology floor to have a chat, and I saw his new wife with him all the time. He did not respond to the treatment and died in the hospital, within one year after his first wife's death.

About two months after Mr. Snow died, I received a letter from his son, who lived in a northern state. In the letter, his son wanted to know if his father had any mental disorder like dementia six months before he passed away. The letter stated that his father, Mr. Snow, married the woman just a few months before he died. At the time, Mr. Snow was already diagnosed with incurable terminal lung cancer, and receiving chemo and radiation. Now his new wife had inherited all of his properties, including Mr. Snow's house. I quickly checked the office notes and hospital records, but I could not find any psychiatric symptoms related to dementia.

I called Mr. Snow's son and told him that I could not find any documented dementia in Mr. Snow's record. I stated that he could request all the medical records to send to him or his lawyer for review. I also informed him that Mr. Snow's new wife accompanied Mr. Snow in the hospital and at the office visits, taking care of him during a difficult time in his life, which lasted eight months. Was it fair for her to take over all of his life savings without anything left to his son, who lived far away in another state and could not come back home to care for his father? It depends on whom you ask. Would the woman still have married him if all the money matters were settled before the marriage? Who knows? I saw Mr. Snow's new wife once at the clinic after Mr. Snow died. She has not come back for medical care since then. In addition, I have not heard anything from Mr. Snow's son ever since that phone conversation five years ago.

Still, some people do undergo planning before the remarriage. Mr. Solomon was an 85-year-old man who married a woman after his wife (also my patient) died of an illness three months earlier. I was a doctor to his whole family. His son told me that they asked their father to sign all the papers to take care of property problems before the marriage. I had never met the newly wed woman and did not know if she was happy about the financial arrangement. This elderly man died just within one year after his wedding.

Often, I have seen many families fight for the inheritance, and I have needed to provide statements to explain patients' conditions from time to time. Luckily, I did not need to deal with this issue for Solomon's family.

Be prepared and you won't be sorry.

Wife Forever

Mr. Keith, 85 years old, looked healthy and strong, with even more hair than me. He told me that he traveled to the beach to perform in a band every other week and was still earning good money. He bragged about still having at least three girlfriends at the same time.

"How can you get to know so many women?" I asked curiously.

"I can meet them anywhere, at churches, at grocery stores, and even on the street," he said. "I can show you some tricks if you want."

"No, thanks," I smiled.

"Just let me know if you change your mind, I'll fix you up," he laughed. "You help keep me healthy. So, I should help you too, Doc."

"Thank you very much," I laughed. "I'll keep it in mind. By the way, how can you deal with so many women at the same time at this age?"

"No problem. You can handle it as long as you manage your time well."

Ironically, Mr. Keith had shown me that he failed to manage his time well on one occasion.

A few years ago, Mr. Keith miraculously escaped death after falling seriously ill. He was admitted to the hospital for fever and abdominal pain. His problem was presumably caused by **diverticulitis**, leading to sepsis and acute renal failure (kidneys stop working).

Diverticulitis commonly affects middle-aged and elderly people, resulting from inflammation of pouches (diverticula) within the bowel wall. The formation of bowel pouches is described as diverticulosis, and it usually occurs within the large intestine (colon) or occasionally in the small intestine. Diverticular diseases usually affect the left side of the colon (the sigmoid colon, 95%) in the west, while it commonly involves the right side in Asian and African countries.

The inflamed diverticula can break open to cause an infection of the lining of the abdominal cavity (peritoneum) and lead to peritonitis, which can be life-threatening. Other complications include bowel obstruction (narrowing of the bowel) and fistula formation (an abnormal connection between an organ and adjacent structure). Treatment for diverticulitis usually requires bowel rest, use of antibiotics, and other supportive measures. Occasionally, surgery is required in severe cases of peritonitis, abscess, or fistula.

In Mr. Keith's case, the bacteria entered the bloodstream from the infected diverticula and caused sepsis, a whole-body inflammation (a systemic inflammatory response syndrome or SIRS). Sepsis can lead to multiple organ dysfunctions, including lung damage (respiratory failure, acute respiratory distress syndrome), brain malfunction (encephalopathy), liver failure (disruption of metabolic functions), kidney failure, heart failure, and potential death. Millions of people in the world die from sepsis each year. Despite Mr. Keith receiving IV antibiotics and other treatments, he developed kidney failure and liver dysfunction with little urine output. His prognosis did not look good at the time.

One day, I was talking to both Mr. Keith and a woman at his bedside about his condition. I assumed this was his wife because she was with him most of the time while in the hospital or at office visits. Then, another woman entered Mr. Keith's room. I recognized her as one of my patients. So I spoke to her, "How are you doing, Mrs. Keith?"

"I'm fine. Thank you," Mrs. Keith said. "I've come here to see my husband."

"Is he your husband!?" All of a sudden, I realized that she had the same last name as Mr. Keith. However, this was the first time she had come to see him after he had been in the hospital for three days.

"Yes. Ha-ha, Dr. Li, you didn't know that?" she smiled.

"How could I know that? You both have never come to see me together."

"I'm here now."

When Mrs. Keith noticed another woman sitting at the bedside with her husband, she shouted to her across the room, "Who are you?!" Mrs. Keith walked toward the other woman angrily. The two women approached each other and stood face to face. Then they started to stare and yell at each other in a language I did not understand. I did not want to get involved and walked out of the room quickly. Even with the closed door, I still heard from the hallway the loud arguments inside the room. I realized that Mrs. Keith was the patient's legal wife and that the other woman was only a girlfriend, whom I had been speaking to about the conditions of her "husband" every day. Fortunately, there was only a civilized verbal altercation between the two women. If this incident had occurred in China, there might have been a physical fight. Ten minutes later, Mrs. Keith walked out of the room with a long face.

Luckily, Mr. Keith did not develop severe peritonitis or bowel obstruction. No surgery was necessary. While he continued to receive IV antibiotics and other supportive treatments, he was put on hemodialysis every other day for two weeks. Unexpectedly, Mr. Keith was so strong and resilient that his general conditions improved gradually, as well as his kidney functions. He started to pass more urine and eat again as his abdominal pain subsided. Eventually, he did not require hemodialysis anymore, and the dialysis catheter located on his neck was removed. He stayed in the hospital for two more weeks for rehabilitation, and then he was discharged home. It took about two more months for his kidney and liver functions to return to normal. It was uncommon for an 80-year-old man to survive sepsis and come out of a kidney machine with a complete recovery. Mr. Keith was truly a lucky and tough man with many girlfriends.

In fact, all three people in the room that day were my patients. When Mrs. Keith, the lawful wife, came to see me again in the office, I joked, "What an exciting moment we had in the hospital that day!"

"It sure was. Dr. Li, you saw it," she laughed.

"I was so embarrassed. I did not know you were his wife until then."

"He moved out of the house many years ago. Now, he lives in an apartment somewhere."

"You didn't know he had another woman, did you?" I asked.

"I knew he might have had somebody. But I never saw any of his women face to face until that day in the hospital."

"Are you still married to him legally?"

"Yes. We have been married for almost 60 years," she said. "We haven't divorced. I keep the house and other benefits. We still talk with each other occasionally. He comes back to the house to pick up his mail once a week."

"That's good, as long as you are both happy," I said. "You have your own life while he has his girlfriends."

"Yes, you are right. My son loves me and supports me too."

Mr. Keith's girlfriend continued to accompany Mr. Keith to the clinic for medical care regularly. Occasionally, she came by herself. I never mentioned anything to her about the hospital confrontation.

Sometimes, things are just better off remaining unsettled.

Although some couples have lived together for many years, they may not trust each other in some ways. Mr. Arthur, 72 years old, was admitted to the ICU because of hypertensive emergency and heart failure. His wife was standing at his bedside in the ICU when I made rounds. Since I had never seen her in the clinic with Mr. Arthur, I asked Mr. Arthur if it was alright to discuss his conditions in front of his wife. I expected that he would be okay with it like most patients. Surprisingly, he said firmly, "No."

His wife became very upset and left the room right away.

After I had finished talking with Mr. Arthur, I walked out of the ICU and saw Mrs. Arthur crying in the hallway.

"Mrs. Arthur, I am sorry that your husband did not want you to hear about his conditions," I said to her. "I can't say anything about his health conditions to you owing to the privacy rule of the HIPAA."

The Health Insurance Portability and Accountability Act of 1996 (HIPAA) is the public law regarding an individual's right to purchase medical insurance, the standard for electronic health records, and the privacy protection of health information. I can be fined or even imprisoned if I violate the HIPAA.

"I understand," she said. "It's not your problem. I'm just upset."

"Maybe your husband just doesn't want you to worry about him. He cares about you."

"Do you think so?"

"He did not actually say that," I said. "At least, you'll feel better if you think that way."

"You might be right."

Mrs. Arthur was lucky. At least, Mr. Arthur admitted that she was his wife. Some women are not this lucky

Mr. Dillon was an 80-year-old man with dementia. His demented status fluctuated. Sometimes, he behaved like a normal person. Every now and then, he was really insane. Three years earlier, he was admitted to the hospital as a result of a new stroke. With a fast recovery, he started to walk again after three days in the hospital. He sneaked out of the hospital at midnight without notice. Having walked six blocks away from the hospital, he wandered around in a downtown parking lot. The policemen found him and brought him back to the hospital.

One day, the secretary asked if I would see Mrs. Dillon as she had walked into the clinic and wanted to talk to me privately. I thought that she must have been concerned about her husband's medical problems.

"No problem," I said to the secretary. "Please put her in a room. I'll talk to her after I finish seeing this patient."

"What can I help you with, ma'am?" I asked Mrs. Dillon (not my patient) when I entered the room.

"Mr. Dillon said that I am not his wife," she cried.

"Are you married to him legally?"

"Not legally. But I have been living with him and taking care of him for more than eight years."

"I don't know anything about the legal issue of your marriage," I said. "You'd better talk to your lawyer about it. All I can do is document in the chart that you have accompanied Mr. Dillon in the hospital and at all office visits. Is that okay with you?" Although I knew that common-law marriage (informal marriage) was still being contracted in this state, I did not know anything about the criteria for it.

"That's okay. Thank you very much."

About one year had passed since then. Mr. Dillon came in for an office visit accompanied by his daughter, instead of his wife.

"Where is Mrs. Dillon?" I asked curiously.

"She died from a stroke recently," his daughter answered.

"Really?" I was surprised.

Mr. Dillon, now 84 years old, was living in an assisted living facility with a stable mental status when I left town. His common-law wife had passed away before him. One time, Mr. Dillon told me that he had a new girlfriend.

"How can you have a girlfriend?" I asked. "You're living in the assisted living facility."

"She doesn't stay there with me," he smiled. "She comes to see me once a week,"

"What do you do when she comes?"

"She takes me out for lunch," he said happily.

As the saying goes, a man makes his plan and then God decides the outcome. Life is unpredictable.

On the contrary, wives tend to continue to care for their loved ones no matter what happens.

"You've lost a lot of weight. What's going on?" I asked Mr. Palmer, a quadriplegic patient who lived at an assisted living facility.

"I don't like the food there," said Mr. Palmer. "My wife only comes to visit me every two to three weeks."

"Does she bring some good food to you every time?"

"Yes. But I can only enjoy her good food once every few weeks. And I want to leave there and go home."

"You can go home anytime if your wife agrees. Please ask her to come here with you next visit."

"Okay."

True to his word, he came in with his wife at the next office visit. Mrs. Palmer was a lovely and intelligent woman.

"Your husband said he only likes the food you cook," I said to her.

"I know that," Mrs. Palmer said with a smile. "I'm a teacher. I'm busy all the time, even taking extra courses for my master's degree."

"Your husband is losing weight. And he wants you to take him home."

"I just can't take care of him at home. Hopefully, I can take him home after I finish my degree courses."

"Then could you try to see him once a week and bring him more good food each time?" I smiled. "Let him eat your delicious food for a few days each week."

"Okay. I'll try, Dr. Li," she smiled too. Since then, Mr. Palmer told me that his wife has seen him every week so far, and he was happy about it.

"You are losing weight. Why?" I asked a patient of mine with diabetes and rheumatoid arthritis, Mr. Ruth, who looked much thinner than before.

"I'm too lazy to cook my meals," Mr. Ruth replied. "I eat only one meal a day most of the time. And I don't like the food I cook either."

"I thought you had a wife."

"Yes. Anyway, we are separate now. She's gone out with another man."

"Does she think somebody is better than you?" I smiled.

"Maybe so," he laughed. "She still comes back to see me and cook for me from time to time."

"Really? Bring her here next time," I said.

"You are right," he said. "Dr. Li, you definitely need to talk to her about this."

"No problem."

As expected, he came in with his wife at the next visit.

"Your husband said he cannot cook the food he likes," I talked to Mrs. Ruth. "He wants you to help him because he has lost a lot of weight."

"Okay," Mrs. Ruth smiled and nodded.

"Could you please go to see him more? He often forgets to inject his insulin. His diabetes has been out of control recently."

"Okay," she nodded again and did not say anything else.

Mr. Ruth told me that his separate wife had come back to him more often since then, and he had been eating better. He gained weight and had better control of his diabetes.

Quite frequently, anxious wives would drag their stubborn husbands to the clinic for a checkup.

"This is my husband, Dr. Li," said Mrs. Howell, introducing a man who came in for a new patient visit.

"Your husband?" I looked puzzled, thinking that Mrs. Howell might have married again. I recalled she came in with another man a few months earlier. At that time, she told me that the man was her husband.

"No. This is my ex-husband!" she giggled when she noticed the puzzling look on my face.

"Oh, I see."

"I still check on him at times. He hasn't seen a doctor for many years. So, I brought him here to see you."

Sometimes, husbands can do the same as wives do.

I asked Mrs. Ingram, "You come in alone today. How is your husband doing?"

"He is doing well," Mrs. Ingram said, "He is at work today. Actually, we are divorced."

"What has happened? He came here with you just three months ago."

"We have divorced for 10 years."

"Ten years already?"

"That is true. He moved out a long time ago, and he lives separately. However, he helps me out often while I live with and take care of his mother. We're still good friends."

Mrs. Marriott came in for a walk-in visit. I asked, "What can I help you with today?"

She said, "I have been congested and coughing for two weeks. Please help me knock it out because I'm going to get married next week."

"So you're going to get married again?"

"Believe it or not, this is the third time I am marrying the same man," she smiled.

"Your husband still thinks you are the best wife in the world."

"You're exactly right," she laughed.

LIFE AND MEDICINE

An old Chinese proverb says, "A day together as husband and wife means endless devotion the rest of your life." Wives are just great!

5. Diabetes

The good physician treats the disease; the great physician treats the patient who has the disease.

—William Osler (1849-1919, Canadian Physician and Professor of Medicine)

The secret of the care of the patient is in caring for the patient.

—Francis Weld Peabody (1881–1927, American Physician)

O ccasionally, patients ask me, "How come you look so fit? Chinese people don't have diabetes, do they?"

"Yes, they do have diabetes," I say.

"Really?"

"Actually, diabetes is now more common in China than in the U.S."

"I didn't know that."

"My mother lives in China, and she also has diabetes," I say. "Since I have a family history of diabetes, I try to keep fit to prevent diabetes."

"You look good then."

"I need to work harder," I smiled. "Look at me... I still have a big belly."

"No way!"

It is estimated that 11.6 percent of Chinese adults (about 113.9 million people) are suffering from diabetes, according to a recent JAMA (Journal of American Medical Association) article published in 2013.[1] Diabetes rates in China have increased significantly over the past decades. Less than one percent of the Chinese population had diabetes in the 1980s. Nevertheless, the rate of diabetes had risen to 5.5 percent in 2001, 9.7 percent in 2007 and 11.6 percent in 2010. China's rate of this disease not only has surpassed that of the U.S. but become the highest in the world.

Statistics about Diabetes in the U.S. quoted from American Diabetes Association: *In 2012, 29.1 million Americans, or 9.3% of the population, had diabetes. Prevalence in seniors (age 65 and older), 25.9%, or 11.8 million seniors. New Cases: 1.7 million new diagnoses/year.*[2]

The rates of diagnosed diabetes by race/ethnic background are:

7.6% of non-Hispanic whites

9.0% of Asian Americans

12.8% of Hispanics

13.2% of non-Hispanic blacks

15.9% of American Indians/Alaskan Natives

Mom Has Diabetes

Mom, Yueyou, has been obese most of her life with a nickname of "Fat Yo." In China, "Fat" is nothing offensive. I remember one of my father's friends was called "Fat Uncle Chen." Mom, a farmer's daughter, had grown up in the country and had never gone to school when she was young. Only her brother had the chance to go to school. Mom and her sisters stayed at home and farmed. It was very common 70-80 years ago that poor families supported only their sons to go to school. However, Mom proudly said to me several times, "I make more money than your father even though your father had read so many books." It was true that Mom earned more money when Dad was politically oppressed and lost his job in his thirties. He had been sent to work at a labor camp earning a minimum wage.

At eighteen years of age, Mom started to work at a department store, which was located very far from our home. She needed to take 1.5-hour bus ride to and from work every day. Even though having attended some classes for illiterates and learned basic Chinese words, she cannot write a letter or read a newspaper. Through hard work, Mom was promoted to manager and awarded the title as "State Model Worker". She retired at the age of 50. This is the normal retirement age of a woman in China. In addition to her regular pension, she receives a monthly retirement bonus thanks to her "State Model Worker" status. Now, at 82 years of age, Mom has retired for 32 years, and she continues to enjoy her retirement.

Mom wakes up at five every morning to go to a nearby park where she meets other elderly people, exercises and socializes. Afterward, the group goes to the tea house together for breakfast about 6:30 a.m. and continues to chat until 8-9 a.m. Later, Mom rests at home and eats lunch at noon. After lunch, she usually walks to her neighbor's apartment to play **Mahjong** until 5-6 p.m. **Mahjong** is a Chinese game played by four people with 144 domino-like tiles marked in suits.

Mom hires a housekeeper to cook and clean for her. The housekeeper is also paid to stay with Mom at night. The housekeeper is her neighbor and has become like a family member through years of friendship. Mom watches TV with the housekeeper in the evening. After finishing watching TV, Mom and her housekeeper sleep in their separate rooms. When morning comes, my mother will enjoy another busy and joyful day.

Mom has experienced chronic knee pain for the past few years. I bought several bottles of glucosamine at Sam's Club and took them to China for her to try. Glucosamine is an amino sugar used as an over-the-counter dietary supplement for treatment of joint pain. This product is distributed by American companies. I suspect the ingredients are possibly imported from China. "American glucosamine is good. I can walk better with less pain," she said after trying those pills for a few months. As long as it works, no one cares who makes it or what randomized clinical trials have shown. At least, she does not need to have a knee replacement. Very few people in China undergo knee replacement surgeries. And, in her 80s, Mom can walk up three flights of stairs many times a day!

Mom is very kind and smiles all the time. It seems that nothing has bothered her in her whole life. And everybody likes her. One of my father's friends said to me, "Your mother is probably the only one person who is liked by everybody. I've never seen her get angry at anyone since I've known her for more than 60 years."

In my memory, Mom got furious once 45 years ago when she came back from work and found some government officials moving valuable items from our home. Back then, my grandfather was said to have committed embezzlement from the store where he worked. There was no legal procedure that proved this. The government officials claimed that my grandfather stole about 400 dollars from the store, and they had come to seize our property. Mom shouted at the officials, "Stop! I won't let you move anymore!" It was funny that those officials did stop removing the items from inside the house without argument. Then they left for good with some items that had already removed from the house.

At the age of 65, my grandfather not only lost his job but also was sent to a remote rural area, where he was forced to do manual farm work. Within six months, he suffered a bad stroke and became paralyzed. He came back to the city and stayed at home for the rest of his life. He could not get his pension since he had been fired for "dishonorable behavior". Grandfather passed away at the age of 70 – only one week after the death of my grandmother. My grandmother passed away, also at the age of 70, during her sleep due to emphysema caused by long-term smoking.

It is unlikely that the facts about my grandfather will be uncovered. I have not seen any official statement on his embezzlement. There were millions of similar cases during the tumultuous period.

Mom came to the U.S. to live with us after my father died. She had stayed in the U.S. for about three years. With her experience in farming, Mom grew a lot of vegetables in the yard. Owing to a more healthy diet and exercise through gardening, she lost at least 20-30 pounds while in the U.S.

Then, Mom went back to China because American life was too boring for her. When Mom returned to China, people said to her, "How did you lose so much weight living in America? You look too thin. You must have had a hard time there."

In the south, if you weigh less than 200 pounds, people may say to you, "Are you sick?" Some of my patients who retired from the northern states said to me at their first visits, "The people here are so heavy."

"Don't worry about it. You will become one of them sooner or later," I told them. These retirees from the north typically gain 20-40 pounds after settling here. Two of my patients had gained up to 100 pounds within three years. One lady, in her 70s, had gained 30 pounds within two years after coming down here from New York. She said to me, "Dr. Li, you've got to do something to help me lose weight. Otherwise, how can I find a man?"

"I don't think I can help too much with your weight," I said. "My mother is also heavy. I can't even help her lose weight."

She asked in surprise, "Your mother is overweight too?"

"Yes. She has diabetes like you. Since you live in the south, where most people weigh the same as you, it is very difficult, maybe even impossible, to lose any weight here."

Mom had regained 30 pounds within one year after returning to China. One day, she looked confused and sluggish while playing

Mahjong. The relatives sent her to the hospital, and she was found to have blood glucose level of over 500 mg/dL (27.8 mmol/L). She was diagnosed with new-onset type 2 diabetes and hospitalized with insulin treatment for about one week. She was discharged home with oral antidiabetic medications.

Diabetes is diagnosed if glucose level is elevated to the diagnostic range of diabetes: fasting sugar levels are equal to or higher than 126 mg/dL (7 mmol/L) or random sugar levels equal to or higher than 200 mg/dL (11.1 mmol/L) with typical diabetic symptoms.[3] **A1C** (higher or equal to 6.5%) test is also used to diagnose diabetes.

There are four types of diabetes: type 1 diabetes, type 2 diabetes, gestational diabetes mellitus (GDM), and uncommon specific diabetes caused by many disorders involving the pancreas (such as genetic defects, cystic fibrosis, surgical removal of pancreas, and adverse drug effects).[3]

Type 2 diabetes mellitus is manifested as hyperglycemia (high blood sugar) resulting from insulin resistance and relative lack of insulin. On the contrary, type 1 diabetes mellitus is characterized by an absolute lack of insulin due to the destruction of pancreatic Beta cells. Type 2 diabetes comprises more than 90 percent of all diabetes cases while the remainder of 10 percent is essentially type 1 diabetes mellitus and gestational diabetes (diabetes during pregnancy).

Insulin resistance refers to the unresponsiveness of cells to the normal actions of the hormone insulin. The insulin cannot be utilized effectively, resulting in hyperglycemia, which is high blood glucose level. Beta cells in the pancreas are responsible for insulin production in the body and subsequently increase their production of insulin to compensate for the insulin resistance. **Metformin**, an antidiabetic drug, not only decreases blood sugar levels by suppressing glucose production by the liver, but also reduces insulin resistance by enhancing peripheral glucose uptake.

When I traveled to China to see Mom, I asked, "How is your diabetes doing, Mom?"

"Don't need to worry about my diabetes," Mom said. "So many people get it in China now. Quite a few of the old people I know in the park have diabetes."

I looked at her outpatient record booklet with laboratory reports inside and her pill bottles. I noted that she was taking glyburide (antidiabetic), irbesartan (antihypertensive), atorvastatin (lipid-lowering drug) and aspirin. Her diabetes was under reasonable control with A1C of 7.4%.

The **A1C** test is a common blood test, which is conveniently done through a finger stick by a hand-held meter in many outpatient clinics. It takes a few minutes to obtain an A1C test result, which can be used to diagnose diabetes and monitor how well one's diabetes is managed. A1C has many other names, including glycated hemoglobin, glycosylated hemoglobin, hemoglobin A1C and HbA1c. The A1C value represents one's average blood sugar level for the past two to three months. High A1C level indicates the poor blood sugar control. When an A1C level of 6.5 percent or higher is found, diabetes is diagnosed. For most people with diabetes, the common treatment target is an A1C level of 7 percent or less. Higher A1C targets should be considered in some patients. Usually, the higher your A1C level, the higher your risk of suffering long-term diabetes complications. But, the A1C targets should be set according to individuals' condition and adjusted accordingly. The lower A1C targets, the higher incidence of hypoglycemia (low sugar level). Hypoglycemia is dangerous and can cause confusion, seizure, loss of consciousness and even death.

"You'd better take metformin because you are overweight," I said to Mom. "And metformin causes less low sugar reaction and better outcomes."

"The people in the park said that my diabetes pill is good," she said. "I don't want to change it."

During the past six years, I noticed that my mother had been taking metformin.

"Now you are on metformin," I said.

"My doctor prescribed it for me, and the people in the park told me that metformin is good," Mom replied, "So, I am taking it now."

It is funny that Mom believed the people in the park more than her own physician son.

"Your diabetes is well controlled." I noticed that her A1C levels were in the range of 6.8 % to 7.2 % without incidence of hypoglycemia.

Diabetes was considered a rich people's disease in China three decades ago. The prevalence of type 2 diabetes has increased from less than 1 percent to 11 percent during the past three decades. It's not likely due to the fault of rice, carbohydrate. I remember that 30-40 years ago, most people consumed about 400-500 gram (about one pound) of rice per day, around 2,000 Calories per day, while few people suffered from diabetes. During that time, I spent more than two hours riding my bike to work daily. And I did not know what "snacks" meant since there were no snacks at all in the house back then. Chinese people have adapted more and more to a Western diet and lifestyle over the past 30 years. When I travel to China now, I can see more McDonald's in the city, more cars on the roads, and fewer bikers.

Chinese people have become heavier, and they suffer from these so called "civilized" diseases such as diabetes, coronary heart disease, stroke, and all kinds of cancers. The rapid economic development in China has brought about not only material comforts but also these diseases and other social problems like drug addiction, prostitution, etc. One of my cousins suffered a heart attack, and another sustained a stroke, both in their early fifties. Every one or two years, I travel to China to visit my Mom and stay with her for three weeks at each visit. Owing to my job, I cannot spend more time with her. Unfortunately, Mom doesn't know how to use FaceTime or Skype. Otherwise, I could see her every day.

I worked at a diabetes clinic, and 80-90 percent of my patients had diabetes. Mom does not like to listen to my advice, but most of my diabetic patients do.

Lifelong Struggle

L ife is not always fair, especially to patients with type 1 diabetes. In this type of diabetes, the beta cells of the pancreas cannot make insulin because of being destroyed by the body's immune system. Type 1 diabetes is usually first diagnosed at young ages, and there is no cure yet. People suffering from the disease have to struggle with it almost their whole life.

While seeing patients in the clinic, I received a call from the emergency department, "Your patient, Mr. Craig, is very sick in the ER again." Mr. Craig, with type 1 diabetes, was 44 years old when this event happened. He also had schizophrenia requiring a monthly intramuscular injection of haloperidol (an antipsychotic used to treat schizophrenia and other behavioral disorders) at a mental clinic. He used to be an illicit drug user, addicted to cocaine, but had not used illicit drugs for many years. I remembered that he was proud to show me his badge, which was issued by the drug rehabilitation facility to celebrate his 6th anniversary of being drug-free.

When I arrived at the emergency room, I found that Mr. Craig was lying in bed lethargically. His face was shriveled with sunken eyes. And his usual cheerful smile had vanished. He was breathing so rapidly and shallowly that he could barely speak. His glucose level was 1,236 mg/dL (68.6 mmol/L), and he was severely dehydrated (the excessive loss of body water). I also noticed that two police officers were sitting in the corner watching him. Mr. Craig was brought in from the county jail when he developed abdominal pain, nausea, and vomiting. He told me that he had not taken insulin for two days after he was put in jail.

Apparently, Mr. Craig developed **diabetic ketoacidosis (DKA),** which is a serious acute complication in patients with diabetes mellitus. **DKA,** which was first described in 1886, is a medical emergency and can be fatal if not treated promptly. DKA occurs primarily in patients with type 1 diabetes, but patients with type 2 diabetes can develop it occasionally. DKA usually led to death before insulin treatment was

117

introduced in the 1920s. Now its mortality has dropped to less than 1% with prompt and appropriate treatment.

The underlying mechanism for **diabetic ketoacidosis** is a lack of insulin accompanied by the elevation of counterregulatory hormone levels, such as glucagon, cortisol, catecholamine, and growth hormone. The deprivation of insulin combined with the rise of glucagon and other hormones increases the release of glucose by the liver through the breakdown of glycogen and generation of glucose. The kidney cannot handle significantly high concentrations of glucose, which passes into the urine and causes osmotic diuresis, leading to dehydration.

The deficiency of insulin results in the release of free fatty acids from adipose tissue and the fatty acids become ketone bodies in the liver. Accumulation of ketone bodies (acetoacetate and β-hydroxybutyrate) will make the blood acidic (metabolic acidosis), leading to a so-called DKA or diabetic ketoacidosis.

Dehydration in DKA can result in average body water loss of 6 liters for an adult (or 100 mL/kg). Additionally, loss of blood solutes such sodium, potassium, chloride, phosphate, magnesium, and calcium can cause severe metabolic abnormalities. DKA symptoms include nausea, vomiting, dehydration, deep gasping breathing, confusion and even coma.

Mr. Craig had episodes of DKA about once a year as a consequence of running out of medications, doing heavy drinking, forgetting to inject his insulin as a result of partying or having pneumonia. I told the police officers that Mr. Craig had brittle type 1 diabetes and could die without insulin treatment for two to three days. They said that they did not know the medical details about Mr. Craig, and they were just assigned here to guard him. Mr. Craig was lucky enough to be sent to the hospital in time for prompt treatment. Otherwise, he might have died from diabetic ketoacidosis due to lack of insulin in a few more hours. There have been some reports about diabetic inmates who died because they were denied insulin treatment.[1, 2]

Mr. Craig was admitted to the ICU and received standard treatment for DKA with IV insulin, IV fluid, electrolyte replenishment and other supportive treatment. Mr. Craig had recovered quickly, and his metabolic abnormalities had almost resolved. His mental status returned to normal the next day, and he started to eat at noon. I asked him why he got arrested.

"I stole a pack of cigarettes and a small pack of potato chips at a 7-Eleven," he said.

"That's all you did?" I was surprised.

"Yes, I swear."

No wonder the United States has the highest incarceration rate in the world, considering the fact that people like Mr. Craig are put in jail when committing misdemeanors such as stealing a pack of cigarettes. Around one percent of U.S. adults are incarcerated. According to the U.S. Bureau of Justice Statistics (BJS), about 2.3 million adults were locked up in U.S. federal and state prisons and county jails in 2011. Therefore, the United States, with 5 percent of the world's population, houses around 25 percent of the world's prisoners. Besides, 4.7 million adults were on probation or parole in 2011. In total, the U.S. correctional systems involved almost 7 million adults who were on probation or parole and in jail or prison in 2011. (For more details on this topic, see *Wikipedia: Incarceration in the United States.*). Annually, taxpayers spend about $60,000 imprisoning a person in New York State, $168,000 in New York City, and $30,000 on average in other states. [3]

Two police officers continued to guard him in the ICU room. When they finished their 12-hour shift, two new officers came in to take over. Thus, four officers were needed to watch over him while Mr. Craig was in the hospital. Mr. Craig was transferred to the regular ward after he was stabilized. I went to the regular ward to make rounds at noon as usual. When I entered Mr. Craig's room, I was surprised to find out that there were no more policemen inside.

"Where are the policemen?" I asked.

"They are gone," Mr. Craig said with a grin, just stepping out of the bathroom.

"Why?"

"I don't know. They just went away."

"Maybe they are tired of you," I said.

"I am happy that they left."

"Me too," I said to myself, for I did not have to sign in whenever I entered the room. It is a rule that any visitors including doctors need to sign their names on the police logbook, and a police officer will write down visitors' names and visiting time.

"What happened? The officers are gone," I asked a nurse when I walked back to the nursing station to write my note.

"They have dropped the case," the nurse replied. "They said that they're not coming back."

"It's good for them," I said.

It is likely that the police considered it too risky to prosecute the young man with many medical problems for this minor misdemeanor. They might have realized that Mr. Craig could fall sick anytime and was a difficult person to take care of in jail, thinking about what I had told them about Mr. Craig' s brittle type 1 diabetes. Furthermore, Mr. Craig could become truly crazy if he did not take his psychiatric medications properly.

Thousands of dollars had been spent hospitalizing Mr. Craig in the ICU and on the regular ward in addition to the cost of guarding him by four officers. The police or jail did not need to pay for Mr. Craig's hospitalization as he had been released within days, and he had maintained his Medicare and Medicaid. Once an individual patient is incarcerated, he or she is removed from the Medicaid plans. The correctional system is responsible for all the health care for inmates. Health care services in prisons and jails are mainly funded by state and local legislative appropriations according to Correctional Health Care by U.S Department of Justice.[4]

Not many people know that inmates have the best medical insurance plan in the U.S. They commonly do not need to pay copayments or deductibles for medications, procedures, surgeries, ER visits or hospitalizations. Their insurance company reimburses the hospitals and doctors at a higher rate than that of Medicare or Medicaid. Thus, inmates are welcomed by all the hospitals and clinics. They come to our clinic to see doctors by free transportation and can enter the exam room directly through the back door without waiting in the waiting room, of course, always escorted by two officers.

Ironically, approximately 20 percent of American adults could not afford medical insurance before Obamacare started in 2013.[5, 6] I felt sad to watch the news that a 59-year-old, unemployed poor man was alleged to rob a bank for $1 in North Carolina in 2011, so that he could get medical care in jail.[7] Nonetheless, similar stories had been reported since then: an Oregon man in 2013, a New York man in 2012, and an Alabama man in 2013 all intended to get arrested for committing pseudo-crimes in order to get free health care behind bars.[8]

Even though Mr. Craig was schizophrenic with brittle type 1 diabetes, he could manage his medical problems sufficiently enough to enjoy an independent full personal life in the society. He had a car to drive around and attended parties sometimes. He smoked cigarettes and did binge drinking occasionally. He came to the clinic for office visits with his different girlfriends. Every now and then, he just stopped by the clinic to ask for Viagra samples. He was cheerful most of the time. One time, he developed a big painful growth on his penis (genital wart). I referred him to a urologist for evaluation and treatment. One month later, he happily told me that the wart had almost gone, and he could function again. He looked upset and regretful one time when he told me that he just lost $150 on the instant lottery at a 7-Eleven.

Mr. Craig was hospitalized for disorders related to his diabetes around one time per year. Unlike some patients, Mr. Craig did not like the hospital and wanted to get out of it as soon as possible to enjoy the outside world. He never asked for narcotic painkillers. He was proud that he had been off illicit drugs for almost 10 years. The worst thing he had done was steal some small items at a convenience store. According to his mother, he had never been violent. He did not contribute to society, but at least he did not do too much harm to it. Tragically, he died in a motel for an unknown reason at the young age of 48. I hope that Mr. Craig will continue to enjoy his life in heaven. I will miss his cheerful face. His story taught me how to remain calm and cheerful and to enjoy life no matter what happens.

On the contrary, Mr. Winston with type 1 diabetes like Mr. Craig's is 85 years old. He is alive and active, without serious complications of

121

diabetes such as heart attack, stroke, and kidney or eye problems. He was diagnosed with type 1 diabetes at the age of 15, and he checks his sugar level six to eight times daily. His diabetes is brittle with frequent severe hypoglycemia leading to coma at least three to four times per year. Still, with his wife's help and his motivation and diligence, he has been able to handle these situations well without any injury or other consequences for 70 years.

I told Mr. Winston to read the diabetes book by Dr. Bernstein, who is a diabetes expert, and also a patient with type 1 diabetes for more than 60 years.[9] I also showed him the news on my computer screen: In June 2011, a San Diego man, at the age of 90, received a medal from the Boston-based Joslin Diabetes Center to commemorate his living with diabetes for 85 years.[10] Mr. Winston was surprised to know that somebody had lived so long with type 1 diabetes. The center has honored long-time diabetes survivors since 1948, and 34 people with diabetes have won the 75-year medals.

"I hope you will continue to stay healthy and become one of the 75-year medal winners in a couple of years," I said to him.

"I hope so," Mr. Winston smiled confidently.

Patients with the same disease may have many different outcomes. Some people are just luckier than others in many ways.

Foot Exam

W hen I examined his feet during the first office visit, Mr. Byrd said, "**No doctor has ever touched my feet since I was diagnosed with diabetes 15 years ago.**" Mr. Byrd, in his 60s, just retired and moved from New York City to this southern state.

"My previous doctor has never examined my feet even though I have seen him for many years. And we go to the same church!" another patient said after I examined her feet at the first office visit.

In fact, foot examination is my routine for a diabetic patient visit, especially for new patients. The American Diabetes Association (ADA) issues an updated "Standards of Medical Care in Diabetes" yearly. It used to recommend **yearly** comprehensive foot examination on diabetic patients: inspection (skin, nails, and contour), palpation of pedal pulses, assessments of ankle reflexes, position/vibration perception, and sensation. Standards of Medical Care in Diabetes—2015 even emphasizes the importance of performing foot exam **at each visit** on all patients with reduced foot sensation, foot deformities, or a history of foot ulcers.[1] It is not surprising that this simple, costless and effective examination is neglected commonly nowadays since more and more nerve conduction devices are used in the outpatient clinics, which can generate revenue while foot exams do not.

Oftentimes, even a simple foot exam takes time and is not easy to perform because a lot of patients cannot bend down to reach their feet as a result of obesity and other health issues. Sometimes, I need to help patients take off and get their shoes/socks back on. Occasionally, their wives or family members have to help them out. The funniest scene, which is commonly seen, is that a man turns to his wife sitting beside him, and uses his finger, without saying a word, to instruct her to take off his shoes and socks. In contrast, few men assist their wives in removing their shoes and socks for a foot exam.

A lot of people relocated from the southern states to the North to seek better opportunities 30-40 years ago when they were young. They move back to the South when they retire. Most of them can live comfortably back home thanks to their better financial status and cheaper housing down here. They are proud of that. A retired firefighter from the North told me that his retirement pension is 50% higher than the salary of a local firefighter. Another patient said he had always gotten union jobs in the north while there are not so many labor unions in the South. Another boasted that he could buy several houses here after he sold his house in New York. However, if they have not reached the Medicare age of 65 years old, most of the retirees from New York have only GHI medical insurance and have trouble finding a doctor who accepts GHI.

Group Health Incorporated (GHI) is a health insurance company based in New York City. GHI and Health Insurance Plan of New York (HIP) merged to form EmblemHealth in 2006. Only a handful of clinics in this southern state accepts GHI insurance plan because it reimburses out of state doctors poorly. Our clinic is one of those clinics. Even Medicaid payments are much better than GHI's. Patients with GHI who are not qualified for Medicare have to drive 30-50 miles to come to our clinic.

One of my patients had to drive 100 miles to see a gastroenterologist for a colonoscopy. Thus, quite a few patients tend to plan regular long trips back to NY for imaging studies, procedures, surgeries or seeing specialists while visiting their family at the same time. Mr. Byrd drove 50 miles to see me for he could not find any nearby doctors who accepted his insurance.

"Until today, I didn't know my feet have no feeling!" Mr. Byrd said after the foot examination. It was found that his feet had lost sensation up to the ankle level. Fortunately, even though Mr. Byrd's feet revealed many calluses, corns, thickened toenails and dry skin, they maintained good pedal pulses and showed no skin breakdown.

"You know that now," I said. "In the future, you need to be more careful. You should check your feet every day and make sure there is no cut or wound in them. Once a diabetic foot ulcer develops, it can be difficult to heal. You can lose your foot or leg because of it."

"I understand it now. Thank you very much."

Before leaving the room, Mr. Byrd pulled out a twenty-dollar bill from his wallet and wanted to give to me, "You are the best doctor I've ever seen. This is a little thing for you."

"It's so nice of you," I said. "I don't accept money from patients like that. Your insurance will pay me for your visit."

"Please take it," he insisted. He picked up my hand and pressed the twenty dollar bill into it.

"Here is not New York, you know," I smiled and returned the money to him.

"Yep, I see it," he giggled.

"Foot exam is my routine. Please keep your money. Thank you very much, though."

Mr. Byrd continued to drive 50 miles to see me every three months even after he was qualified for Medicare, and he could see any doctor close to his home.

Praise for good service from my patients makes me more humble and committed to providing them with the best possible care.

Although the simple foot exam costs nothing to perform, it can save a patient's foot or leg sometimes. Mr. Fisher, 50 years old, came in for an office visit after he had not been to the clinic for a regular checkup in three years. He was diagnosed with diabetes 10 years ago, and his diabetes had been under good control until he stopped coming to the clinic. He had run out of medications for two years, and his sugar level was 430 mg/dL (23.9 mmol/L) on that day.

"Why did you stop coming here for your diabetes treatment?" I asked.

"I'm feeling good," Mr. Fisher. "I am just too busy to come."

"Look at your sugar... it is so high. Your diabetes was good three years ago."

"I know my sugar is not good," he said. "That's why I'm here now."

"Could you take off your shoes and socks? Let me look at them to make sure they are okay."

I already smelled the bad odor from his feet before he took off his shoes. As I expected, I noticed blood and pus oozing from a large ulcer on the bottom of his left foot. I knew that it was his bad foot that had forced him to come to the clinic today. He had difficulty pulling the sock off his foot as the sock and the wound stuck together with pus and bloody fluid. The room was filled with foul odor as soon as he pulled his sock off. His whole left foot was red, warm and swollen up to 10 centimeters above the ankle.

"How long has this been going on?" I asked.

"About a week," he replied sheepishly.

"I think it may have been much longer than a week. You need to be admitted to the hospital right now for IV antibiotic and surgical intervention because of the large foot ulcer along with cellulitis, fever, and uncontrolled diabetes. Or you may lose your foot or your leg."

"Let me call my girlfriend first," he hesitated.

After talking with his girlfriend on the phone, Mr. Fisher agreed to an admission to the hospital. He was started on IV (intravenous) antibiotics after admission and received surgical debridement on the second day. His sugar level was well controlled with insulin treatment. However, his wound did not heal well, and he had an intermittent fever. And the imaging study showed signs of osteomyelitis (bone infection). His surgeon recommended amputation of his fourth and fifth toes, and Mr. Fisher refused. In the meanwhile, his kidney function deteriorated as a result of infection and adverse effects of vancomycin (an antibiotic), which was discontinued after the renal test showed abnormal values.

"Why do you refuse the surgery?" I said. "You still can walk well without the fourth and fifth toes. If you don't have surgery, the infection won't be under control, and the wound will never heal. And your kidney will get worse. You may lose your whole foot and end up on a kidney machine."

"My girlfriend doesn't like the amputation," he said.

"I suppose you should make your own decision."

"I'll think about it myself then."

Mr. Fisher received one more week of conservative treatment without significant improvement. Finally, he decided to undergo the amputation. Mr. Fisher had recovered very well from the surgery. After the surgery, the wound on his foot was healing rapidly with the assistance of a vacuum pump (a portal device can suck out fluid from the wound and augment blood flow to the affected area). He was discharged home one week later and received home health care. He went back to work one month after the amputation and his kidney function returned to normal too. Since then, Mr. Fisher had kept his appointments to come to the clinic for the treatment of his diabetes, which was under control with oral medications. And he had not had any more diabetic complications.

Sometimes, you have to make the right decisions in life. Overtreatment is bad, but denial or non-adherence is not good either. Fortunately, Mr. Fisher lost only two toes owing to his denial. He was able to walk normally after the toe amputation.

Denial, most common in men, can cause serious consequences in some diabetic patients like Mr. Brandt. Mr. Brandt was 50 years old when he came to the clinic for the first visit with his wife. He saw an ophthalmologist one day before this office visit because he could not see well.

"How can I help you today?" I asked.

"My eye doctor urged me to see a medical doctor right away because my eyes are bad," he answered.

"How bad are they?"

"I can see very large letters only. I can't drive anymore. The eye doctor said I must have diabetes."

"I can check your sugar right now." His sugar turned out to be 290 mg/dL (16.1 mmol/L) according to a glucometer.

"You surely have diabetes," I continued. "Your sugar is above 200 with typical diabetic symptoms: blurry vision, thirst, and frequent urination. How long have you been feeling sick?"

"I have felt bad for two to three years, and I knew there was something not right...probably diabetes. It runs in the family. My parents also see you for diabetes. Do you remember them?"

"Oh, yes. They are over 75 years old and doing well without bad outcomes of diabetes. What made you decide not to see a doctor even when you felt something wrong?"

"You know, I just don't like seeing doctors."

"Unfortunately, you've learned a bitter lesson this time. You have to see doctors all the time from now on."

"I know, I know."

"How are your feet?" I told him to take off his shoes and socks to have a foot exam.

"They're perfect," he smiled. "Do you really want to look at them?"

"Sure," I said. It was true that I did not find anything wrong with his feet during the foot exam.

"One more thing you need to tell Dr. Li," his wife pushed his shoulder to remind him.

"What's wrong?" I asked.

"I have some problems with erection," Mr. Brandt replied with embarrassment.

"How long have you had that problem?"

"At least two years."

"You're having so many uncontrolled medical disorders now," I said. "Let's try to handle one at a time. How about we take care of this issue in one to two months after your sugar gets better and your eye condition stabilizes."

"Sure, no problem."

Mr. Brandt suffered severe diabetic retinopathy that had damaged his vision badly. Diabetic retinopathy is a complication of diabetes involving the blood vessels of the light-sensitive tissue at the back of the eye (retina). Diabetic retinopathy can impair vision and cause blindness. I started him on metformin simply to lower his sugar level gradually. Metformin is the only oral diabetic medication that has been proven to reduce diabetic complications and does not decrease glucose level rapidly. Rapid reduction of glucose level in patients with severe retinopathy may further impair their vision.

Mr. Brandt's glucose level reduced to the 100-150 range in about one month. In the meantime, the ophthalmologist had performed many procedures on him in order to improve his vision and stop the progression of his eye problems. His vision remained very poor after one year of eye treatment though it had not gotten worse according to him.

His diabetes was easy to treat and under good control with metformin only (A1C was 6.5–7%). Nevertheless, he developed heart failure one year later and needed to see a cardiologist regularly since then. His heart failure was presumably due to diabetic cardiomyopathy, which is characterized by the weakened heart muscle without evidence of coronary artery disease.

The denial caused him to have a weak heart, severely impaired vision, and erectile dysfunction. Mr. Brandt had to quit his job as a truck driver because of his poor health. He was 100 percent disabled, and surely, he got his disability approved fast. He had tried Viagra, Cialis and Levitra (drugs used to treat erectile dysfunction) without satisfactory results. He could not climb up one flight of stairs and could watch TV programs only two to three feet from his new 70-inch TV set.

"I can watch TV now, Dr. Li. I bought a 70-inch TV set a couple days ago," Mr. Brandt told me happily.

"I'm happy for you," I said.

Sometimes, medical non-adherence can lead to premature death. Mr. Davidson, about 50 years old then, had had diabetes at least 10-15 years and stopped seeing doctors for three to four years. When Mr. Davidson came in to see me as a new patient, he did not complain of anything. The medical assistant checked his glucose level using a glucometer. The meter displayed "HI", indicating the blood glucose was over 600 mg/dL (33.3 mmol/L).

On exam, his feet revealed many calluses and corns with reduced sensation, fortunately, no skin breakdown or sores. I restarted him back on his insulin treatment, giving him insulin samples and a new glucometer. Since he did not have symptoms, and his vital signs were normal, I let him go home. Next morning, I found that his blood test came back with glucose at 1,120 mg/dL (62.2 mmol/L) and A1C at 25%. I was concerned and called him.

"How are you doing, Mr. Davidson?" I said. "Your blood test shows your sugar was very high yesterday, more than one thousand. I am concerned about you."

"I am fine," Mr. Davidson replied. "I started to use insulin again. I have been working all these days. You know, I am doing my job right now." I heard some noises that sounded like a construction site.

"Please come to see me as soon as possible if you have any problems. Please make sure to take your insulin and see me in two weeks."

"I will."

Mr. Davidson came back to the clinic two weeks later without any complaints. His sugar level was down to 450 mg/dL (25 mmol/L). Sadly, Mr. Davidson did not return to the clinic since then, despite the secretaries and medical assistants calling him to remind him of the appointments numerous times. About one year later, I received his death certificate from the county coroner. I had to check the emergency department record to find out what happened to him before I could sign the certificate. The ER note stated that Mr. Davidson suffered a cardiac arrest at home, and he was pronounced dead after cardiopulmonary resuscitation. Most likely, he died of a heart attack.

All the above patients have jobs with health insurance, but denial and non-adherence had cost their health, their jobs, and even their lives. Moreover, a lot of other factors, particularly social issues, can contribute to poorly controlled diabetes or other chronic diseases. For instance, Mrs. Heyward's diabetes had never been under control even though she kept her outpatient appointments and received extensive inpatient care.

Mrs. Heyward was about 50 years old when I saw her as a new patient in the clinic 15 years ago. Her diabetes had been out of control for years, and her A1C was 22% at the first office visit, most likely still the clinic's second highest record. Frequently, her sugar levels were too high to measure at office visits.

She was admitted to hospital for gastroparesis, skin infections, and asthma attacks every two to three months. However, her glucose, blood pressure, and other disorders were under good control when she had a good hospital environment and care. She told me that her house was so noisy that she felt nervous and anxious all the time and could not fall asleep because there were many young grandchildren in the house. On several occasions, she was discharged to her uncle's home. She had to go back to her own home after a while. Then she would get sick again sooner or later.

Of course, she was also on anti-depressants and sleeping pills. She had lost sensation not only in her feet but also in her fingers due to diabetic neuropathy. Sometimes, she had difficulty injecting insulin owing to hand stiffness and numbness. She could not get the help she needed even though there were many people in the house.

Her feet were severely burned when she splashed boiling oil onto her feet accidently. She was transferred to a burn care center out of state and stayed there for more than one month. Afterward, she continued to receive wound care at a medical center 90 miles away for one more year until her wound healed.

Mrs. Heyward had undergone a knee replacement in her forties. A few years later, her left leg was amputated above the knee level after recurrent infections around her artificial knee. Thus, she had only one foot left, which did not feel anything, and she was confined to her wheelchair most of the time. She is lucky to able to see well and have functioning kidneys. Sometimes, I felt helpless for the only thing I could do was to keep her alive.

Metformin as Herbal Medicine

A t times, patients asked me, "Do I need to take some herbal medicine to help my diabetes?"
        "You're taking herbal medicine now," I said.
"Really?"
"Metformin, which you are taking, originated from a plant called French Lilac. People started to use it as an herbal medicine in medieval Europe."

Galega officinalis (French lilac or goat's rue) was used to treat symptoms of diabetes for centuries. A review article tells the interesting story of the scientific development of Metformin.[1] According to the article, *G. officinalis* was found to be rich in guanidine in the late 1800s. Guanidine was shown to lower blood glucose level in animals in 1918, but it was too toxic for clinical application.

A less toxic extract of *G. officinalis*, galegine (isoamylene guanidine), was used briefly as an antidiabetic drug in the 1920s. Then two biguanides, Synthalin A and Synthalin B, were synthesized and used clinically with better tolerance and efficacy in the 1920s. Because of their toxicity and limited efficacy, they were discontinued by the early 1930s (although Synthalin B was used in Germany until the mid-1940s.)

Several biguanides including dimethyl-biguanide (**metformin**) were synthesized in 1929. They were shown to lower blood glucose in animals without significant toxicity. Jean Sterne (1909–1997) was the first to conduct a clinical trial of metformin in diabetic patients. His trial results were published in 1957. He made the name "Glucophage" (glucose eater) for dimethyl-biguanide (metformin). The trial with **phenformin** was also published by Ungar G in 1957 and studies on **buformin** were reported by Mehnert H in 1958.

Phenformin and **buformin** had stronger antidiabetic effects, and they were discontinued in most countries by the end of the 1970s because of their association with lactic acidosis. **Metformin** can also cause lactic acidosis, but with much lower incidence (less than 0.01 to

0.08 case per 1000 patient-years).[2] The most common adverse effects of metformin are gastrointestinal symptoms including abdominal discomfort, nausea, vomiting, diarrhea, and flatulence. Metformin started to be sold in the UK in 1958 and was approved in Canada in 1972. Finally, Metformin (brand name called Glucophage) was approved by FDA in 1994 and came on the market in the United States in 1995. (For more details on this topic, see *Wikipedia: Metformin*.)

I feel fortunate to have witnessed the progression of treatment for diabetes over the past twenty years. Before metformin was introduced in the United States in 1995, only one type of oral antidiabetic medication (sulfonylurea) and the injected insulins were used in the U.S. At present, there are more than 10 types of antidiabetic drugs and several types of insulin preparations.[3] I still remember I handed out metformin samples to diabetic patients in the resident clinic when metformin just hit the shelf in 1995.

Metformin is the only antidiabetic medication that has been proved to improve diabetes outcomes and is still the most prescribed antidiabetic medication in the world. It also helps lower LDL (low-density lipoprotein) cholesterol and triglyceride levels, and usually does not cause weight gain or hypoglycemia. According to a recent study, diabetic patients treated with metformin can live longer than the untreated individuals without diabetes.[4] Metformin is recommended as the initial therapy of choice in most diabetes guidelines. However, in the real world, only 58% of patients with type 2 diabetes are put on metformin as their first oral antidiabetic drug.[5]

I saw Mrs. McGee as a new patient one year ago. Mrs. McGee, 68 years old, was diagnosed with type 2 diabetes two years earlier. She was on dapagliflozin (an oral antidiabetic), saxagliptin (another oral antidiabetic) and exenatide (an injectable antidiabetic) with normal kidney function.

"Doc, you've got to stop my exenatide," she said. "It is expensive and makes me sick all the time."

"Have you tried metformin before?" I asked.

"Nobody has mentioned it to me. I have been on these three medications since I got diabetes."

"Metformin is the first choice for type 2 diabetes," I said. "I can stop your exenatide and start you on metformin. I'll adjust your other medications later."

Mrs. McGee tolerated metformin well, and her dapagliflozin and saxagliptin were discontinued a few months later. Her diabetes was under excellent control with metformin only.

Another patient said. "Can you change my saxagliptin back to metformin?"

"Why do you want to switch?" I asked.

"It is too expensive. Now I'm paying $40 copay a month for saxagliptin. But next month, I'll fall into the Medicare '*donut hole*' and I need to pay $300 each month for it." ("**Donut hole**" is a coverage gap existing in most Medicare Prescription Drug Plans. For more details on this topic, see *Wikipedia: Medicare Part D coverage gap*.) A 30-day supply of Metformin costs $4 at Wal-Mart.

"What's the reason you were put on saxagliptin in the first place?" As a matter of fact, saxagliptin was found to be associated with more heart-failure hospitalizations.[6]

"I was told that I don't need to take saxagliptin with food," he replied.

"Did you have any problem with metformin in the past?" I asked.

"Not at all. And my diabetes was under good control with metformin."

Even if patients do not tolerate metformin initially, they can try it again after a while, starting at a low dose and increasing the dose gradually. This is the case for Ms. Spencer. The next story is about Ms. Spencer, who, in her 30s, was born with spina bifida.

Spina bifida is a developmental congenital disorder called neural tube defects resulting from incomplete closure. Spina bifida is one of the most common birth defects, which is seen in one to two cases per 1000 births worldwide. In the U.S., the incidence of spina bifida is lower, on average 0.7 per 1000 live births. The lumbar and sacral regions of the spine are most commonly involved. Neurological impairment caused by spina bifida include: muscle weakness, bowel and bladder problems, seizures, orthopedic problems, such as deformed feet, uneven hips, a curved spine (scoliosis) and psychiatric problems. Daily folic acid supplements are proven to significantly decrease the risk of spina bifida and other neural tube defects if taken in supplement form at least one month prior to conception. It is unknown how folic acid can reduce the incidence and the severity of spina bifida.

Ms. Spencer had many of complications induced by spina bifida including paralysis of legs, urinary incontinence, deformed feet and scoliosis. She lost her right leg as a result of numerous infection and needed to see a podiatrist for the care of her left foot, which had recurrent ulcers or infections. As a consequence of bladder dysfunction, she had repeated urinary tract infection and received many bladder surgeries at a university medical center. Finally, she was placed with a suprapubic urinary catheter. With unhealed bedsores in the sacral areas, she needed to see wound specialists regularly.

She was confined to a wheelchair. The impairment of her mobility contributed to her obesity. She, weighing 275 pounds (124.7 kilograms), developed type 2 diabetes at age 20 because of multiple risk factors: obesity, immobility, and family history. Additionally, she needed to take care of her young baby without help from a husband. Without a good home and societal environments, it was even harder for her to fight diabetes and other diseases. You can imagine how much Ms. Spencer was suffering at this young age.

She used more than 300-400 units of insulin per day: insulin glargine 100 units twice per day and insulin aspart 40-60 units three times per day. Still, her diabetes had never been under control with this dose of insulin. She saw an endocrinologist regularly with numerous visits to a dietician and diabetes education nurses. In addition to pioglitazone (an oral antidiabetic, its brand name is Actos), she was also put on other injectable antidiabetic medications and oral phentermine (a diet pill), which worked for her for three to six months and lost their efficacy. She said she could not take metformin because of nausea and vomiting and abdominal pain.

As she had Tricare insurance (a health care program of the United States Department of Defense Military Health System), I was her primary care doctor (called care manager), and I took care of her in the hospital and occasionally saw her in the clinic. When she was hospitalized for skin or urinary tract infections, her glucose levels were in the range of 400-500 mg/dL (22.2-27.8 mmol/L) on admission. I always cut her usual home insulin dose (300-400 units) in half on the admission order. Her glucose would gradually improve and fall in the range of 100-150 mg/dL (5.6-8.3 mmol/dL) within four to five days with reduction of daily insulin dose to 40-50 units.

"Why do you use more than 300 units of insulin per day at home when you need only 40-50 units with good control in the hospital?" I asked.

"I probably eat a little bit more at home," Ms. Spencer said sadly. "You know, I am stressed out at home too."

"I understand. You have so many doctors to see, a baby to care for, and difficulty moving around. I am very sorry for you. At least, you understand you can do well in the hospital. Of course, the hospital provides more care, proper diet, and a better environment. I hope you can continue your diet and be relaxed at home as you are in the hospital. And I'm going to put you on metformin again while you are in the hospital, starting at low dose: 250 mg twice per day with food."

"It's okay. I'll try," she said. She tolerated metformin well in the hospital and continued to take it at home after she was discharged from the hospital.

Ms. Spencer's mother, Mrs. Spencer, was also my patient. Mrs. Spencer had type 2 diabetes, coronary heart disease with several stents, knee and back pain, and depression. She was definitely stressed out, for she needed to take care of five people at home, three grandchildren, one daughter (Ms. Spencer), and her sick husband with stroke-induced hemiparesis. She would always come with complaints of not feeling good, fatigue and pain. Her diabetes was out of control with A1C of 13-15% all the time no matter how much insulin she injected and how many diabetes or nutrition classes she took. Of course, she was on metformin and tolerated it well.

Home or societal problems cannot be solved with medications, gene therapy, robot microsurgery, advanced imaging, wireless medicine or human genome mapping. Using A1C as a parameter for the quality of medical care is significantly flawed since some patient's diabetes is just uncontrollable. Additionally, A1C is affected by many factors, and it varies in different ethnic groups.

Life is just so hard for some people, even harder with diabetes.

I have been involved in clinical medicine in the U.S. for more than 20 years, and I had worked at a diabetes treatment facility for 15 years. The majority of my patients had diabetes mellitus. I have learned so much from taking care of them, and I have seen their struggle, success, endurance, and disappointments.

During the first few years after pioglitazone (an oral antidiabetic, its brand name is Actos) or rosiglitazone (an oral antidiabetic, its brand name is Avandia) hit the market, numerous patients had been put on pioglitazone or rosiglitazone as a result of powerful pharmaceutical promotion. Many of them had gained so much weight with edema after they were started on pioglitazone or rosiglitazone.[7] I had admitted dozens of them for pulmonary edema, for I was their primary care doctor though pioglitazone or rosiglitazone was not started by me. I recall that I admitted a patient for pulmonary edema and fluid retention three times on night calls. I stopped his pioglitazone on each admission. Unbelievably, the patient was restarted on pioglitazone again at every discharge by his attending doctor.

By looking back all the development of diabetic medications during these twenty years, it seems to me that the treatment for diabetes has returned to how it was twenty years ago: sulfonylurea and insulin with the addition of metformin. All the later new antidiabetic medications have not been proven to provide long-term efficacy and improve clinical outcomes since metformin came on the U.S. market in 1995.[7, 8, 9] Therefore, I seldom use new fancy antidiabetic drugs except for metformin and injected insulins.

As in the case of Ms. Spencer, how could she have time, energy, and motivation to give herself a few more shots (other injectable antidiabetics such as exenatide) in addition to insulin treatment four times per day? She had achieved better control over her diabetes only with insulin and metformin, and led a simpler life.

Recently, I received a consultation report about a diabetic patient. This patient has already been on five diabetic medications including metformin, sitagliptin, pioglitazone, insulin aspart and insulin glargine (4 insulin injections per day) for quite some time. I noticed that the patient was started on two more antidiabetic medications: dapagliflozin (oral antidiabetic) and exenatide (subcutaneously injected antidiabetic) by the consultant. In addition to these seven antidiabetic medications, she took carvedilol, digoxin, lisinopril, spironolactone, and furosemide for her heart failure and hypertension, and warfarin for atrial fibrillation (irregular heartbeat). Her treatment regimen consists of 13 medications totally including one of the most dangerous medications on the earth, warfarin, which is the number one cause of emergency hospitalizations resulting from adverse drug effects.[10] If I were her, I could not handle the complicated regimen myself even though I am a physician.

"... for most patients older than 50 years with an HbA1c level less than 9% receiving **metformin** *therapy, additional glycemic treatment usually offers at most modest benefits. ... and even small treatment adverse effects result in net harm in older patients."* [11]

Some of the diabetic patients not only have many hardships in their lives but also are overwhelmed by their diabetes treatment. Too many medicines will make their lives even harder without better clinical outcomes. I have learned that simplicity is pivotal, at least in the treatment of type 2 diabetes. Life is easier and more enjoyable with simplicity.

Current Antidiabetic Medications [3]

1. **Metformin**
2. Sulfonylurea
3. Insulin
4. Thiazolidinediones (TZD)
5. Dipeptidyl Peptidase 4 Inhibitors (DPP-4 inhibitor)
6. Sodium–Glucose Cotransporter 2 Inhibitors (SGLT2 inhibitor)
7. GLP-1 receptor agonists
8. Repaglinide/nateglinide
9. α-glucosidase inhibitors
10. Colesevelam
11. Bromocriptine
12. Pramlintide

6. Seeing Doctors in China

The practice of medicine is an art, not a trade; a calling, not a business; a calling in which your heart will be exercised equally with your head.

—William Osler (1849-1919, Canadian Physician and Professor of Medicine)

Peace begins with a smile.

—Mother Teresa (1910 –1997, Roman Catholic Religious Sister and Missionary)

Sometimes the questions are complicated and the answers are simple.

—Dr. Seuss (1904-1991, American Author)

Take Mom to See Doctors

I took Mom to an outpatient clinic to see a doctor for knee pain three years ago. We left home around 7:45 a.m. The clinic, only 15-minute walk from home, was located in the outpatient building within a nearby municipal hospital. We walked through the old streets and lanes in this historic district (Xiguan, 西关). The lanes were paved with granite. The covered pedestrian arcades along the streets or roads created long shaded pathways, providing protection from wind, rain, and sunshine. The familiar structure and smell of these streets reminded me of my childhood. In 1962, I entered an elementary school that was located a few blocks away from home. All the students in my class lived on the same lane. This lane, where Mom lives, is claimed to be the longest lane in Guangzhou (also called Canton).

Patients usually do not have a primary care doctor in China. You may not see the same doctor at each visit. You can go to see a doctor at an outpatient clinic without a prior appointment. In order to obtain an appointment on the same day, what you need to do is to register at the reception counter. Your family member or friend can register for you in the morning, and you can see a specialist without a referral. The majority of the doctors working in large hospitals are specialists. Even though there are few formal specialty fellowship programs in China, doctors can become specialists after working for years in the same department.

Mom and I arrived at the hospital around 8 a.m. The outpatient registration and the outpatient pharmacy were located on the first floor of the outpatient building. There were about 8-10 register counters. People were standing in lines waiting for their turn in front of the counters. The doctors' names and their specialties were posted on the wall above the register counters. You could choose any specialist on the wall as long as there were openings. If the doctor you preferred was fully booked that day, you could come back early the next day to register, or you could choose another doctor that was available. Nevertheless, you could not register in advance. Medical doctors are mainly classified into

143

attending physicians, associate chief physicians, and chief physicians. Some senior doctors are designated as expert physicians by the hospital administration or the health department. You need to pay a higher fee to see an expert physician.

Lines were not very long that day. My turn came after about a 10-minute wait. I pointed to the name of an orthopedist and said to the registrar, "I'd like to register my mother to see this doctor." I was surprised that Mom's appointment time would be at 9:00 a.m. Mom could see an orthopedist within one hour after the same day registration.

In the U.S., it sometimes takes days to see a primary care doctor, and you have to wait weeks (even months) before you can see a specialist, which requires a referral by your primary care doctor in most cases. In my clinic, I need to type in a referral order on the computer if I refer a patient to see a specialist. The front desk secretary will print out the referral on paper and tell the patient, "I'll notify you after I obtain an appointment for you." Sometimes, the staff at the front desk is too busy to call the specialist's clinic to get an appointment. Most of the time, they do not even bother to call before the patient checks out, as the majority of specialist clinics do not give you an appointment right away. Some specialist clinics need to review the patient's record before offering an appointment. I know one clinic does not even accept phone calls for a referral. This clinic only accepts fax or email referral materials, saying they will notify the referred patient after reviewing the patient's information. The supporting staff in the clinic spends a lot of time printing, faxing or emailing office notes and other laboratory or imaging reports in order to get a consult. More errors are likely to occur as a result of this tedious communication. Furthermore, patients in my new clinic need to wait six months to see an endocrinologist.

Mom and I took the elevator to the surgery clinic on the third floor. There was only one patient ahead of us. Before long, Mom was already sitting on one side of the doctor's desk. The orthopedist ordered a knee x-ray after examining Mom's knee. I took Mom back to the radiology department on the first floor. After I had paid the fee, I waited. Mom waited about 15 minutes and then entered the x-ray room for the test. After the test, Mom and I waited about 40-45 minutes in the waiting area before the x-ray report was signed by a radiologist.

We brought the report and the x-ray film back up to the third floor to see the orthopedist again. I also looked at the x-ray film myself. In fact, the orthopedist had already reviewed the digital image of Mom's knee on his computer. Mom's knee x-ray revealed only mild to moderate osteoarthritis.

"Try some medicine, ma'am," the doctor said to my mother while entering the prescription into the computer without looking up again. The doctor prescribed some anti-inflammatory drugs, plus several boxes of herbal medicine for Mom. Mom had tried numerous herbal medications, Chinese massages, and acupuncture without any improvement. I had seen many unopened boxes and bottles of herbal drugs in her apartment.

"Is it okay to give her a cortisone injection in her knee?" I suggested.

"That's fine. Let's do it," the doctor said without looking at me.

The doctor entered new orders into the computer. He printed out the prescription by the printer next to him and handed the paper to me. Mom waited on the third floor while I took the prescription to go to the pharmacy on the first floor. Since I knew those herbal medications were useless or harmful, I filled only the prescription for injection medications. I paid the medication and injection fee at the cashier, who transferred the information to the pharmacy electronically. The pharmacy was located 30 yards away on the same floor. (In the past, you needed to take the receipt yourself to the pharmacy and then wait until your name was called.)

Within 10-15 minutes, Mom's name appeared on the large screen above the pickup windows at the pharmacy. After picking up the medications at the pickup window, I walked back up to the third floor and handed over the medications to a nurse, who notified the orthopedist. The orthopedist came to perform the knee injection on Mom within 15 minutes. Then Mom and I left the hospital for home. The whole ordeal lasted less than three hours, and it was not bad compared to seeing doctors in the U.S. The only difference was that I did not see a smile on the face of any healthcare personnel, and the doctors had little eye contact with patients. Mom's knee pain showed some improvement after the knee injection.

In 2014, I accompanied Mom to the same hospital clinic for her diabetes. The outpatient building was much more crowded than three years earlier. Mom and I arrived at the registration area at 7:30 a.m. I stood in line for about 30 minutes before I got to the registration counter. I told the registrar that Mom wanted to see a doctor for her diabetes. I was given a registration slip for internal medicine. Mom and I took the elevator to the fourth floor, where the department of internal medicine was located. I was surprised to find out that there were many offices inside the department of internal medicine. There was a sign posted at the front of each office indicating specialties, general medicine, diabetes care, cardiology, nephrology, etc. You could choose to see any doctor within the department. There were two doctors working in each office.

Mom told me to put the registration slip at the door of the office for diabetes care. There were more than 10 people ahead of Mom. Mom sat in the waiting area, waiting for her turn. All the office doors were wide open. The people waiting outside could see and hear what was going on inside the office. According to my observation, it took about three to five minutes for the diabetes doctor to finish seeing one patient. Mom and I waited about an hour and a half until Mom's name was finally called. Mom entered the room and sat down in the chair. She handed her medical record booklet to the doctor, who started to look at the record and his computer without looking at or talking to Mom. Then he pulled out his automatic blood pressure meter to check Mom's blood pressure.

"Your blood pressure is too high. I'm going to increase your blood pressure medication," he said while entering data on the computer and printing out a prescription slip, which included all the medications Mom needed to take. He did not explain to Mom which medications had been adjusted. The whole office visit lasted about three minutes without any eye contact or physical exam. The doctor spent most of his three minutes dealing with his computer.

Since Mom can only get 30 days of medication without refills at each visit, she has to come to the clinic monthly to get her medications. Even though no optimal follow-up interval has been defined in terms of clinical outcomes, a monthly routine office visit seems unnecessary for patients with stable chronic diseases like my mother.[1] The news says that China plans to double the number of its general doctors by 2020 in order to improve its health care system.[2] In my opinion, if routine office visits can be scheduled for stable patients every three or six months instead of every month, then the number of general doctors will be increased by more than 200 percent immediately! Most importantly, doctors can see fewer patients per day and provide higher-quality patient care.

Sometimes, I take Mom to see my parents-in-law, who moved to a nursing home a few years ago as they were getting weaker and required more care. My father-in-law, Mr. Wang, is now 87 years old and a World War II veteran. He has suffered chronic back pain for more than half a century. Mr. Wang has a good memory and can handle his financial issues without signs of dementia. He can do calculations and read newspapers, magazines, device instructions, and details of drug information. However, he has a bad temper, has a strange personality, and is extremely difficult to get along with. He has fired numerous medical aids.

The cost of nursing homes varies with the quality of the facilities in China. The nursing home where my parents-in-law live costs around $1,000-1,500 per person per month. However, the government health insurance doesn't cover nursing home care. My parents-in-law pay for it by their savings. The nursing home is located on the top two floors of a hospital building and is considered to be high-end. The nursing home residents can be conveniently transferred to the acute hospital wards within the same building when they get sick. Additionally, doctors can be called to come up to see nursing home residents when they do not feel well. How much care they receive in the nursing home depends on how much money they want to pay. The nursing home provides different levels of care to residents: routine, intensive, or 24-hour maximum care on the basis of their payment. The nursing home residents can change the level of care at any time according to their health conditions, or they can hire private medical aids to supplement the nursing home care. As in the U.S., powerful or wealthy people can live in luxury in medical facilities with all the care.

In the U.S., nursing home residents receive their care according to their needs. As far as I know, American nursing homes charge each patient at the same rate unless a resident pays extra money to get a private room. Of course, the cost of nursing home living varies in different areas, in the range of $40,000 to $100,000 per year. Medicare only pays for the first 100 days of nursing home care. Beyond that, the residents or Medicaid will take over. However, most nursing home residents cannot afford to pay for the nursing home cost. The majority of my nursing home patients were supported by Medicaid.

Mr. Wang fell one year ago and fractured his right hip, resulting in severe pain. His doctor recommended surgical treatment for his hip fracture. However, he refused to undergo surgery.

"Please shoot me with some medicine and let me die. My hip hurts like hell!" he spoke to his doctor. He signed a DNR (Do Not Resuscitate) and "no artificial feeding" document many years ago.

"We doctors don't kill people," his doctor replied firmly.

There is no palliative or hospice service in China. Many people suffer a lot before they die. There is a curse word in China: "die like a dog!" To die peacefully is considered a blessing in China. Mr. Wang continued to decline the surgery. He had a lot of pain, lying in bed and moaning all day. A family member or a surrogate needed to sign the consent for the surgery. There was no preoperative medical evaluation. His surrogate called us about the situation. His children could not persuade him to have surgery. I was not sure if his doctor had talked to him about the benefits of the surgery. Anyhow, Mr. Wang was willing to speak with me over the phone.

"I don't want surgery. I just want to die," he said, seemingly in pain.

"Without surgery, you'll keep having pain for a long time," I said. "Besides, you won't be able to walk anymore and will stay in bed all the time. Have you thought about that?"

"Not quite like that."

"I know that you are not afraid of death," I said. "They're going to put you to sleep during surgery, and then you won't have pain and won't know what happens. If you get over the surgery, your hip pain will improve, and you can walk again and live better. If you die during surgery, God bless you. Is that what you want?"

"You're right," he replied. "I'll take the surgery."

148

Initially, we thought the surgeon was going to pin the broken bones back together. Actually, Mr. Wang underwent total hip replacement. He got a new American artificial hip, which cost three times as much as a Chinese hip. He not only survived the surgery but also was able to walk with a walker again after three months of rehabilitation. Recently, he has learned to shoot pictures using his new smartphone.

There is always a way out as long as you dare to try.

IV (Intravenous) Tonic

One time, Mom took me to see her old friend and her friend's son, Mr. Liu, who helped Mom a lot in the past. When we got to their house, Mr. Liu was not at home. Mom's friend said her son (Mr. Liu) had just walked to a nearby clinic to receive tonic treatment. We stopped by the clinic to see him on our way home. This was a small neighborhood clinic. We found Mr. Liu lying on a hospital bed and receiving IV (intravenous) treatment in a therapy room. There were 10 beds in the room, which was so crowded that people had difficulty walking through it. Amazingly, all the 10 beds were occupied by patients receiving IV infusions. This kind of scene only takes place in oncology clinics or hospital infusion facilities in the U.S.

"Why do you come here for an IV?" we asked.

"I just want to take some tonics because I've been feeling tired recently," Mr. Liu replied.

"Do you feel better after the IV?"

"Sure."

When Mom and I passed by the clinic two years later, I was surprised to find that there were no patients there at all. The clinic with glass doors was wide open so that I could see inside: two medical doctors were reading newspapers at their desks while a dentist was taking a nap in the dental chair. I guess the patients must have gone to large hospitals for care.

China's doctors provide one kind of IV treatment that is unique in the world. According to the theory of traditional Chinese medicine, even healthy people need to take tonics from time to time to stay strong and prolong life, instead of doing exercise, eating a healthy diet, and having good rest. The tonics consist of medicinal herbs. In the old days, people used to consume them by mouth. However, in modern times, more and more people take tonics by intravenous infusion. The intravenous tonic solution usually contains herbal extracts, vitamins, amino acids, glucose, and saline. Doctors will add some western medicine to the solution according to patients' symptoms.

There is no scientific evidence that tonic treatment improves health. Some tonic manufacturers claim that their products are made of secret ingredients used by emperors and royal family members. Ironically, most of these emperors died young. Nowadays, people think IV tonics work even more quickly and better than oral therapy. This kind of tonic treatment is not always benign. It may make you sick or kill you. Here are two tragic stories about IV tonic therapy.

Mr. Tang, 82 years old, was my father-in-law's next room neighbor in the nursing home. He was still actively enjoying his life before he died. His wife, Mrs. Tang, went to receive IV tonic treatments regularly even though she was not ill. She urged her husband, Mr. Tang, to take IV tonic therapy too, for she felt better and stronger after IV drips. Mr. Tang was not sick at all and did not want to take it initially. Finally, he listened to his wife's advice and took IV tonics. If you wish to pay for IV therapy, you'll get it in China. Regrettably, Mr. Tang died from cardiac arrest during an IV tonic therapy, which was witnessed by my cousin who was taking care of my father-in-law in the same therapy room. I guess Mr. Tang might have suffered from an allergic reaction to the herbal extracts or from fluid overload (the infusion rate is too fast for elderly people). The tonic therapy had left Mrs. Tang with loneliness and remorse for the rest of her life.

When my sister-in-law traveled to China a few years ago, she went to see her former colleague, who was a stroke patient in a nursing home. Her former colleague was in her fifties and had gone to take IV tonics without any medical reason. As soon as she walked out of the clinic, she developed a massive stroke. She became bedridden in a vegetative state for three years and then died. I think her stroke might have been due to brain embolism caused by an intravenous accident or herbal extract particles.

There have been many reports that people die from allergic reactions to IV herbal extracts in China. Herbal extract IV drugs are not rigorously tested before being used in humans in China. IV injection of herbal medicine causes much more and serious adverse reactions than oral administration does.[1] The government continues to allow the production and clinical use of IV herbal extracts due to political and economic reasons. There are numerous chemicals and proteins in an herbal extract solution, compared with only a few chemicals in an IV solution in western medicine. Thus, the risk of allergic reactions to IV herbal extracts is much higher. Although China's doctors prescribe numerous IV tonics or IV herbal extracts for their patients, I don't think that the doctors themselves want to have a taste of this "good stuff." And few people dare to say something bad about it in public.

I had met quite a few patients in the U.S. who were interested in Chinese medicine. One of them came to see me as a new patient.

"I want to see a doctor who knows Chinese medicine," he said.

"You have come to see the right doctor then," I said.

"Do you offer Chinese herbal medicine or acupuncture?"

"No."

"Why?"

"Because they are neither effective nor better than existing treatments. Some herbal medications are even harmful."

"How do you know that?"

"I studied Chinese medicine and acupuncture in China, and I'm familiar with the scientific research on them."

"Then I don't think you can help me."

"I can't help you if what you want is only Chinese medicine. You'd better look for another doctor who offers alternative medicine treatment."

I remember two of my patients walking out of the office after the above conversation. But most of them stayed and said, "I still like you even if you don't give Chinese medicine."

For more than 10 years, I have been giving this answer to patients or their families who are interested in Chinese medicine. I would liken Chinese medicine to a horse, and modern medicine to contemporary transportation. People have used horses to do all kinds of things for thousands of years, such as carrying things/people and fighting battles. You can still see police officers ride horses to patrol, and we watch horse races. Nonetheless, modern transportation provides us with cars, planes, ships, and trains that carry us much farther away at higher speeds. You will surely get to your destination almost all the time. Undoubtedly, there are numerous traffic accidents that cause injuries and deaths. About 40,000 people die from motor vehicle accidents in the U.S. each year. In the same way, modern medications have adverse effects, and procedures or surgeries cause complications. Still, we know about those bad outcomes and are trying to reduce them. You cannot go too far by riding a horse, and horses cannot carry thousands of people to work every day as subways do. People can fall from horses and become paralyzed. In the U.S., more people watch car races than horse races.

A lot of people argue that Chinese people have used Chinese medicine for several thousand years and that there are so many people in China thanks to the effectiveness of this medicine. But the fact is, most Chinese people, including emperors, died young until western medicine like vaccinations was introduced into China, along with improved public health care. Actually, the population density of China is ranked as the eighty-second in the world.

If Chinese medicine were a viable and effective medical modality, then it should keep progressing and treat more and more diseases the same way modern medicine does. However, the opposite is happening. For instance, when there was no effective treatment for HIV or AIDS twenty years ago, Chinese traditional medicine doctors had claimed to be able to treat AIDS. Nonetheless, they have stopped talking about it ever since effective treatments for HIV/AIDS became available. Thus, most herbal medications, acupuncture, and other alternative therapeutics are proven to be either ineffective or minimally effective in a handful of conditions (most related to pain), but not better than modern medical treatments. They also tend to be more costly. Back in the 1970s, acupuncture anesthesia was touted as a miracle through political propaganda both in the U.S. and in China. Nowadays, you would be considered insane if you wanted to have any surgery under acupuncture anesthesia.

It has been known that acupuncture works better for Western patients than for Asian patients. When patients with chronic pain are told to be referred to a pain specialist, they may get better even before they are seen by the pain doctor. The mind and brain influence how one perceives pain. People are familiar with the phantom limb phenomenon, i.e., one feels pain in his leg even after the leg has been amputated. Quite a few patients told me they felt pain in their amputated legs, especially during sleep. On the contrary, wounded soldiers sometimes experience no pain in the battlefield. The "belief" in alternative medicine will affect the result of interventions, at least in the area of pain control.

Acupuncture is popular in the U.S. even though it has been proven to produce only a placebo effect or little or no beneficial effects in most circumstances. I can say it cannot achieve better outcomes than the existing treatments, and it tends to be more expensive. For instance, recently, a Medscape article quoted two studies on GERD (gastroesophageal reflux) treatment by acupuncture.[2,3,4] One of the studies showed: six weeks of daily acupuncture treatment had achieved beneficial effects similar to a daily treatment, with a combination of PPI (proton-pump inhibitor like omeprazole) and H2-receptor antagonists such as ranitidine. This kind of treatment is not cost-effective in the U.S. One session of acupuncture costs about $50-$125. A patient may pay about $2,000 for 30 sessions ($75 x 30 = $2,250). Furthermore, the patient may spend at least two hours on each session of therapy, including transportation time, waiting time, and actual therapy time. If one's wage is just $20 per hour, the working hours lost during the treatment course can generate $1,200 ($20 x 2 x 30 = $1,200). Namely, one needs to spend about $3,000 on GERD treatment with acupuncture to achieve a similar benefit with PPI treatment. PPI treatment of one-year duration costs less than $300. PPI drugs can be bought over the counter at $20-30 per month. For example, Nexium 24HR Capsules (42 Count) are available for just $23.68 ($0.56/Count) at Amazon.com on August 23, 2015.

"Do you do acupuncture?" a new patient asked me.

"No," I replied.

"I have been receiving it three times a week for the past five years in another state," he said.

"Why do you want to continue to do it? Look, you still use a cane to walk after five years of acupuncture treatment."

"That's the reason I need to keep doing it. My insurance paid for it. My doctor was so nice that she did not even want me to pay the copayment." (According to Medicare regulations, waiving copayments or deductibles is a fraud.)

"You can look up the names around this area. I don't refer my patients for acupuncture."

By the same token, acupuncture cannot regrow the damaged cartilage of the knee, and the acupuncture for knee pain requires about ten to twenty sessions in most cases, which are costly in the U.S. When acupuncture treatment ends, pain tends to come back very soon so that patients have to keep going to acupuncture clinics. The latest original investigation published in the Journal of the American Medical Association in 2014 states: *In patients older than 50 years with moderate or severe chronic knee pain, neither laser nor needle acupuncture conferred benefit over sham for pain or function. Our findings do not support acupuncture for these patients.* [5]

Chinese medicine represents an early stage of the conventional medicine (also called: modern, mainstream, or Western medicine). The theories or concepts in traditional Chinese medicine reflect the thinking of ancient people, which are not unique and have existed in medicine in many other countries for a long time. Human beings all over the world started to try herbal medicine thousands of years ago. Even my cat will lick and chew plants or grass when he feels bad. If some components of herbs or plants have been proven to be effective, they have already become members of conventional medicine like aspirin, metformin (antidiabetic), statins (cholesterol-lowering drugs), and so on. For example, the anti-malaria drug (Qinghaosu, artemisinin) was discovered and isolated from a Chinese herb by Tu Youyou, a Chinese scientist using scientific methods in the 1970s. The success of artemisinin has nothing to do with Yin Yang or the Five Elements theory in traditional Chinese medicine. Similar elemental concepts or theories about medical disorders and human beings were already used in medieval Europe and ancient Greece.

In summary, Chinese medicine is like a horse in many ways. A horse cannot run faster than a plane, and a horse-drawn carriage cannot carry more people than a train no matter how hard you try to train the horse. Besides, breeding horses is expensive too. Namely, it is impossible for

Chinese medicine to develop and flourish as conventional medicine does. Herbal medicine is much more costly with little or no beneficial effects or even harmful effects. For decades, Chinese medicinal herbs have been known to cause liver damage.[6] Taiwan is found to have the highest rate of end-stage renal disease in the world.[7] One of the causes is probably associated with the widespread use of herbal remedies.[8]

Let a horse be a horse. We can continue to use horses for horse races, horse sports, patrolling the streets, carrying tourists for sightseeing, or even mountaineering. In the same way, minor ailments can be treated with dietary supplements (vitamins, minerals, herbs, etc.), home remedies, and even nothing at all. When you're in an emergency, you should call an ambulance, not a horse-drawn carriage. Whenever you fall ill, you should see your medical doctor first. An alternative medicine or Chinese medicine clinic is the last resort, where you will be given hope only if you can afford to buy the hope.

I haven't found any statement that describes alternative medicine better than this: "*It is time for the scientific community to stop giving alternative medicine a free ride... There cannot be two kinds of medicine — conventional and alternative. There is only medicine that has been adequately tested and medicine that has not, medicine that works and medicine that may or may not work. Once a treatment has been tested rigorously, it no longer matters whether it was considered alternative at the outset. If it is found to be reasonably safe and effective, it will be accepted...,*" which was written in 1998 by Dr. Marcia Angell, the former editor-in-chief of *New England Journal of Medicine*.[9]

If people understand the simple concept: *medicine that works and medicine that may or may not work*, as described above, then there won't be any arguments about alternative medicine or Chinese medicine.

Yi Nao (医闹-Medical Disturbance)

Recently, my medical school classmates had a heated online discussion about the event concerning a doctor who was beaten up by an unsatisfied patient in China. It is true that some Chinese people use their fists, knives, or demonstrations to solve the conflicts between patients and doctors. A lot of western media has reported that violence against China's health care personnel has been rising in the recent years. From 2002 to 2012, assaults against health care personnel increased by about 23% per year, as stated by the China Hospital Management Society. On March 22, 2014, the Lancet published an editorial titled, "Violence against doctors: Why China? Why now? What next?"[1]

I had thought that it was very safe to practice medicine in the U.S. until I started to write this section and did some research on this issue. I found out that violence against health care workers occurs all over the world and is also on the rise.

An article in British Medical Journal (BMJ) states, *"(In China)-Over the 10 years to the end of 2011, details of 124 incidents of serious violence in hospitals have been collated. The incidents included 29 murders and 52 serious injuries, most of which were caused by stabbing or head injury."*[2] In summary, about three doctors are killed by patients or patients' relatives in China each year. According to the Ministry of Health, more than 17,000 incidents against hospitals and their personnel occurred in China in 2010, while there were only around 10,000 incidents five years earlier.[3]

On another note, physicians kill themselves at the rate of one per day in the U.S.[4] About 300-400 physicians commit suicide in the U.S. each year. The suicide rate of American physicians is two times higher than the general population. That means the physician's job itself kills many of them. Two young doctors died prematurely in the small town where

I worked during my first five years of practice. One of them killed himself using a gun, and another died mysteriously in his office.

According to the U.S. Bureau of Labor Statistics, 16,849 assaults in the workplace occurred in 2007.[5] Nearly 60 percent of all nonfatal assaults and violent acts by persons in the workplace occurred in healthcare settings in 2003-2007. That means around 10,000 assaults occurred in healthcare settings each year. Nearly three-quarters of these assaults were by patients or residents of a health facility. The most common victims of assaults were nursing aides, orderlies, and attendants.

Twenty physicians and fifteen nurses were killed at work in the U.S. from 1997 through 2007.[6] Moreover, eight health care providers, including four doctors, have been killed by anti-abortion violence over the past twenty years.[7] There are twice as many physicians in China as in the U.S. I could not obtain the information about how many physicians commit suicide in China each year. It seems that physicians are murdered in healthcare settings in the U.S. at the same rate as in China. I heard the news from the radio while revising the draft for my memoir: a doctor was fatally shot at a VA clinic in Texas on January 6, 2015, and Dr. Michael Davidson, a 44-year-old cardiac surgeon, was killed by a gunman at Boston's Brigham and Women's Hospital just two weeks later.[8, 9]

The violence against China's doctors stands out because of an emerging phenomenon called Yi Nao (medical or hospital disturbance). Yi Nao incidents are commonly initiated by patients, patients' relatives, and friends. In recent years, more and more Yi Nao activities are handled by Yi Nao companies. In fact, Yi Nao companies do business just like the injury law firms in the U.S. The difference is that they seek compensation from the hospital on behalf of patients by using threats or assaults instead of standard legal procedures. When medical disputes occur, Yi Nao companies will send their personnel to approach hospitals, which are often forced to settle the cases outside the legal system. In the U.S., anti-abortion activists use similar tactics against health care personnel, but more violently. They carry out not only demonstrations but also murders, assaults, threats, arsons, bombings, kidnappings, etc.[7]

American lobbying companies follow the law to influence politicians, and American people like to seek help from lawyers for any medical-legal issues. In the U.S., injury law firms advertise their businesses on TV, in the newspaper, and on huge roadside billboards. The majority of the advertisements for legal services are paid by injury law firms, which handle cases of medical malpractice, compensation from drug companies, car insurance, etc.

During a routine office visit, I mentioned to Mrs. Atkins that some lawyers on TV had advertised about bladder cancer being caused by Actos, an antidiabetic drug. Mrs. Atkins misheard my words: Actos causes "breast" cancer instead of "bladder" cancer. She acted so fast that she went to see her lawyer about it after the visit, without asking me for more information. She had been diagnosed with breast cancer while on Actos a few years earlier. At the next visit, she told me that her lawyer did not have any clue about the breast cancer induced by Actos. She laughed loudly when I explained to her that there was data showing that Actos might increase the risk of "bladder" cancer, not "breast" cancer.

"It is my fault. My poor English," I smiled.

"There is nothing wrong with you," she giggled. "I just acted too quickly."

"Dr. B lost one million dollars in the malpractice lawsuit."

This was the headline on the front page of our local newspaper a few years ago. In a small town, the local hospital is usually the largest employer and has a considerable impact on the local economy. Anything that happens to doctors will appear in the newspaper. A lot of doctors get sued during their lifetime of practice. By age 65, 75% of physicians in low-risk specialties and 99% of physicians in high-risk specialties will have been involved in a malpractice lawsuit, according to the estimates in an article published in the New England Journal of Medicine.[10]

Surely, medical violence cannot be completely prevented in China or the U.S. Nevertheless, I think that the appearance of Yi Nao companies can be seen as favorable progress. I have yet to see any report of a doctor being killed by a Yi Nao company in China. If angry patients or relatives hire Yi Nao companies to settle their cases, they will not resort to their fists or knives without first thinking of the consequences. The problem is how the Chinese government will regulate and supervise Yi Nao companies and make them legal businesses like law firms in the U.S. As in medicine, preventing or reducing conflicts would help more than hiring security guards or establishing Yi Nao companies.

In spite of some Yi Nao (medical disturbance), China's health care system has greatly improved over the past six decades. A recent article published in the New England Journal of Medicine states, *"By 2012, a (Chinese) government-subsidized insurance system provided 95% of the population with modest but comprehensive health coverage."* [11] Chinese hospitals or clinics accept most insurance plans. There are not that many programs to choose from, and most people have the same insurance card throughout the cities.

It is common in China for people to use their insurance cards to get medicine for their friends or relatives. They talk about it openly without embarrassment. When a patient is hospitalized in China, the family frequently needs to hire a nursing aid to help the patient. American hospitals take care of almost everything for inpatients. However, hospitalization in the U.S. is much more expensive, probably 5-10 times more than in China.

China's doctors may earn bonuses for prescribing more medications, tests, or procedures. The hospitals usually own the equipment and pharmacies. My cousin complained to me in China, "Son of a b...! My doctor always prescribes expensive medicine for me. I have to spend more than 150-200 Yuan (about $30-$40) filling my prescriptions every month." His retirement payment is around $500 monthly.

In China, IV (intravenous) therapies are used extensively in treating even minor illnesses, such as upper respiratory infections. Hospitals or clinics are crowded with people receiving IV antibiotics, especially in the winter. Chinese people receive two to three times more IV infusions than the world average.[12] Even the Chinese Health Department and medical experts recognize that a lot of these IV treatments are inappropriate. According to the state-run Xinhua News Agency, antibiotic use in China is 10 times the level in the U.S.[13] The good news is that the overuse of antibiotics in China has reduced in recent years.[14]

China's doctors tend to look serious without smiling or making eye contact when talking with patients and families. Before a surgery in China, a patient tends to give his or her surgeon an envelope filled with money as a gift. The envelope is called *hongbao* or "red packet," containing something like 1,000 Yuan (around $160).[15] The Chinese government has been implementing anti-corruption policies in the healthcare system in the recent years.[16] Hopefully, the *hongbao* phenomenon will disappear soon.

I have never heard of any surgeon accepting such monetary gifts from patients in the U.S. However, some doctors do get paid by drug or device companies to be speakers or consultants. *The New York Times* reported that one of the doctors at Harvard University had received $1.6 million in speaking and consulting fees from drug companies.[17] An orthopedic surgeon allegedly claimed the fee for five major procedures from an insurance company, when in fact, the patient stayed in the operation room for less than 10 minutes, according to a report at Medscape.com.[18]

What I described above and in other chapters is just a reflection of the differences between China and America in terms of cultural background, stage of economic development, government health policies, health care environments, and educational systems. I am amazed that many large hospitals in China have better facilities than their American counterparts. Residency training programs have started in recent years and, hopefully, will soon be implemented everywhere in China. Then there will be fewer variations in clinical knowledge and skills among Chinese doctors. In the future, patients do not have to crowd the large hospitals in China.

The United States of America has the best medical education, technology, and science in the world. Most American physicians possess standard medical competence thanks to supervision systems like licensure, board exams, board certifications, strict uniform residency/fellowship training, and so on. However, American medical care is the most expensive (about $8,000 per person per year) in the world, and its health delivery system does not produce favorable health outcomes, with possibly more than 100,000 deaths per year due to medical errors.[19]

According to *The New York Times*, after undergoing his three-hour neck surgery for herniated disks, Mr. Peter Drier had received a bill of $56,000 from the hospital, a bill of $4,300 from the anesthesiologist, a bill of $133,000 from his orthopedist, and (surprisingly) another bill of $117,000 from a surgeon he did not meet.[20] The whole medical bill consisted of $310,300, which is the average price for a new house in the U.S.[21] It was unbelievable that the three-hour neck surgery had cost so much. It is no wonder that medical bills are the number one reason why American people file for bankruptcy.[22]

"America is the greatest place in the world to get care for a complicated but treatable disease, if you have the ability to get the care and pay for it. It's not a great place to be sick if you are poor and uninsured or want consistent, basic care," Dr. Otis Webb Brawley stated in his book, *How We Do Harm.* [23]

At the end of the day, many health care problems need to be solved in China and in the U.S., as well as in other countries. The first change I would like to see: China's doctors having a warm smile on their faces, and American medicine becoming less like a business.

7. End of Life

The greatest human freedom is to live, and die, according to one's own desires and beliefs.

—Melissa Barber
(The Electronic Communications Specialist, the Death with Dignity National Center)

己所不欲，勿施於人。
(What you do not wish for yourself, do not do to others.)

—Confucius (551-479 B.C., Chinese Philosopher)

I feel guilty for not being able to help Mom more, as I only get to spend two to three weeks with her in China each year. Whenever I am in China, I always ask her, "Where do you want to go? I can go with you to see your relatives, friends or doctors." Mom lives in Guangzhou (广州, also known as Canton), which has become a huge city with a population of around 12 million in the recent years. It is the third largest city in China. Traffic is usually heavy most of the time, even though there are buses, cabs, and an underground railway system. Mom will make arrangements for our trips on each day. We usually go to our destinations by taking a cab, with each trip costing about $5-15. We always go to her hometown and see my uncles, aunts, and my cousins. We eat dinner together with relatives at the same restaurant every year. Mom has three sisters and one brother. All her sisters are healthy in their 70s. Her brother, my uncle, was the oldest and died four years ago at the age of 82.

We went to visit my uncle at a hospital two months before he died. My uncle had suffered from dementia for years, most likely due to heavy drinking and aging. This time, he had been hospitalized for more than six months as a consequence of recurrent infections and failure to thrive. I almost did not recognize him when I entered the room. He was semi-comatose with a nasal feeding tube and was moaning all the time. He was extremely skinny and bony with soiled clothing and bed sores. His two sons, my cousins, were standing at the bedside. They had hired a nursing aid to take care of their father. One of them stepped out into the hallway to criticize the aid for not taking good care of their father, pointing out issues such as not turning the body regularly, not keeping the body clean, not feeding him well, etc.

My uncle was terminally ill with severe dementia. The feeding tube and antibiotics would prolong the dying process so that my uncle would suffer more. Most Chinese people were unfamiliar with the concept of comfort treatment, palliative care, and hospice. In the U.S., patients and families tend to choose palliative therapy or hospice service in this situation. My cousins did not ask me for advice; therefore, I could not offer any recommendation. They would have been unhappy if I said to them, "Please ask the doctor to withdraw all the treatments and do something to keep your father comfortable." Palliative or hospice therapy was not widely available in China then. Even if my cousins had asked for comfort treatment, their doctors would not have listened to them.

The scene was very depressing. "I can't look at this anymore," Mom said sadly, wanting to leave the hospital as soon as possible. My uncle's dying process lasted two more months after our visit.

"Die in Your Hand"

Long before she passed away, Mrs. Peterson spoke this to me several times, "I'd like to die in your hand." I initially thought Mrs. Peterson simply meant that she liked my service and had trust in me. Unexpectedly, in the end, she did pass away in my hand according to her "plan."

Mrs. Peterson was about 80 years old then, slim, of medium height, with blues eyes and still looked beautiful when I met her the first time. She was a widow of a government official and used to work as a manager at a department store. She suffered from numerous chronic conditions: rheumatoid arthritis with persistent joint pain, osteoporosis, chronic neck and back pain, hypothyroidism, muscle spasm, insomnia, anxiety, depression, chronic abdominal pain with more than 10 abdominal surgeries, GERD (gastroesophageal reflux disease), chronic constipation, urinary incontinence, chronic fluid retention and heart failure. Her generalized weakness and unsteady gait had resulted in many falls and fractures.

She had seen many other specialists, including orthopedists, gastroenterologists, rheumatologists, endocrinologists, general surgeons, and many internal medicine doctors. It is very common to drive 30-50 even 100 miles to see a specialist in this rural area. Mrs. Peterson had undergone at least twenty surgeries. Her daughter, Emily, was her main care provider. You can imagine how much work Emily had done for her mother all those years.

The first time I saw Mrs. Peterson was in the emergency department. I was admitting another patient in the emergency room when Emily (her daughter) came up to ask me if I was willing to take care of her mother, Mrs. Peterson. Mrs. Peterson came to our clinic to see Dr. Vaughan, an endocrinologist for osteoporosis regularly. When she got sick, she would be admitted by her internist from another clinic in town. Emily saw me in the hallway at the clinic and knew that I was an internist working with Dr. Vaughan there.

In the emergency room, I told Emily that I would review Mrs. Peterson's record to decide what I could do. After I had finished the admission of my patient, I reviewed Mrs. Peterson's record and found out that she was a frail woman and had been hospitalized countless times and received many surgeries. Furthermore, she had seen almost all the internists in town except for me. She presented to the ER this time because of recurrent abdominal pain, and she had been seen by her internist and was waiting for transporting to the ward.

I entered Mrs. Peterson's room and noticed that she was groaning in bed, accompanied by Emily. I asked Mrs. Peterson why she wanted me to take care of her. She said she did not like her present internist and wanted to change to another doctor. Emily added, "We have heard a lot of good things about you. We choose you to be her doctor."

"Your doctor has written all orders to admit you and completed his dictation of history and examination," I said to Mrs. Peterson. "It's inappropriate for me to take over your case right now. You can come to the clinic to see me as soon as you are discharged from the hospital. Is that ok?"

"That's fine. I'll see you at the clinic then," Mrs. Peterson replied.

Keeping her promise, Mrs. Peterson came to the clinic to see me after being discharged from the hospital. She had been in my care for about eight years since then. Her daughter, Emily, also became my patient afterward. Initially, Mrs. Peterson took more than 20 medications daily, including subcutaneous injection of Forteo (a drug for osteoporosis). I gradually reduced her medications and adjusted her doses. Finally, I successfully decreased the number of her medications to about ten. She stayed away from the hospital most of the time for the first seven years. She needed hospital care only about once a year during this period.

She had all kinds of complaints when she came in for office visits. Frequently, she showed up as a walk-in patient on Friday afternoon. Her office visits lasted at least 30 minutes or even longer. I always asked her questions one by one patiently. On most occasions, I did not prescribe any new medications or recommend any procedures. She was often satisfied when she left the clinic. Her daughter told me that her mother complained about everything at home, but she looked normal again after seeing me.

Nowadays, more and more people have realized that a hospital is a dangerous place. Some bad things happened to Mrs. Peterson during her hospitalizations. One night, she was admitted because of abdominal pain and back pain. She was given IV fentanyl (an opioid pain medication) by the on-call doctor, who did not review her allergy history. Subsequently, she collapsed with hypotension and confusion. She was transferred to the ICU to receive supportive treatment, and she recovered.

Another time, she fell off the bed face down in the ICU at midnight. I drove back to the hospital to look at her right away and ordered a head CT, which did not show bone fracture or intracranial hemorrhage. Luckily, she suffered only soft tissue contusion, abrasions of her face, and lacerations of her scalp. Her right forehead had looked deformed and concave for years. She had complained of a headache all the time since then.

The ICU is supposed to provide the highest level of supervision. This kind of accident is considered unacceptable. The family members were so angry that the hospital president and other administrators had to come to the ICU to explain things to them. Mrs. Peterson told me that her grandson, a lawyer, spoke to the hospital administrator, "Don't mess with my grandma."

These unfortunate incidents also happened to her daughter, Emily, in the same hospital. Emily was about 60 years old and suffered similar medical problems as her mother did, including rheumatoid arthritis and chronic neck and back pain. Emily was hospitalized for new-onset right sided weakness, which was maybe due to stroke or cervical spine problems. Her CT scans in the emergency department were normal the day before. A nurse called me that Emily still complained of not being able to move the right side of her body and that she had a worsening headache and neck pain. I was seeing patients at the clinic at that time. So I gave an order over the phone to perform an MRI of head and neck without contrast, knowing that Emily had a bad reaction to MRI dye in the past.

However, the nurse called me again later, saying: "Emily is not doing well after coming back from the MRI. She is probably allergic to MRI dye."

"I ordered an MRI without contrast," I said. "Why did they inject the dye into her?"

"You had ordered an MRI with contrast, according to the order on the computer."

I gave some treatment orders over the phone to stabilize her. Then I stopped seeing the patients in the clinic and drove to the hospital immediately. It took 15 minutes for me to drive from the clinic to the hospital. When I arrived at the hospital, I found that Emily was restless, hypotensive, and anxious with rapid breathing. She complained of burning and itching of her whole body as if it were on fire. Still, she was alert and awake, answered my questions correctly. I ordered IV Benadryl, hydrocortisone, IV fluid, oxygen, and nebulizer breathing treatment. Emily was transferred to the ICU for close monitoring.

I looked at my order in the chart: MRI of the head and cervical spine without contrast, which was correct. I showed the order to the nurse in charge. The nurse said, "We are sorry. We found out your order is right. But the secretary entered the incorrect order into the computer."

"I think you need to talk to the administration and take some measures to prevent this kind of error from happening again."

"We will."

Fortunately, Emily's mental status, blood pressure, and breathing had improved gradually overnight. All her symptoms, including weakness, resolved in the morning. Her MRI images did not show abnormalities either. She was transferred out of the ICU at noon, observed one more day in the regular ward, and then discharged home uneventfully. Remembering that her son was a lawyer, I was so relieved and happy when Emily was ready to go home.

Mrs. Peterson often complained about retention of fluid and shortness of breath. During the examination, she was always found to have crackles at the lung bases, but without signs of swelling of legs or feet. She pointed to her abdomen, "My water builds up in my belly, not in my legs or feet." When her symptoms of dyspnea could not be alleviated by oral diuretics, she would be hospitalized for two or three days to receive intravenous diuretic treatment. The transthoracic echocardiography (an exam of the heart using ultrasound) revealed diastolic dysfunction of the heart (abnormal relaxation of the heart). The consulting cardiologist did not recommend invasive diagnostic procedures and advised supportive medical treatments. After three hospitalizations for fluid retention, I added an intramuscular injection of furosemide (a diuretic) to supplement her oral diuretics. Her daughter was shown how to inject diuretic intramuscularly so that she could give Mrs. Peterson an injection of furosemide when Mrs. Peterson felt more dyspnea.

Ever since the addition of intramuscular injection of diuretics, Mrs. Peterson was not admitted for fluid retention and heart failure anymore. Her daughter called me whenever there was something wrong with Mrs. Peterson. I gave instructions over the phone, and Mrs. Peterson responded well most of the time. As a result, she was able to avoid a lot of hospitalizations.

During the last year of her life, Mrs. Peterson was hospitalized for pneumonia, urinary tract infection, and heart failure every one or two months, and she was discharged to nursing homes for rehabilitation many times in addition to home health care. She was confined to a wheelchair most of the time and could walk only two or three steps even with a walker. Mrs. Peterson's final admission was due to pneumonia with fever, chills, and shortness of breath. She requested a **DNR** (do not resuscitate) order whenever she was hospitalized.

DNR means that a person does not want health care professionals to perform cardiopulmonary resuscitation (CPR) on him or her when one stops breathing, or one's heart stops beating. **CPR** includes heart compression, cardiac defibrillation (electric shock across the chest), using a ventilator after endotracheal intubation, and applying medications. Patients do not need to have an advance directive to request a DNR order. Moreover, patients commonly do not have to sign any paper to demand DNR order in the hospital. A physician can obtain a DNR request from a patient's surrogate (proxy) even over the phone.

171

Usually, the next of kin of a patient makes medical decisions for the patient when the patient is unable to do so, unless a durable power of attorney for health care has been chosen in an advance directive (e.g., a living will).

It is very helpful to have a living will or advance directive if you want to have control over your treatment near or at the end of your life. It is also important to express to your spouse or children what treatments you wish to have at the end of life while you are still healthy with a clear mind.

After two days of treatment, Mrs. Peterson showed some improvements. Her fever subsided, and she breathed more comfortably. She was able to sit up in bed and eat some food, occasionally choking. Mrs. Peterson had had difficulty swallowing her food for more than a year, which probably resulted in her pneumonia by aspirating food into her lungs. She had been evaluated by gastroenterologists and speech therapists many times and was recommended NPO (no oral intake) with gastric feeding tube placement. However, Mrs. Peterson refused it.

Unexpectedly, Mrs. Peterson spoke to me quietly, "I have been sick for so long, in and out of the hospital almost every month... I always feel short of breath and tired. With many broken bones and bad joints, I have terrible pain all the time. And I can't even enjoy my food anymore because I choke whenever I swallow."

"Apparently, you have been suffering so much and so long," I said.

"You're right. I have lived a good life. Now, I'm tired of the hospital and nursing home. Even if I can recover this time, soon I'll be right back in the hospital and continue to suffer. I have prayed to God these days. I think I'm ready to go home now. I'd like you to stop all the treatments and just make me comfortable."

"What does your daughter think about this?" I was surprised, thinking that Mrs. Peterson was improving clinically.

"I have had this plan for quite some time. I told my daughter about it a long time ago. She supports me."

"I understand what you mean. I'll talk to your daughter first, and then I'll decide what I'm going to do. Is that okay?"

172

"Okay. Thank you very much. I'll be waiting."

I walked out of the room to call her daughter, Emily and discussed Mrs. Peterson's decision with her.

"Mama is a fighter and has struggled with her illnesses for so many years," her daughter said calmly. "Mama knows it's her time to rest now. The whole family honors Mama's wish. Dr. Li, please just do whatever Mama wants you to do. I agree with Mama."

Then I talked with Mrs. Peterson again, who expressed the same wish firmly. Mrs. Peterson had numerous medical problems causing her to be confined to a wheelchair, and she had frequent hospitalizations due to pneumonia, urinary tract infection and heart failure, and many nursing home rehabilitations. She had continuing fatigue, chronic pain, shortness of breath, and difficulty swallowing - all resulting in poor quality of life. She was competent to make her medical decision, which was also supported by her family. **Palliative care** was indicated for Mrs. Peterson because of her serious illnesses leading to physical and psychological distress.

Palliative care (also called palliative medicine) can be described as comfort care concentrating on alleviating the suffering of seriously ill patients by pain and symptom management. Palliative care services can be offered to patients in all disease stages, without restriction to disease or prognosis. Therefore, Mrs. Peterson was an appropriate patient for palliative care since she suffered serious, complex illnesses even if she might fully or partially recover. Mrs. Peterson had the right to make her treatment choice, which is patient autonomy.

I discontinued all the therapeutic treatment orders and started Mrs. Peterson on intravenous (IV) morphine treatment, which was titrated to her comfort. The intravenous administration of morphine could alleviate her ongoing shortness of breath and pain, for she had difficulty swallowing her oral medications and did not tolerate fentanyl skin patches (opioid patches used for relief of pain). And I asked the hospital hospice service to check on her daily. Mrs. Peterson stopped eating her food and lay in bed comfortably with IV morphine for seven days. During the first few days, she woke and slept in cycles. She slept more and more as the days passed by. On that Friday, I went to the hospital to round on my patients as usual. With closed eyes, Mrs. Peterson was unresponsive to verbal and other kinds of stimuli. She was breathing comfortably with some rapidity.

After finishing examining Mrs. Peterson, I was sitting at the nursing station and writing my notes in the chart when a nurse came up to speak to me, "Dr. Li, I think Mrs. Peterson is dying now."

I headed back quickly to Mrs. Peterson's room and found that she was completely comatose with episodic breathing efforts. I felt her carotid artery and could not detect any pulse. So I held her hand and watched her. She remained beautiful even at the age of 88. A gentle smile spread over her face, and she was peaceful with closed eyes. Her breathing became shallower and shallower, and it finally stopped two to three minutes later. Clearly, God had taken her home.

Mrs. Peterson had been a strong fighter, and she knew when she should stop the fight. She had left for a better place with dignity. Although her physical life had ended quietly, her spirit would live on in the hearts of the people who knew her. Her touching life story will inspire all of us to think about what we want and what we should do near the end of our lives. That was Friday afternoon, just one day before I traveled to China for vacation.

I called her daughter, Emily, to inform her that Mrs. Peterson had just passed away.

"I saw Mama this morning, and I knew she was departing," her daughter said sobbingly, "I know she sensed you were leaving for China tomorrow. She said she wanted to die in your hand. She really did. Thank you very much for all that you have done for her."

I am surely gratified by patients' trust and relationship, and I have experienced the joy of being a doctor through caring for patients - it has made me a better human being. I hope that my doctor can do the same for me and help me leave this world peacefully when I am ready to die.

A few years ago, I thought that I would enjoy leisure time by traveling and reading when I retired at 66.7 (my Social Security age). After writing this story, I have changed my mind. I wish I could work until the day I die, for I can help patients relieve some sufferings with my knowledge and skills while finding joy and happiness in my work. I understand that I have gained knowledge and skills from my teachers, colleagues, and society...but most importantly from my patients. I should pay all the people back by continuing to serve patients.

LIFE AND MEDICINE

DNR (Do Not Resuscitate) Order

DNR means that a person does not want health care professionals to perform cardiopulmonary resuscitation (CPR) on him or her when one stops breathing, or one's heart stops beating. CPR includes heart compression, cardiac defibrillation (electric shock across the chest), using a ventilator after endotracheal intubation, and applying medications. (See more details in the previous section, **"Die in Your Hand"**)

Mr. Schultz, 75 years old, was brought in for the first clinic visit by his sister, the only care provider. He had suffered a bad stroke with significant left side weakness and needed to walk with a walker. He had been diagnosed with schizophrenia since his twenties. Now he was taking four psychiatric medications and could not speak a full sentence. Even though he could eat by himself, he needed assistance with his grooming, toileting, and dressing.

"Since Mr. Schultz cannot make decisions, and you are the care provider, can I talk to you about his end-of-life care?" I asked his sister.

"Yes, please," she replied.

After I had explained the JAMA (Journal of American Medical Association) Patient Page on decisions about end-of-life care to her, I asked, "Do you want Mr. Schultz to have CPR and a feeding tube if he needs these in the future?"

"Yes, I want everything for him."

"Would you want the same thing for yourself if you were in his situation?" I asked.

"No, I wouldn't if I were him."

"Then why do you want CPR for your brother if you don't like it yourself?"

"I've never thought about it that way," she said. "Thank you, I want a DNR order for him."

"This is the first time we have talked about this issue. You don't have to rush. You can think about it and tell me your decision at the next visit."

"I don't need to think about it anymore," she said firmly. "Please write DNR in his chart."

"Okay, I'll write down DNR in his chart. We can talk about this again at the next visit."

In non-critical situations, people have more diverse opinions about end-of-life care. Mrs. Anthony is a 93-year-old retired nurse and still active. She can drive a car and travels around the country two or three times per year. She refused to discuss end-of-life care, saying, "It is too early to discuss this issue."

On the contrary, Mrs. Gibbs, 80 years old, mentioned to me at her first office visit as a new patient that she wanted a DNR order and preferred to donate her body to the nearby medical school after she died.

"Dr. Li, please make sure to put all my wishes into my medical record," Mrs. Gibbs said.

Although Mrs. Gibbs smoked heavily, she did not suffer any lung diseases or lung cancer. As usual, I advised her to quit smoking during the visit.

"No, I don't want to quit smoking as I like it," she said.

"You know, smoking is bad for your health," I said.

"I know that," she smiled. "I don't have children and don't have any hobby. Smoking is my only enjoyment. You know, people said I killed my husband."

"Why did they say that?"

"He was 10 years younger than me and died of lung cancer 10 years ago. He had never been a smoker. I smoked around him all the time. His lung cancer must have come from the second-hand smoke I gave off."

One day, Mrs. Gibbs presented to the emergency room because of passing black stool. She requested a DNR order when she was admitted. She received blood transfusions and other treatments.

Unfortunately, she was diagnosed with metastatic gastric cancer by endoscopic and imaging studies. She did not want to have any treatment for her stomach cancer. She continued to enjoy her cigarettes and told her friends, "Dr. Li said it is okay for me to keep smoking."

Mrs. Gibbs was lucky to have a clear mind and be able to decide herself what she wanted near the end of life. She stayed at home all the time and received hospice service without hospitalizations. She passed away peacefully nine months later.

Even though some elderly dementia patients cannot make decisions themselves, their families request DNR and no hospital care for them so that these patients can die peacefully with dignity at home or in nursing homes. This is one of the humane methods used to avoid prolonging the dying process. Patients on hospice service usually die at home.

However, some of my patients were not that lucky, and their destinations were decided by other people. Mrs. Rose was admitted to a nursing home at the age of 80 because of Alzheimer's disease, and she stayed there for five years until her family took her back home. When she could not eat, her family requested a feeding tube for her. Mrs. Rose received her nutrition through a feeding tube and did not have the ability to speak. She lay in bed all the time with contracture of arms and legs.

Mrs. Rose had seven daughters and one son. Three of her daughters were in town and were my patients. Her other children lived outside of the state. Mrs. Rose's children had requested a DNR order for her, but they wanted her to receive hospital care whenever she got sick. Mrs. Chapman, one of the daughters in town, was the main care provider. Every day and night, Mrs. Chapman had been taking care of her mother at home with the assistance of home health services all these years.

"Dr. Li, your patient, Mrs. Rose, is here for respite care. Please make sure to see the patient when you make rounds," called a nurse from the sub-acute floor of the hospital.

Mrs. Rose was admitted to the sub-acute floor twice per year for respite care, which was paid for by Medicare. **Respite care** is a service that provides short-term and time-limited breaks for the caregivers who are taking care of sick family members. It has been proven beneficial to the health of caregivers. Patients can receive respite services at home, in licensed residential facilities, nursing homes, hospital sub-acute units, etc.

In between respite hospitalizations, Mrs. Rose was admitted for pneumonia or urinary tract infection two or three times per year. Mrs. Rose was so bony (weighing about 60-70 pounds) that she looked like a

179

skeleton with stiff contracted arms and legs. She had developed multiple bedsores. I tried to persuade the family to give up the futile treatment whenever I had the chance.

"Your mother does not look like a human anymore," I said to Mrs. Chapman (the main care provider). "You know that your mother is suffering. You should have a family meeting to decide on having no more hospital care and no more tube feeding, and then start hospice care."

"I understand," Mrs. Chapman said. "All siblings except our brother in Boston did not agree to the withdrawal of treatment."

"Not only does your mother suffer, but you don't have your own life either," I said. "You can't go out to work and are stressed out at home taking care of the sick. And you are sick too." Mrs. Chapman was also struggling with diabetes, obesity, and chronic joint and back pain.

"My brother is far away in Boston and doesn't do the actual caring job," she said helplessly. "However, he wants everything done by the others. We have had several meetings already. He sticks to his decision. Recently, he even stopped talking with us on the phone."

Mrs. Rose continued to be hospitalized twice for respite care and two or three times for infection every year. Finally, she passed away at 93 after being bedridden and speechless at home for eight years.

No wonder one of my patients, a 66-year-old lady, cried during an office visit, "I take care of my 90-year-old mother at home day in and day out. My mother doesn't like me and blames me all the time. Mom says that my brother is the best child. Anyway, my brother doesn't even see her once a year."

That explains why it is often said: if you have a daughter, she will care for you when you become older. Occasionally, some caring daughters manipulate DNR orders liberally. A daughter of a patient requested a DNR order for her mother while her mother was in the hospital, but she demanded full code while her mother was in the nursing home. She said that her mother would receive better care if not in DNR status.

Mrs. Dean was 79 years old then and had been severely demented for more than fifteen years. She had received home health care service during that period. She had been bedridden and speechless for 10 years and relied on a gastric feeding tube for nutrition. Her daughter would call the ambulance to transport her mother to the emergency room whenever her mother did not look right to her. This included her urine smelling bad or having a dark color, her body jerking like a seizure, or sleeping all day without opening her eyes. Most of the time, Mrs. Dean was evaluated and treated in the ER and then discharged back home.

When Mrs. Dean was admitted, her daughter changed the DNR status of her mother from time to time. During one of her mother's hospitalizations, she wanted a DNR order for her mother initially. Then, she called back in an hour to change DNR to full code. She decided DNR status for her mother according to the nurses' attitude and service. She said, "I want DNR status for my mother if the in-charge nurse is nice, but I request full code if the nurses are not doing their jobs well."

Indeed, one of the nurses did perform a poor job: giving Mrs. Dean IV antibiotics that belonged to another patient. I was making rounds in the evening when her daughter came up to me.

"Please come here to have a look, Dr. Li," she said with anger. "They gave the wrong medication to Mama!"

I went to the room to look at the already empty IV bag, indicating the medication had been given to Mrs. Dean. Another patient's name was on the IV bag. Fortunately, Mrs. Dean was not allergic to that antibiotic. Her daughter notified the head nurse and the administration about the medication error. Since then, I have witnessed the hospital taking measures to reduce medication errors. Nowadays, every nurse carries a handheld computer with a barcode reader at work all the time. A drug needs to be scanned to match the barcode on a patient's wristband before it can be given to the patient.

On one occasion, a miracle happened after a DNR order was placed. Mrs. Miller was a 95-year-old demented woman who was admitted to the ICU and placed on a ventilator because of pneumonia, sepsis, and respiratory failure. She did not have a DNR order. After having been on the ventilator for more than one week, she still did not meet the criteria to be removed from the ventilator. I talked with the pulmonary specialist and respiratory therapist, and they both declared that Mrs. Miller was not ready for ventilator removal. I held a family meeting to explain her condition to the family members, and I asked if they wanted to continue the current treatment for Mrs. Miller. The family members also held their own meeting after I left the conference room.

The daughter, the representative of the family, spoke to me, "We have made up our mind. We request a DNR order for Mrs. Miller and approve of taking her off the ventilator. But we would like to keep all other treatments except the intubation and ventilator."

"Now I can say this is the right decision. I'll do as you request."

Afterward, Mrs. Miller was removed from the ventilator by the respiratory therapist. I expected that Mrs. Miller would have passed away within minutes after discontinuation of the ventilator treatment. However, Mrs. Miller amazingly started to breathe comfortably on her own without any assistance. She continued to improve gradually and was discharged back to the nursing home. Even her family was surprised by Mrs. Miller's recovery. Since then, her family had requested a DNR order for her, both in the hospital and in the nursing home. Mrs. Miller was demented and able to say only a few meaningless words. She was bedridden, slept most of the time, and acquired her nutrition through a gastric feeding tube. Her family continued to request hospital care whenever she got sick. Mrs. Miller died at 97 years of age after seven more hospitalizations. Was her life extended or her death prolonged for two more years? It depends on how patients or their families regard the quality of life.

"I Don't Want to Die."

According to the Quality of Life Research Unit at the University of Toronto, the quality of life is described as "the degree to which a person enjoys the important possibilities of his or her life."[1] Typically, this means the individual's perception of his or her physical and mental well-being, such as activities of daily living and pain. Activities of daily living (**ADL**s), basic and instrumental, are referred to as daily self-care activities. Basic ADLs include dressing/bathing, eating, ambulating, toileting, and grooming. Instrumental ADLs, which are required for one to live independently in the community, consist of shopping, housekeeping, accounting, preparing meals, taking medication as prescribed, and using transportation and the telephone. (For more details on this topic, see *Wikipedia: Activities of daily living*)

A measurement of an individual's functional status, especially in the elderly, is how much he or she can perform ADLs. Nevertheless, people have different opinions about what a meaningful and enjoyable life is. Thus, people have different ideas when it comes to making decisions about end-of-life care. Some people want to fight to the last minute. I have seen one breast cancer patient with untreatable metastases to her whole body, including the head and lungs, wanting everything done to keep her alive, even though she was so sick with pneumonia that she was in the ICU. Finally, she died after prolonged CPR.

Oftentimes, the patients do not want all these life-sustaining procedures, but their children request all the aggressive and painful treatments for their parents. Children of patients can have different views on what to do. Some patients or family members even change their decisions about end-of-life care as the disease progresses.

People make significantly different choices when facing life and death issues. "Life" is not the same to everyone. And one's attitude toward life may change from time to time.

Mr. Fuller was a 69-year-old man who lived with a bad heart for many years. He had struggled to survive with advanced technology, medications, and hospital care. He had end-stage heart failure with an implantable cardioverter-defibrillator (ICD, implanted in patients to prevent death from heart arrhythmias) and many stents in the heart. He was also on home oxygen and used a BiPAP machine at night. **BiPAP** (Bi-level positive airway pressure) is a device that delivers a preset positive airway pressure during inhalation and exhalation to assist a patient's respiration. He was not a candidate for heart bypass surgery or heart transplant.

During the last year of his life, he was hospitalized almost every month for exacerbation of heart failure. He developed severe shortness of breath, swelling of the legs and pleural effusion (fluid in the chest cavity). While in the hospital, he received many thoracentesis procedures (removing fluid from the chest cavity by inserting a needle through the chest wall) and required BiPAP treatment all day except while eating. He requested a DNR order every time he was admitted, until the last three months of his life. Cardiologists stopped seeing him, as his heart was end-staged and they did not have anything to offer. Mr. Fuller had been evaluated at several tertiary medical centers many times. When he was admitted again, I asked him if he wanted to maintain his DNR status.

"No. I want everything done to keep me alive," he answered, to my surprise.

"You know you have a very bad heart that can't be fixed, and you have been sick all the time," I asked. "You have requested a DNR order at each admission in the past. Could you tell me the reason why you changed your mind this time?"

"I don't know myself. **I just don't want to die**. It's possibly due to my daughter."

"Your daughter has been sick for years, and I know she was admitted on the fourth floor last night. Is there anything unusual about her?"

"No. I just worry about her."

Mr. Fuller's daughter, Ms. Klein, was an unlucky 35-year-old woman who had been on hemodialysis for 10 years, suffering other numerous medical disorders, including coronary heart disease, diabetes, hypertension, and several strokes. She had undoubtedly broken the hospital record for the number of ER visits and admissions within one year. Owing to her 58 ER visits and 20 admissions during that year, she was well known in the hospital. Ms. Klein usually presented to the ER with complaints of pain in the chest or inability of moving her arms and legs. Many times, she was admitted for observation of questionable acute coronary syndrome, or hospitalized for a new stroke due to her serious underlying diseases. Last night, she was admitted because of severe hyperkalemia (high potassium level in the blood) requiring emergent hemodialysis, which was not unusual for her.

During the last hospitalization, Mr. Fuller developed cardiac arrest and received CPR, for he was full code (i.e., not DNR). He passed away after a lengthy CPR process. His daughter, Ms. Klein, continued to frequent the hospital after her father's death. When reflecting on this case, I have realized that Mr. Fuller had changed his DNR decision because he did not want to leave his family. That will be further demonstrated in the next story.

Mrs. Copeland relocated here from a northern state. She was recommended to see me by one of the medical assistants working at our clinic, who also came from that state. They were family members. When Mrs. Copeland came in as a new patient, this medical assistant helped take her vital signs and enter the clinical data into the computer. I was surprised to find out that Mrs. Copeland was on five psychiatric drugs and on long-term narcotic painkillers. I asked the medical assistant, "How come your relative takes so many psychiatric drugs?" The medical assistant replied, "I don't know why. Anyway, several of my cousins in the north take as many mental drugs as her."

Mrs. Copeland was 53 years old and had numerous medical problems, including diabetes, chronic obstructive pulmonary disease (COPD), depression, hepatitis C, and chronic back pain. She continued to smoke one to two packs of cigarettes per day and refused to try anything to quit. She had severe COPD and was on home oxygen therapy. I could hear her wheezing during the examination of her lungs at every office visit.

"Don't need to worry about it," she said. "I've had wheezing all the time for years. I've seen many lung doctors in the north. Nobody can fix it."

"It may improve if you quit smoking."

"Maybe. Well, I'm not ready to quit yet."

But then, something happened that made her decide to quit smoking. One night, she went to the emergency room with worsening shortness of breath caused by acute exacerbation of COPD. She was intubated and put on the ventilator as a result of acute respiratory failure. Then she was admitted to the ICU.

"Dr. Li, please remove my wife from the ventilator," her husband spoke to me on the second day of hospitalization.

"Why?" I asked in surprise.

"My wife told me in the past that she does not want to be on the ventilator. I was not in the emergency room when they put her on the ventilator."

"Anyway, she's already on the ventilator. And she is young and improving. I think she can be taken off the ventilator in a few days."

"How many more days does she need to be on the ventilator?"

"I can't be 100 percent sure how many more days she will require mechanical ventilation. I suppose you'd better wait at least two to three days before you make the final decision."

"I'm okay with just three more days."

Fortuitously, Mrs. Copeland was removed from the ventilator on the fifth day of hospitalization and had done well since then. She had been out of psychiatric drugs for one week. I restarted her on one of them after she began to eat again. She was doing well mentally, and her diabetes was under control, even without insulin. She used to inject 180 units of insulin per day.

When Mrs. Copeland came back to the clinic for the follow-up visit after being discharged from the hospital, the chest examination revealed only minimal scattered wheezing.

"Hey, your lungs sound much better," I said.

"I quit smoking since I left the hospital," she smiled. "I can breathe better now. I won't smoke anymore." It is fairly common that smokers quit smoking after a stroke, heart attack, or ventilator treatment.

"Good job! I hope you'll continue to be this way."

"I hope so."

"Your husband wanted to have you removed from the ventilator when you were in the ICU, since you did not wish to be on the ventilator," I said. "Do you remember?"

"Yes, I do."

"Do you want to be on the ventilator if you need it in the future?"

"Yes, I want everything done, including the ventilator, to keep me alive," she replied.

"It seems that you have changed your mind after that."

"Yes. I'm a new person now. Quitting smoking has made me feel much better. After having gone through the ventilator, I know what it's like, and I think I can take it again. I want to continue to see my family."

Being with family is doubtless the most enjoyable moment in life. I will never forget Mr. Knight's happy smiling face when he was holding his grandson to his chest while lying in a hospital bed. Mr. Knight was 60 years old at the time. He was diagnosed with type 1 diabetes as a teenager and had struggled for more than forty years since then. I could sense the light of joyfulness emitting from his closed blind eyes.

Mr. Knight had suffered almost all the complications of diabetes: blindness, coronary artery heart disease, multiple strokes, end-stage kidney disease on hemodialysis, and bilateral above-the-knee amputations due to infection and poor circulation. Additionally, he could neither eat nor drink because of diabetic gastroparesis (paralysis of the stomach) and stroke-induced dysphagia, receiving his nutrition through gastric tube feeding. He had been hospitalized almost every month for the past three years. Without signing a DNR order, he chose to fight to the very end, most likely for this reason: he was still able to hold, touch, and hear his children and grandchildren.

A 92-year-old woman was transferred from a nursing home to the hospital after she had fractured her hip. She was blind, on gastric tube feeding, and bedridden for years owing to multiple strokes. The family requested full code for the patient. I asked her daughter why she did not request a DNR order since her mother's quality of life was poor and had a high risk for perioperative complications.

"Dr. Li, I understand what you mean," her daughter said. "Well, my mother said, 'I don't want to die. If I die, I can't see you all anymore. I want everything done to keep me alive.' I have no choice but to respect her wishes."

I admire these patients' determination and endurance. By taking care of them, I have learned to appreciate and enjoy each of the family moments whenever possible.

"I am not afraid of death. But I am not ready to go to heaven yet," almost all the patients say to me when we talk about end-of-life care issues.

Sometimes, I say to my patients, "Everybody says that heaven is good, yet nobody wants to go there alive. Is that right?"

"You are right. Nobody has come back to tell me how heaven is," some of them respond.

Life is a miracle, and the afterlife is a mystery.

8. Fight for Life

Life is a series of natural and spontaneous changes. Don't resist them - that only creates sorrow. Let reality be reality. Let things flow naturally forward in whatever way they like.

—Lao Tzu (老子) (571 BCE, Chinese Philosopher)

Don't cry because it's over, smile because it happened.

—Dr. Seuss (1904-1991, American Author)

Hemodialysis

Hemodialysis is a medical treatment that helps remove waste products and extra water from the body when the kidneys stop working. The other two renal replacement therapies are renal transplant and peritoneal dialysis. Patients with ESRD (end stage renal disease) cannot live without one of the above three renal replacement therapies. The majority of patients with kidney failure are on hemodialysis, which can be conducted in outpatient or inpatient settings. Hemodialysis is infrequently performed at home. The first hemodialysis for a patient was performed by Hass in 1924, and the artificial kidney was developed into clinically useful equipment by Willem Kolff during 1943-1945. The world's first outpatient dialysis facility was established by Belding H. Scribner in Seattle, Washington, U.S.A. in 1962. (For more details on this topic, see *Wikipedia: Hemodialysis*.)

Hemodialysis evolved into a big business in America when the U.S. Congress passed a bill on dialysis coverage in 1972 and when Medicare started to cover dialysis in 1973. It costs $50,000 to $100,000 per year to take care of a dialysis patient in the U.S. Approximately 370,000 Americans undergo dialysis, with 100,000 new cases added each year. Dialysis patients without a kidney transplant will live about four years on average. Younger patients on dialysis can have a much longer life expectancy.

After dialysis is initiated, all end-stage renal disease patients are entitled to Medicare, which pays for the expenses of hemodialysis or peritoneal dialysis and transportation to outpatient dialysis facilities. Most dialysis facilities are run by commercial for-profit dialysis companies. Nephrologists are the medical directors for these dialysis facilities.

I worked at a kidney and diabetes clinic and would share night and weekend calls with nephrologists and endocrinologists. There were not many emergent endocrinology consults besides the occasional ones about nutrition or gestational diabetes, and they were easily handled. The challenging cases were mostly related to patients on hemodialysis.

Most of the dialysis patients presented to the emergency department at night because of pulmonary edema (abnormal accumulation of fluid in the lungs) and hyperkalemia (an abnormally high concentration of potassium in the blood), which commonly resulted from missing dialysis therapy. Patients with end-stage kidney disease (ESRD) cannot remove excess fluid and potassium from the body without dialysis therapy. Pulmonary edema causes difficulty breathing. Hyperkalemia can lead to weakness, cardiac arrhythmia, and even death. Missing dialysis treatment and illicit drug use are especially common among younger dialysis patients.

Whenever I received calls from the ER at night, I got up and turned on my computer to access the hospital medical record. I could review the patient's lab, x-rays, CT, and vitals while speaking with the ER doctor, who usually told me how sick the dialysis patient was. Then I would talk with an ER nurse to give orders to admit the patient. I needed to decide if the patient required an emergent dialysis or if he or she could wait until the morning. Sometimes, I needed to put in a dialysis catheter if the patient's fistula or grafts were not functioning.

One night, I was woken at 2:00 am by a call from the ER, "Mr. Dickson came to the ER again."

"Him again?" I said to myself.

Mr. Dickson was a 45-year-old man who had been on dialysis treatment for 8-10 years. Once again, he came to the ER with chest pain, severe high blood pressure (250/120 mmHg), fast heart rate, pulmonary edema, and hyperkalemia. I specifically had to call a dialysis nurse out to dialyze him in the hospital dialysis unit. I drove to the hospital to see him at three o'clock in the morning.

"Did you take cocaine again?" I asked, after reviewing his record. His urine had always been positive for cocaine a few years earlier. We could not do a urine drug screen as he was unable to pass urine anymore. Nonetheless, he showed typical cocaine-induced signs and symptoms.

"A little bit…a few days ago," he replied.

"How long do you feel high after you smoke cocaine?"

"Just a few minutes."

"Then back to hell, right?"

"Yes."

"You have been admitted almost every month for the past year. Cocaine can cause a heart attack or stroke. You don't want to die, do you?"

"No."

"Do you want to quit?"

"Yes."

Unfortunately, he died of a massive stroke within a year. As far as I know, the majority of younger male dialysis patients take illicit drugs or are dependent on (or addicted to) prescription opioid medications.

One Friday around 6:30 p.m., I received a message on my pager saying that one family member wanted to talk to me. I dialed the phone number.

"Hello," someone answered.

"It's Dr. Li on call for the nephrology service," I said.

"My son needs his pain pills filled today!" the man said, sounding very upset.

"What's the name of your son?"

"Davis."

I turned on my computer to pull up the electronic medical record.

"What pain pills is your son taking?" I asked.

"Oxycodone."

"This is a controlled drug, and it is Friday evening. Why didn't you call the clinic before five?" I looked up his son's record: Davis was 23 years old and had been on hemodialysis for more than five years after a kidney transplant failure. He had also been on long-term narcotic pills for years. It seemed that it was time for him to refill the pain pills today.

"I called Dr. George at two in the afternoon," he said. "He didn't answer me. No staff at the clinic called me back!"

"Oxycodone is a Schedule II controlled drug," I said while thinking. "The clinic is closed now, and I can't call it into the pharmacy. Let me see what I can do about it..."

"Where do you live?" he got more upset. "I'm going to your home right now to pick up the damn prescription!"

"No, I don't think you can come to my home," I said. "How about I meet you at the emergency room and give the prescription to you there?"

"Okay."

"I'll see you there at seven."

When I met the patient's father in the ER, he looked much nicer than he sounded on the phone. He said thanks to me with a smile when I handed the prescription to him. I empathize with the frustration of parents who have chronically ill children. These parents are constantly occupied by taking care of their sick loved ones. They have to watch their loved ones suffer all the time. I would do whatever I could to help my children as this patient's father did. Sometimes, I even wonder whether I would end up doing drugs just like the younger dialysis patients if I had to undergo hemodialysis in my 20-30s.

No doctor likes getting up and going to the hospital at two o'clock in the morning. However, serving patients is our calling. One of the night calls had given me unforgettable inspiration. On that night, Miss Sandy, a 40-year-old woman who had been on hemodialysis for more than 10 years, was admitted due to bleeding from the arteriovenous (AV) graft in her arm. An AV graft is an artificial blood vessel that is placed in the arm or the thigh for hemodialysis. Her bleeding finally stopped after a prolonged compression treatment. I saw Sandy in the hospital and found that the compression gauze showed a small spot of clotted blood with no oozing blood, indicating that the bleeding had stopped. Then I left the hospital for home.

"Sandy is bleeding again!" a nurse called nervously around two o'clock in the morning.

"What's going on?" I asked.

"I checked her dialysis graft five minutes ago and found that the compression gauze was completely soaked with blood. I tried to shift the gauze slowly in order to place a new one when the blood spilled out like a geyser. I compressed the bleeding site immediately. We placed more new gauzes on it, but the graft is still oozing blood. Sandy seems to be losing a lot of blood."

"Please transfer Sandy to the ICU and inform the on-call surgeon about it. I'll be on my way."

After I had arrived at the ICU, I found that Sandy was sitting up on the bed nervously. Two nurses were compressing her left arm with their hands. Some blood was still oozing out, and the nurses' gloves were covered with blood. Sandy's hemoglobin had dropped by three grams from her previous level. The floor nurses did a great job to compress the ruptured dialysis graft promptly on the regular floor. Otherwise, Sandy could have died within minutes. Fortunately, Sandy was clinically stable, for she was a young lady and could tolerate the rapid drop in blood count.

Right then, I was told that Dr. Hertz was on call and on his way to the hospital from his home. Dr. Hertz, a vascular surgeon, had relocated from a northern state to this small town hospital. He was so friendly to patients and health professionals that everybody in the hospital liked him. I felt relieved as soon as I heard Dr. Hertz's name, for other surgeons might not have acted as quickly as him.

As expected, Dr. Hertz appeared in the ICU within five minutes after I arrived. He entered the room to check on Sandy right away. His appearance had dispelled Sandy's anxiety and fear. Kindly and calmly, he talked to her with a smile. Dr. Hertz lifted the corner of the compression gauze gently and located the ruptured site of the graft, from which blood continued to ooze out. He told the ICU nurse to give him the suture kit, and then he started to tie up the ruptured graft. Because of the emergent situation and the requirement of continuous compression, he could not give Sandy any anesthetics. He said, "I'm sorry" to Sandy each time when he put a stitch in her arm. Sandy replied with a tearful smile, "I'm okay, Dr. Hertz. Thank you very much." Finally, the bleeding stopped after about six to seven stitches were put in.

"I just tied up the graft to stop the bleeding, and I'll be back early in the morning for further management," Dr. Hertz said to Sandy with his usual smile.

"Thank you very much, Dr. Hertz." Sandy's eyes were filled with tears. What a moving scene at 3 am in the ICU!

After watching Dr. Hertz working, I felt that I would prefer to die in Dr. Hertz's hand. From that moment, I resolved to become a doctor like him. I still think that Dr. Hertz is the best doctor I have ever met. He had never given me a hard time when I asked him for help. When he had finished a consult for our group or me, he always called me and discussed the case with me. He would tell me what time he was coming to see my patients if he was stuck in the operation room. During lunch breaks, I enjoyed listening to him in the doctors' lounge as he knew many medical and political stories. I had watched him smile most of the time unless he talked with patients or their families about life and death issues.

"I have confidence in him as soon as I see Dr. Hertz's smiling face," a patient said to me.

One time, I referred one of my patients to see him. When the patient came back to see me at the office after the consultation, I asked her, "How did it go with your consultation with Dr. Hertz?"

"Oh, my God! Dr. Hertz is such a warm, kindly person that he looks like the doctor God has sent here to take care of me!" the patient said excitedly.

It's certainly true that we don't have to go to heaven to see God. The Bible (1 John 4:12, NLT) says, *"No one has ever seen God. But if we love each other, God lives in us, and his love has been brought to full expression through us."* Nobody can see God's real face, for He expresses His mightiness and kindness in many different ways. God is everywhere and in our hearts as long as we love and help each other.

Unfortunately, Dr. Hertz left for another state after working in town for a few years. He had inspired me to become a better doctor. I will never forget his kind, smiling face, and gentle gestures.

When it comes to hemodialysis, the hospital does not always make the best economic decisions, even ignoring common sense. There was a medical ward in the hospital, where most dialysis patients were usually admitted, and they always occupied more than 70-80 percent of the beds. The hospital dialysis unit was located at the entrance of the ward. Therefore, it was very convenient to transport dialysis patients to the dialysis unit for dialysis treatment, usually happening three times per week and occasionally once per day. After a renovation, this ward became an overflow ward that was frequently empty. The dialysis patients had to be admitted to another ward one floor below. The dialysis patients needed to be transported in the elevator to another floor where the dialysis unit was located. How much time or labor was wasted by the long elevator wait times in addition to the high electricity bills?

Nevertheless, the cost of transporting dialysis patients within the hospital was essentially trivial, when compared with the cost of the out-of-hospital patient transportation. When I made rounds on the subacute floor on weekends, I occasionally could not find dialysis patients in the room. I asked a nurse, "Where is the patient?" The nurse replied, "The patient is out for hemodialysis." The subacute floor at the hospital was considered an outpatient facility by Medicare. After being admitted to the subacute ward for rehabilitation, a dialysis patient could not receive hemodialysis therapy at the hospital dialysis unit, even though it was only **20 yards** away from the subacute floor. Instead, dialysis patients were transported out of the hospital by ambulance to an in-town dialysis facility (**five miles** away) or even to out-of-town facilities (**20 miles** away). The ambulance service would take them back to the hospital after dialysis treatment. This practice has been going on for more than 20 years and will possibly continue in the years to come. It is amazing that Medicare is willing to cover this type of expensive and unnecessary ambulance transportation. As it involves only the government's money, nobody seems to mind.

Sadly, while we are wasting our precious resources in the U.S., end-stage renal disease (ESRD) patients in many parts of the world cannot afford dialysis therapy or kidney transplant, and their lives are cut short.[1] It is estimated that over one million people die from untreated kidney failure every year around the world. As a matter of fact, without money to pay for dialysis or kidney transplant, the best way to obtain medical care is to stay in or come to the U.S.

Mr. Mitchell was an undocumented worker from Mexico, who suffered from end-stage renal disease and had been started on hemodialysis by our clinic's nephrologists more than 10 years beforehand. Back then, he was a 20-year-old young man and did not know how to speak English at all. After being together with us all these years, he could communicate with us in simple English. Being undocumented, he was not qualified for Medicare or Medicaid and could not be on the kidney transplant list, and he was denied access to a

197

commercial outpatient dialysis facility. The only option was to admit him to the hospital for dialysis treatment every one or two weeks through the emergency room.

The emergency room has to treat anyone who needs emergency care under any circumstances. In 1986, the United States Congress passed the law, the **Emergency Medical Treatment and Labor Act (EMTALA)**, which requires Medicare-participating hospitals to provide emergency medical assistance to anyone, regardless of citizenship, legal status, or ability to pay. This law applies to almost all hospitals since most hospitals accept payments from Medicare. Thanks to this law, everybody can have a health care safety net in the U.S. However, the emergency room is overcrowded, and 55 percent of emergency care is unpaid. (For more details on this topic, see Wikipedia: Emergency Medical Treatment and Active Labor Act).

Recently, a few more undocumented Mexican patients with the end-stage renal disease had moved to our area and became patients of our clinic. They had already been started on hemodialysis in Mexico. However, they could not afford regular hemodialysis therapy there and entered the U.S. illegally in order to receive dialysis treatment. All of them were young (around 30-40 years old), and they could undergo hemodialysis only in the hospital. The hospital could not reject them while none of the commercial outpatient dialysis facilities accepted them.

The hospitalization for hemodialysis increases medical costs, infection rates, and medication errors. Nevertheless, nobody seems to be interested in changing this situation. Maybe nobody can. Sometimes, I cannot help but wonder why there is so much human suffering for the Mexican people when Mexico has the richest man in the world.[2] Inequality is everywhere, and it is undoubtedly more widespread in developing countries.

A dialysis patient needs to go to an outpatient dialysis facility to undergo hemodialysis three times per week, and each therapy lasts three to four hours in addition to transportation time. About 5-10 percent of dialysis patients are hospitalized for infections, cardiovascular diseases, malfunctioned dialysis access, etc. – resulting in poor quality of life.

There are some ESRD patients who would rather die than go on dialysis, and there are some who decide not to continue dialysis after being on dialysis for a period of time. These patients usually receive hospice service in the hospital and then come to die after the dialysis stops for two to six weeks.

In contrast, I remember a dialysis patient who was a 70-year-old woman in a coma. With tracheostomy (the construction of an artificial opening through the neck into the trachea) and a gastric feeding tube, she had been on the ventilator most of the time and had stayed in the hospital for over a year. The nursing home did not accept her since she had a tracheostomy and was on the ventilator. Her family refused to stop the futile treatment, no matter how much the ethical committee of the hospital tried to persuade the family.

Another ESRD patient could not be accepted by an outpatient dialysis facility because of tracheostomy due to chronic respiratory failure. He had been in a persistent vegetative state for more than a year and was on gastric tube feeding. His wife insisted on the continuation of all treatments, including hemodialysis. He had to be admitted to the hospital for dialysis every 10 days: staying in the hospital for three or four treatments of dialysis, being discharged home for three or four days, and then being readmitted. This cycle lasted more than a year, and it still continued after I quit the hospital practice. I currently do not know the status of the patient.

Kidney transplants provide a better quality of life and longer life expectancy. Numerous ESRD patients (about 100,000 people) are on the waiting lists. However, only a small percentage of them are lucky enough to receive donated kidneys: approximately 14,000 people underwent kidney transplants in 2013.[3] A patient with poor kidney function said, "I want my daughter to donate her kidney to me." The son of an ESRD patient stated that he would give his kidney to his mother. A patient of mine bravely donated her kidney to her friend. Some people even go to developing countries to buy kidneys if they can afford to.

I decided 20 years ago I would donate all my organs or my whole body to people who need them when I die. My wife and children have also signed up as organ donors. While writing this chapter, I was deeply touched by the story that Dr. Rita McGill, a nephrologist, donated her kidney to a patient who was unknown to her.[3] Dr. Rita McGill is alive and healthy and continues to work after recovery from the donation. How noble and heroic a deed she has done! To be honest, I don't think I can do the same. Hopefully, future medical technology will soon generate useful biological organs, so that ESRD patients will suffer less.

Optimism

When I saw her again after she moved back from a northern state, Ms. Tina was 45 years old. She was still pretty with a bright smile most of the time. Twenty years earlier, she suffered a serious car accident that caused a spinal cord injury involving the thoracic region. She was paralyzed from the waist down and had lost control of bowel and bladder (paraplegia). She used a manual wheelchair. In contrast, most of my paralyzed patients ride their motorized wheelchairs.

Ms. Tina had done well the first 10 years after the accident. During the next 10 years, she had been struggling with complications resulting from her paraplegia. In my memory, she still had both legs and no artificial holes in her body five years earlier before she moved to the northern state. When she came back to see me five years later, I was surprised to notice that she had a colostomy bag attached to her abdominal wall and a suprapubic catheter with a urine bag tied to her left leg. Her right leg was gone after the above knee amputation due to frequent infections. She still had her strong upper arms and could push her manual wheelchair. And I was glad that she had kept her optimism without taking any psychiatric medication. Of course, she continued to be on long-term opioid painkillers like many other paralyzed patients.

"Dr. Li, I'm back. Nice to see you again," she said cheerfully at the first office visit after coming back from the north.

"Nice to see you too," I said. "You look like you have gone through a lot of things in the north these years."

"I was hospitalized almost forty times during the past five years. I have had many infections and bedsores. They just closed the bedsore at my bottom two months ago."

Pressure ulcers (also called decubitus ulcers or bedsores) are localized injuries to the skin and underlying tissue resulting from prolonged pressures on the skin. Pressure ulcers commonly develop over bony areas of the body, such as the elbows, heels, ankles, knees, hips, and tailbone. If constant pressure on the skin impairs local blood flow to soft tissue for an extended period, pressure ulcers will develop. Muscle tissue can sustain irreversible changes from as little as two hours of uninterrupted pressure. Skin can cope with poor blood supply induced by direct pressure for up to 12 hours. People with paralysis, stroke, dementia, etc. have impaired ability to change positions so that they are at high risk for pressure ulcers, which are often difficult and expensive to treat.

Pressure ulcers are common among patients in hospitals and long-term care facilities like nursing homes. It has been estimated that approximately one million people suffer from pressure ulcers in the United States. The most common major complication of pressure ulcers is an infection, which develops as a result of the loss of skin barrier against microorganisms. Each year, about 60,000 people die of complications of pressure ulcers including infection of the skin and connected soft tissues (cellulitis), bone infections (osteomyelitis), joint infections (septic arthritis), and sepsis. Even "Superman", the late actor Christopher Reeve, was brought down by pressure ulcers. He became paralyzed from the neck down after a horseback riding accident 10 years earlier. In 2004, he died from complications associated with an infected pressure ulcer at 52 years of age.

"I hope you'll do better down here," I said.

"I hope so," Tina said.

Unfortunately, things did not happen as we wished. Home health care was arranged for her, and she had got an air-fluidized bed to sleep on. The air-fluidized bed mattress contains small ceramic spheres that are continuously blown by temperature-controlled airflow to distribute the patient's weight evenly, keeping pressure off bony prominences in order to promote skin integrity and prevent skin breakdown. Tina had been doing well for the first six months until one day she was admitted for urinary tract infection and a bedsore in the sacral region. The sacral bedsore was small initially, about two to three centimeters in diameter. She was discharged home after her infection, and her wound was treated. She continued to receive wound care at home by the visiting nurse.

Also, a port-a-cath was placed for her because of frequent hospitalization. A port-a-cath is a small medical appliance that is installed beneath the skin. A catheter connects the port to a large, deep vein. Drugs or fluids can be injected into the vein through the port, and blood samples can also be drawn from there. The port is usually used by patients with difficulty accessing peripheral veins or patients receiving chemotherapy, and it can stay in the body for years if not infected or malfunctioned.

She was hospitalized one month later for urinary tract infection with nausea and vomiting. However, her sacral bedsore was found to have extended to the perineal and genital region. The plastic surgeon was consulted and had performed several debridement surgeries. Then she was admitted a few weeks later by the plastic surgeon, who closed her open wound with a skin graft from her left leg. But the perineal and genital region broke open two months later, and the abdominal cavity was exposed. When the wound care nurse and I examined her, we noticed that the open wound had enlarged to 10-12 cm wide, and her pelvic organs just melted away.

"I hope the surgeon can close the area completely," she smiled and made a cross. "Anyway, I don't use that area anymore." The surgeon closed the open wound again two months later with the skin graft from her thigh after antibiotic treatment and wound care. Unfortunately, the wound broke open again within one month. The open wound looked like a deep cave, 12 cm in diameter at the opening and 10-12 cm deep with multiple tunnels inside. The plastic surgeon said that he could not close the wound anymore and recommended continuation wound care leaving the wound open.

Ms. Tina kept asking for the closure of her wound, "I just want the wound closed, and then I'll be satisfied." She had undergone many wound closure surgeries in the north. We tried to transfer her to the university medical center. As you know, the transfer to the university medical center was not an easy job. The medical center finally accepted her once, and she stayed for almost one month. She came back happily with the closed wound. However, once more, her wound broke open two months later and all the work done had been wasted again. She could not follow up with her surgeon at the university outpatient clinic because the clinic did not accept her Medicaid managed plan.

Ms. Tina requested a transfer to a large hospital in the capital city. She had become such a burden to the hospital that the vice president of our hospital helped call a surgeon there, who was a specialist in wound care. The surgeon declined to accept the transfer but agreed to see her at the clinic. The case manager had tried hard to secure an appointment for her to see the surgeon when she was discharged from the hospital. She went to see the surgeon 50 miles away by ambulance. Still, this surgeon recommended leaving the wound open with long-term antibiotic treatment to prevent infection.

The large open wound had become the entry port of bacterial invasion for Ms. Tina. When she was discharged home with a clean wound, she would continue to receive home health care and home IV antibiotic. However, she would end up in the ER within three to four weeks, and her wound looked like a mess with bad odor and foul secretions. The wound culture revealed MRSA (Methicillin-resistant Staphylococcus aureus) or Pseudomonas infection that was resistant to most of the antibiotics and difficult to treat. The infectious disease and wound care services were involved in the care during each hospitalization. Ms. Tina stayed in the hospital for about 8 to10 days with improvement and was discharged home. Then again she would be back in the hospital in a few weeks.

"I think my bladder or bowel is leaky as a lot of water comes out from the hole," Tina said to me during a hospitalization.

"I'll look at it with the wound care nurse when she comes in," I said.

A nurse also informed me that they needed to change Tina's diaper every two to three hours for two days. When examining with the wound care nurse, I found that the open wound at the perineal region looked like a large and deep cave with little odor due to the good wound care and antibiotics. Looking inside the cave 12 cm in diameter and 10 cm deep, I could see only pink muscular structures with clear fluid flowing out. It was sad to see that Tina did not have an anus with no sign of female genital organs inside and outside. The suprapubic urinary catheter was attached to the abdominal wall and connected to the collection bag, which was half filled with urine. It seemed that the urine was drained out of the bladder smoothly. The clear fluid did not look like bowel material or wound secretion. I had guessed that there might have been a leak in the bladder or somewhere in the urinary system. So, I consulted the urologist, who was familiar with the case, and I talked to him about what I found on the exam.

The urologist had ordered a CT scan of the bladder before he saw Tina. The radiologist could not find any leaky contrast coming out of the bladder. The urologist ordered another CT scan in different positions. The second CT still revealed no leakage from the bladder. The urologist called me to consult GI service after he looked at the CT scan. Nonetheless, the gastroenterologist did not think there was anything to do with GI tract after examining Tina. I told the urologist about GI's opinion. Finally, the urologist came up to see Tina and found out that urine leaked out of the bladder through the loose insertion of the suprapubic catheter. The leaky problem was solved within a few minutes after tightening the insertion site. Apparently, this five-minute physical exam was superior to the two CT scans and a GI consult.

Tina's admissions had become a nightmare for the case manager. The Medicaid managed care company called the hospital daily to check on Tina. The case manager had to explain why the patient was still in the hospital. Sometimes, the insurance company refused to pay for her hospitalizations.

"Dr. Li, the Medicaid company, wants you to talk to the insurance medical director about the case." the case manager spoke to me when I made rounds at noon.

"No problem. Please get him on the phone." I said.

"They said the medical director is out of the office, and he will call back. I have given your phone number to him." the case manager said after a while.

"That's fine. I'm waiting."

Interestingly, the medical director had never called me back. That happened not just one time, but at least four to five times. In the end, I had not talked with the medical director even once. I guessed that the director wanted to avoid talking to me on purpose. He should have known this case well since the case manager faxed all the medical records to the insurance company whenever Tina was admitted.

"Dr. Li, good job," the case manager said happily one day later. "They have approved this admission."

"Really? Actually, the medical director has never talked to me. I think he doesn't want to waste his time." I sighed.

Truly, the Medicaid managed care company had become tired of this case after three years of trouble. Finally, they managed to change Tina's managed care Medicaid to non-managed care Medicaid, which is run by the government Medicaid office. This kind of Medicaid plan is usually given to the nursing home patients and would cause much less trouble to the hospital. Both the case manager and Tina were happy to know the good news. With this new insurance plan, Tina could see her surgeon again at the university clinic, and the case manager did not need to deal with the picky Medicaid managed care company anymore.

"Hey, Dr. Li, I can see the surgeon at the university again with the new Medicaid!" Tina said cheerfully. She was reading a novel with a smile when I entered her room.

"I'm happy too," I said. "I'll have less trouble with your insurance in the future."

"All I want is just to close the damn hole. This is the only surgeon who would try to close the wound for me."

The case manager arranged an appointment for Tina to see the surgeon at the university clinic, which was 100 miles away. Tina went to see the surgeon every two or three months since then for almost two years. There, she saw other specialists including an infectious disease specialist. Tina had fewer hospital admissions during these two years. But her wound remained wide open, for the university doctors thought Tina's nutrition status was not good enough to have the closure surgery. The problem was that Tina still looked thin no matter how much she ate.

"Look at me, I'm eating all day, cheesecakes, burgers, butter, and ice cream." Tina showed me all the food on her table.

It seems that paralyzed patients just cannot absorb or utilize the nutrients they eat. Most of my paralyzed patients are thin and bony. At home, Tina could not get enough care or even nutrition. She refused to go to a nursing home, and no nursing home would accept her Medicaid plan.

When she became sick and was admitted, her albumin level was always in the range of 2.6-2.7 g/dL (normal range human serum albumin in adults is 3.5 to 5 g/dL). Albumin is the most abundant plasma protein, which is produced in the liver. Low levels of albumin are associated poor clinical outcomes. According to *The Washington Manual of Medical Therapeutics,*[1] plasma albumin level should not be used for evaluation of nutrition status. Her albumin level would rise to 3.3 to 3.4 g/dL at discharge, which is close to the normal range.

Whenever Tina was hospitalized, the case manager would fax the best lab results to the university medical center. We hoped the university medical center would take Tina there for further care, but it had never happened. They always stated that the albumin level is 0.1 or 0.2 g/dL below the target. When I left for another town, Tina's wound was still open.

I had never heard Tina complain of feeling down. She smiled like sunshine and never looked sad. Although she took opioid painkillers like many paralyzed people, she did not need any antidepressant or antianxiety medication. She remembered to ask a nurse to give one more injection of morphine before each discharge. Fortunately, she had never overdosed with pain medications.

Whenever I admitted her, I thought what I would do if I were in her situation. Tina carried a colostomy bag and a urine bag all the time, sustained a large open wound that could not be closed, had only one leg that was too weak to support her body, and lost all her pelvic organs. And she was in and out of the hospital numerous times. However, she looked cheerful most of the time and managed to maintain her optimism. I admire her for having an indomitable will to keep fighting and a great desire to enjoy the remaining good things on earth. Tina was brave and strong because she was adamant that she would have the "damn hole" closed soon. I have nothing to complain of whenever I recall her smiling face. Hopefully, her wound will be closed one day and stay closed forever.

Resilience

During the second year of my practice, **Mrs. Long** came to see me as a new patient when she was 87 years old. She had already had Alzheimer's disease with moderate severity for a few years. She could say a few words and eat her food by herself then. As her condition worsened three years later, she was admitted to a nursing home, where she stayed for 10 years until she died. Her family signed the DNR (do not resuscitate) paper for her when she was admitted to the nursing home.

As her Alzheimer's disease progressed, Mrs. Long had difficulty eating and drinking, leading to significant weight loss. Her family requested that a gastric feeding tube (PEG tube) be put in her. A PEG (percutaneous endoscopic gastrostomy) tube is inserted into a patient's stomach through a small cut in the abdominal wall. Thus, the patient can receive liquid nutrition and medications through the PEG tube. It is known that declining to eat and drink is a natural, non-painful process near the end of life. Studies have shown that PEG tube feeding does not help patients with dementia live longer.[1] However, Mrs. Long seemed to be an exceptional case because she had not only regained and maintained her weight, but also lived 10 more years after the PEG tube placement.

She did not recognize people and was bedridden for years. Even though she was hospitalized several times per year, her family continued to request hospital care whenever she got sick. She had one daughter in town and one son who lived in New York. Her daughter went to check on Mrs. Long in the nursing home just about every day. Whenever she found something wrong with Mrs. Long, her daughter called me or came to the clinic to talk to me.

Mrs. Long had suffered almost all the common medical disorders seen in the nursing home. She fell many times in the nursing home with only one fracture of her left forearm. Falls are so common in the nursing home or in the hospital that you can get frequent reports about falls from nurses when on night calls. One of my nursing home patients fractured her hip even during transferring from her bed to the chair by care workers. Two patients of mine developed cardiac arrest and died after falling in the hospital.

She was admitted numerous times for dehydration with BUN level up to 130-150 mg/dL(normal range 5-20 mg/dL) and sodium level up to 188 mEq/L (hypernatremia, normal range 134-144 mEq/L) and sugar level up to 1200-1300 mg/dL (hyperglycemia, normal range 65-100 mg/dL). She could overcome all the extreme metabolic abnormalities and be discharged back to the nursing home after hospital treatments. And she survived pneumonia, urinary tract infection, congestive heart failure, and three weeks of *C. difficile* diarrhea (*Clostridium difficile* colitis, commonly caused by exposure to antibiotics). She recovered from gastrointestinal bleeding with blood transfusions. During one of the hospitalizations, she developed drug-induced skin rashes that involved 70-80 percent of her body surface. Amazingly, the rashes had resolved after discontinuation of the culprit medication, and she was discharged back to the nursing home.

One time she developed a large bedsore at the sacral region, which was more than 11-12 cm in diameter and looked like a deep cave revealing bones and muscles inside.

"Dr. Li, make sure to document the pressure ulcer is pre-existing (it exists before admission). Otherwise, the hospital won't get paid and will receive a bad quality score," the case manager talked to me when Mrs. Long was admitted to the hospital. According to the Medicare rule, the hospital won't get reimbursement if a pressure ulcer develops during hospitalization. Medicare considers hospital-acquired pressure ulcer as an indicator of poor hospital care. The surgical service had to operate on Mrs. Long for debridement of the ulcer several times during the hospitalization. Amazingly, her ulcer had healed well after one year of wound care at the nursing home.

One year she was hospitalized three months in a row for dehydration. She received three liters of food supplement and water daily through a feeding tube, which should be adequate for her normally. It was likely that her digestive system was too weak to absorb the nutrient and fluid adequately. In order to avoid frequent hospitalizations, I ordered intravenous fluid treatment once a week in the nursing home. She had not been admitted for dehydration anymore since then. And she did not need the weekly IV fluid treatment six months later. Surprisingly, she had had even fewer hospitalizations (once a year) during the last three years of her life.

Mrs. Long yelled loudly occasionally. Otherwise, she was lying in bed or sat in the chair quietly with closed eyes. She might shout and try to hit nursing home staff when they changed her diaper or cleaned her. It is likely that she did not want to be awoken from her sweet dreams. She did not recognize anybody in the last five years of life. When I entered her room in my white coat, she occasionally could say to me, "Doctor." She died from pneumonia complicated by sepsis at the age of 101. She was DNR and was never put on life support.

I had learned every aspect of geriatric medicine from taking care of Mrs. Long. After Mrs. Long had died, her family thanked me for taking care of Mrs. Long for thirteen years. Although Mrs. Long became ill frequently, she was so resilient that she had defeated one after another illness. She had become even stronger during the last three years of her life with fewer admissions. I am amazed that she was so strong and unpredictable. I am not sure if modern medicine should be applied to extend her life in this way. Undeniably, modern medicine can keep people alive if it is available, and somebody pays for it.

***

"**Ms. Steele** is very sick in the ER, and she is on the ventilator now," the ER doctor called me late in the afternoon. When I rushed to the ER, I noticed that Ms. Steele presented to the emergency department with bilateral pneumonia and respiratory failure. She was intubated and put on the ventilator. I could not recognize her when I entered the ER room. She had lost almost 100 pounds over the past one year. Weighing about 80-90 pounds, she looked gaunt and exhausted.

I started to see Ms. Steele soon after I began to practice in this town. She was 60 years old with diabetes, hypothyroidism, and schizophrenia. Her schizophrenia was under control as long as she took her medications.

211

She often ran out of medications and missed appointments with the mental clinic. Sometimes, she might end up in the emergency department because of unstable mental status or suicidal ideation.

Ms. Steele was admitted to the hospital for pneumonia one year earlier. During the hospitalization, she was found to have AIDS (acquired immune deficiency syndrome). AIDS is a severe immunological disorder caused by HIV (human immunodeficiency virus, transmitted primarily through body fluids, especially blood and semen). Patients with AIDS are susceptible to numerous infections as a consequence of their weakened immune system. Nevertheless, she was at the early stage of AIDS with a good appetite and stable weight. Her pneumonia was resolved with antibiotic treatment, and she was started on and tolerated anti-HIV drugs. One of her daughters wanted to take Ms. Steele to Atlanta to live with her when Ms. Steele was discharged. I wrote all the prescriptions and collected all medical records for her to take to Atlanta. I told her daughter to take Ms. Steele to see a medical doctor as soon as they arrived in Atlanta. Apparently, they did not follow my instruction.

During this hospitalization, it was found that Ms. Steele's CD4 cell count was down to 46 cells/μL (normal range, 600 to 1,500 cells/μL), indicating her body had a very poor defense against infections. **CD4 cells** are a type of white blood cells that play a major role in preventing infections. HIV virus can kill CD4 cells in the body. Thus, the CD4 cell count is an indicator of the progress of AIDS. She suffered many AIDS complications including bilateral pneumonia, malnutrition with a significant weight loss of 100 pounds, yeast infection of the esophagus (candida esophagitis), anemia, and general weakness. Her diabetes was gone as a result of weight loss. She had severe hypothyroidism with TSH level of 200 μU/ml (thyroid stimulating hormone, normal range 0.5 to 5μU/ml), which was treated with IV thyroid hormone. Her infection and AIDS were handled by an infectious disease specialist.

"Why does Ms. Steele look like that? How long has she been sick?" I asked her daughter, who was at the bedside.

"She's just got sick for a few weeks," her daughter said. "She doesn't want to see any doctor but you. So I brought her back from Atlanta to see you." (Atlanta is 250 miles from here.)

"Is she taking her HIV drugs?"

"Not anymore for a few months after she had finished the prescriptions you gave to her."

"Why didn't you take her to see a doctor there?"

"We just did not have a chance."

"Now, your mother is so sick that I don't know if she can make it or not," I sighed.

"Really?" she said.

Amazingly, Ms. Steele came out of the ventilator after one week of the treatment. She could not eat because of swallowing difficulty due to esophagitis and muscle weakness. Therefore, a gastric feeding tube (PEG tube) was placed to supply nutrients to her. She was too weak to stand up owing to muscle atrophy. Marvelously, her condition improved gradually and was discharged to a nursing home after two weeks of hospitalization.

Ms. Steele could not stand up and eat when she arrived at the nursing home. She could walk with a walker and started to eat in three months with weight gain. By the sixth month in the nursing home, she had already gained forty pounds and could walk with a cane. She had regained all her weight and could walk without any assistance by the ninth month. Then her feeding tube was removed and discharged home. The CD4 cell count had returned to normal, and her HIV virus had become undetectable with HIV medication treatment.

Ms. Steele had never missed her appointments or run out of medications since. One time, she came in for an office visit with another man who was the same age as her.

"This is my boyfriend. Please take care of him," she said.

I remembered that Ms. Steele used to have a boyfriend who was twenty years younger than her. I mistook him for Ms. Steele's son and talked with him many times about the conditions of his "mother". Luckily, both of them were never upset with my mistake.

"I will," I said.

Ms. Steele and her new boyfriend came to the office together since then. I am glad that Ms. Steele has a happy new life.

I am amazed that AIDS used to be a deadly disease three decades ago, and now it has become a treatable chronic disease with appropriate treatment. However, thousands of people with HIV infection cannot afford the effective HIV treatment in many parts of the world. We human beings can almost certainly cure or produce a vaccine for AIDS sooner or later. Nonetheless, the environment where AIDS or Ebola arises is much more difficult to improve.

***

Mr. Todd fought in Vietnam. He was wounded several times and awarded with many medals. He told me he knows many generals and politicians, and that his war story was portrayed in a movie. Ten years ago, he was diagnosed with prostate cancer, which had metastasized to his lungs, abdomen, and brain. He has difficulty breathing all the time as a consequence of COPD complicated by metastatic tumors in the lung. The distention of his abdomen has caused pain all the time. He has frequent seizures due to the metastatic brain tumors.

Now, he is 62 years old. He is tall with a large frame. One time he complained of worsening fullness of the abdomen. I thought he might develop ascites due to metastasized colon cancer. He was too weak and too breathless to lie on the examination table. However, the ultrasound study revealed no ascites, but multiple masses within the abdominal cavity. He also has severe COPD (chronic obstructive pulmonary disease) on home oxygen and has had several minor heart attacks, which has resulted in heart failure.

He has seen many cancer surgeons and medical oncologists in the North and the South. He decided not to undergo any more surgery or chemotherapy five years ago after the last abdominal surgery. Then he was enrolled in hospice, which was discontinued two years later as he did not show signs of dying. Even the medical director of the hospice company called me to find out why the patient is still alive.

"Dr. Li, I'm still alive because of you," he said to me one day.

"I have done nothing unusual," I said. "You are just a tough guy. To be honest, I thought you would have died two years ago."

"I thought so too." He does not like the local internist, whom I recommended to him. Mr. Todd continues to see me from time to time after I started to work at the new clinic, which is 65 miles from his home. Every time he comes in, he brings his retired military dog with him. All the office staff like his lovely big and strong dog, which wears an American flag uniform.

Mr. Todd relocated here from New York. He has been applying for disability for six years and failed. He was evaluated by the VA system to be 100 percent disabled 10 years ago.

A few months ago, he was decorated as a wounded warrior. He was happy to show me his new car, which was subsidized by the VA. Her wife, 69 years old, has to keep working as a teacher to maintain her commercial insurance to cover Mr. Todd. It is unbelievable that he, a wounded warrior with scars all over his body, could not be approved for disability with metastasized cancers, COPD, heart failure, and even enrollment to hospice. On the contrary, others can get Medicare and Medicaid because they have some psychiatric illnesses such as antisocial personality disorder or they know how the system works.

Recently, Mr. and Mrs. Todd were planning to buy a 5,000 square feet house. They showed me the pictures of the house, which is huge and beautiful with six rooms.

"Why do you need this large house?" I asked. "Both of you are getting old without children around. How can you take care of the house?"

"I like the big house," Mrs. Todd replied. "I'll close most of the rooms in the house so that I don't need to clean them. I just feel happy whenever I look at the house."

"I'm too weak to walk through the house, you know," Mr. Todd said. "Anyhow, I'll enjoy sitting in the big kitchen."

I hope that they will enjoy their new house together for a long, long time.

I have seen many of my veteran patients suffer from a variety of illnesses associated with wars. Miserably, people living in war zones continue to be exposed to war-related toxic materials and fall ill. War will create human misery, and it is not the only way to resolve conflicts in the world. Pressing a button on the remote to set off an IED (improvised explosive device) or launch a missile will injure and kill people. Their families will be destroyed, for all the people wounded or killed in wars are sons, daughters, husbands, wives, fathers, and mothers.

I wish every leader in the world dare to say not only "*No boots on the ground*" but also "No boots to anywhere forever." Hopefully, world leaders will focus on *investing in books, not bullets*, as called on by Nobel Peace Prize winner Malala Yousafzai.[2] That way, soldiers or any people, no matter which side they are on, will suffer less, and the world will become more peaceful and prosperous.

The care of human life and happiness and not their destruction,
is the first and only legitimate object of good government.
−Thomas Jefferson
(1743-1826, the third President of the United States)

9. Medicine as Art and Business

Care more for the individual patient than for the special features of the disease. . . . Put yourself in his place . . . The kindly word, the cheerful greeting, the sympathetic look — these the patient understands.

You are in this profession as a calling, not a business; ... Once you get down to a purely business level, your influence is gone and the true light of your life is dimmed.

—William Osler (1849-1919, Canadian Physician and Professor of Medicine)

Even when walking in a party of no more than three, I can always be certain of learning from those I am with. There will be good qualities that I can select for emulation and bad ones that will teach me what requires correction in myself.

—Confucius (551-479 B.C., Chinese Philosopher)

The Art of Medicine

It's not what you say, but how you say it that matters. In the U.S., oftentimes some celebrities say things the wrong way on TV or behind the scenes. For this, they lose their jobs or contracts or campaigns. For example:

"The fundamentals of the economy are strong," Mr. John McCain (the United States Senator) said during his 2008 presidential campaign.[1] He was mocked by the media as "out of touch" because America was suffering from the worst economic collapse since 1929.

In contrast, Mr. Michael Bloomberg (the New York mayor at that time) said, "The U.S. economy is resilient and diverse."[2] This statement sounded similar to Mr. John McCain's, but it was impeccable and conveyed the same message that American economy could recover because its foundation was strong.

By the same token, some of my patients were not happy with the way some doctors spoke to them. Mrs. Cook was a 72-year-old woman, who, unfortunately, suffered severe COPD (chronic obstructive pulmonary disease) and uncontrolled diabetes. For the past a few years, she had been in and out of the hospital at least five to six times per year. This time, Mrs. Cook was admitted to the ICU due to ankle fracture and COPD exacerbation. An orthopedic surgeon evaluated her and recommended surgery.

"She is probably going to die during surgery," an anesthesiologist said to Mrs. Cook's family during the preoperative evaluation. Mr. Cook, her husband, was very upset with what the anesthesiologist said and complained to me, "I know my wife is sick, but this doctor should not say it this way, and she did not explain things like you." People usually do not like to hear something negative. A patient will accept a surgery or procedure if he is told of a 90 percent success rate. However, the patient may hesitate if he hears he has a 10 percent chance of dying from the operation.

219

Mrs. Cook was really sick on that day with severe pain from the ankle fracture complicated by her COPD exacerbation and uncontrolled diabetes. Because of her poor lung function, she was prone to retain CO_2 (carbon dioxide) in her blood. She was lethargic and barely arousable as a result of her extremely high CO_2 level (her pCO_2 was above 100 mmHg) and pain treatment (the pain medication can sedate patients and suppress respiratory drive). The normal partial pressure of carbon dioxide (pCO_2) is 35-45 mmHg. The accumulation of CO_2 in the blood can reduce mental status and even lead to coma and death. Despite this, Mrs. Cook could recognize me and answer my questions correctly. I talked to her about treatment options of her ankle fracture.

"Surgery will make you recover faster with better functional outcomes, but pose a higher risk to complications because of your serious medical condition," I said. "Non-surgical treatment has a lower risk, but it takes longer time for you to recover with possibly poor function. Which one do you prefer?"

Mrs. Cook replied, "I choose to have the surgery."

I continued, "You are susceptible to complications of anesthesia and surgery such as infection, blood clots, bleeding … But we'll try our best to help you get over it."

She said firmly, "I understand the risk, and I accept it."

In the meantime, an operation room nurse called me to ask if the patient was ready for the operation. I told the nurse that Mrs. Cook was too sick to undergo the surgery on that day. Obviously, the orthopedic surgeon was unhappy with it. Even though Mrs. Cook had severe COPD with acute respiratory failure, she was not on a ventilator (lung machine), instead on **BiPAP** treatment. Besides, Mrs. Cook received other treatments including steroid, antibiotics, insulin, and nebulizer medications.

BiPAP (Bi-level positive airway pressure) is a device that delivers a preset positive airway pressure during inhalation and exhalation to assist a patient's respiration. BiPAP has been used effectively to manage chronic obstructive pulmonary disease and acute respiratory failure without the need for intratracheal intubation and ventilator, which can cause a lot of complications including tracheal stricture, vocal paralysis, and ventilator-related pneumonia.

Mrs. Cook became more alert and comfortable next morning. Her CO_2 level (pCO_2) dropped to 60 mmHg, which was her CO_2 baseline. Her vital signs were normal. The operation room was notified that Mrs. Cook was medically stable for the surgery. Mrs. Cook successfully recovered from the surgery and was moved out of the ICU to the acute care unit, then to the rehabilitation unit, and finally was discharged home.

Language is powerful, especially in medicine: life and death are at stake.

Although obesity is one of the most common issues in medicine, it needs to be handled the right way. Mrs. Price was a 63-year-old woman with diabetes and chronic kidney disease, who was hospitalized with pneumonia. When Mrs. Price was eating her dinner in the room, Dr. Daniel entered the room and said, **"You are eating too much."**

During the follow-up visit after discharge, Mrs. Price complained to me that she felt humiliated by the way Dr. Daniel spoke. She said, "It was just an insult!"

Food is a basic human need. Eating is not only an instinct to survive but also one of the major enjoyments in human life. Patients receiving bariatric surgery for weight loss were found to have a two to three time higher rate of suicide than the general population.[3]

I have learned to approach the patient in this way, "The food smells good and makes me hungry too. You are improving and eating better now. Congratulations. Could I adjust your diet tomorrow in order to see if your sugar level will improve while you are in the hospital?"

Of course, some patients of mine said to me like that, "Why do you want to change my diet? I'm going to eat whatever I want anyway after I leave the hospital."

When asking a patient if she or he eats a lot of food, you can expect that most of the patients will answer something like: "I don't eat that much." Even the patients asking for diet pills would say the same thing. It will be more effective to try and express ideas or present information in a positive manner. Instead of criticizing a patient, I would rather say,

"How about try to eat this or drink that because doing this will make you healthy or be good for your diabetes and your heart."

When talking with a patient about smoking cessation, you can say, "Do you think you will be healthier and feeling better if you quit smoking? And you'll be saving a lot of money too!" But you need to say it at the right time.

Mr. Jackson came in for a follow-up visit after he was discharged from the hospital. He was hospitalized for pneumonia a few weeks earlier.

"How are you doing, Mr. Jackson?" I asked.

"I'm doing okay now," Mr. Jackson said unhappily. "I do not like the doctor who treated me in the hospital. He is just nasty."

He continued, "Guess what that doctor did to me? He criticized me for smoking cigarettes as soon as he walked into my room. I had a fever and trouble breathing, and was feeling really terrible at that time, you know. He did not ask me how I was doing, and he just blamed me and blah-blah..."

Apparently, it would have been better to talk with Mr. Jackson about the diagnosis and the treatment plan first when the patient was suffering. Smoking is a long-term issue, which can be tackled later when a patient is improving and recovering. The smoking cessation can be emphasized again when the patient is being discharged or when the patient comes to the clinic for follow-up visits.

In China, I have had similar experiences. Mrs. Wang (my mother-in-law) was hospitalized for a possible stroke a few years ago. She had improved gradually and was happy that all her children and grandchildren came back from the U.S. to see her. One day, Dr. Zhong, a chief attending neurologist in his 50s, walked into the room to see her. The room was full of people including all children and grandchildren. We expressed thanks to Dr. Zhong for treating Mrs. Wang, who had a good recovery.

"Thank you very much for taking care of my Mom," Jo (my wife) said to Dr. Zhong. We expected some pleasantries, for every family member was excited and happy at the time that Mrs. Wang had recovered.

"**Just a piece of cake**," Dr. Zhong said, looking up at the ceiling. Then he strutted toward the door emotionlessly. All of a sudden, the atmosphere in the room became tense, and we were speechless after we heard what and how Dr. Zhong said.

As a physician myself, I understood what Dr. Zhong meant by saying "Just a piece of cake": it is his routine job, nothing special. It is obvious that treating patients and alleviating patients' sufferings are the routine job of a doctor, who sees patients day in and day out. However, getting sick and hospitalization are significant events for patients and their families, which will affect their daily lives and can cause anxiety and unease in addition to the financial burden. Regarding patient care as "a piece of cake" will be not only interpreted as a lack of empathy and sincerity, but also devalues a doctor's hard work. If you have been a patient or a family member of a patient, you will profoundly experience how important a doctor's language is.

Not only the way you say, but also where or when you say it that matters. It is crucial to say the right thing to the right person (not just the computer) in the right place at the right time. At the same time, it is important to do the right thing and give the right answer to patients.

When coming in as a new patient, Mrs. Lamb walked hunched over with a walker slowly and unsteadily, and could not even stand straight. Mrs. Lamb, 73 years old, underwent two neck surgeries and took strong painkillers for chronic neck, back, and joint pain. I reviewed her medications with her during the visit.

"You're taking two types of pain pills," I said.

"Yes, I need them to maintain my daily activities," she said. "They can't get rid of all my pain. Anyway, if I don't have these pain pills, I have to stay in bed all the time."

"How long have you taken these pain pills?"

"Almost 10 years. I have to see my pain doctor once a month for refilling my pills."

"The pain clinic is 50 miles from your home. Do you drive your car to go there every month?"

"How can I drive a car? I have difficulty even pushing my walker. My children are not around. I have to pay my neighbor $25 to drive me there."

"That's tough," I said.

"Believe or not. One time I was late for six minutes, the doctor refused to see me. It was due to the bad traffic. I could not do anything about it."

"Did you tell the office staff that you came from far away and you had to pay somebody to get there?"

"Yes. I did," she said. "They know me well since I have been there so many years. A receptionist went to talk to the doctor and returned to tell me that the doctor could not see me. I almost cried. However, I had no other choice than to go home. I paid my neighbor again to take me there the next day.

"That's bad," I said.

"I spend two hours sitting in the car and two hours in the waiting room every month. I feel exhausted after each visit."

In the meantime, a nurse had already finished checking the drug monitor record, confirming Mrs. Lamb had been obtaining the same pain pills from the same clinic for two years. I said to Mrs. Lamb, "I'll try to help you out. From now on, I can prescribe the same medications for you. You only need to see me every three months. It's going to make your life much easier, isn't it?"

"Sure. I'm so happy to hear that. Thank you very much."

"I feel happy too if I can make you happy."

One of my patients told me about her similar experience with another pain clinic. These are not isolated cases, and a couple of doctors have even told me similar events they have witnessed. Unfortunately, I've heard some more striking stories. Mr. Baker came in for an office visit in one afternoon because of upper respiratory infection. I noticed that he kept looking at his watch.

"What happened?" I asked. "You look like you are in a hurry."

"I run out of my pain pills today. After I leave here, I need to go to the orthopedic clinic for my prescription. It is 30 miles from here. I have to get there by five." Mr. Baker underwent a shoulder surgery three weeks ago and was still wearing a sling.

"What pain pills are you taking?"

"Oxycodone (an opioid painkiller)." He showed me the pill bottle.

"You don't have to drive 30 miles to refill your pain pills. I can prescribe for you."

"Thank you very much. How helpful you are! You save me a lot of time and money." Mr. Baker had a legitimate pain due to the recent shoulder surgery.

"I understand it's not easy to see a doctor in the rural area," I said. "I try to help my patients as much as possible. My patients can schedule same-day or next-day appointments to see me. No matter how late it is, I'll see my patients as long as they are in the clinic. A few months ago, an elderly lady told me her sad story: her pain doctor didn't see her because she was just six minutes late for her appointment."

"Tell you the truth, this kind of thing happens a lot," he said. "One time, I drove 25 miles to see a doctor. I got to his office at 4:00 p.m. as I had an appointment for 4:30 p.m. But, the office staff asserted that my appointment was 2:30 p.m. Do you know what? Their computer was down, and they could not confirm that. They asked me to show my appointment paper. I had left my appointment paper back home. How could I show it to them? The receptionist walked inside to ask the doctor and came out with this: 'Dr. M said he didn't have time to see you.' When I got home, I found my paper, which showed that my appointment was at 4:30 p.m. I called the office about it the next day, reluctantly they apologized to me. Since that incident, I've never gone back to that clinic."

"That's an amazing story," I said.

"This is nothing, and I have seen worse things," he continued. "I went to a clinic 90 miles away two years ago. A woman came in when I was sitting in the waiting room with several other patients. Unluckily, this woman was one hour late for her appointment. She drove more than an hour to get there. The staff told her that she was too late to be seen by the doctor even though they knew she lived 70 miles away. One woman in the waiting room watched what was happening. She volunteered to give her appointment spot to the woman who was late. 'I live locally and have no emergent issues,' she spoke to the office staff. 'I can come back in a few days. Please let her take my spot to see the doctor.' Surprisingly, the office staff still insisted that the doctor could not see the woman who was late. I saw the woman walk out of the clinic in tears."

"This is the most incredible story I have ever heard," I shook my head sadly.

"Now you know it, Doc," Mr. Baker said, who read and verified the above story after I wrote it.

When writing these sad stories, I was also in tears. Where is Dr. Hertz now?! (See his story in **Fight for Life: Hemodialysis**) Nevertheless, I do know Dr. Leonard is just right here and always available to his patients. (See below)

"Even when he was out of the country, Dr. Leonard called and gave me advice about my illness," a patient said to me when I saw her in the hospital one weekend. That's absolutely true. Dr. Leonard was on call 24 hours a day, 365 days a year for three decades, taking care of patients using insulin pumps and pregnant patients with diabetes. Whenever I needed him for assistance in life and work, he has never hesitated to offer help. His unparalleled work ethic still challenges me to this day.

"Dr. Leonard worked so hard that he came to see me at 1:30 in the morning!" another patient said to me when I made rounds. I said, "Dr. Leonard is so devoted to his patients that he sleeps only four to five hours a night. I really admired his hard-working spirit." Dr. Leonard has been the chief of staff for the hospital once and has been the chairman of the department of medicine twice. Furthermore, he travels around the country to give lectures, organizes the annual diabetes fair in town and many other diabetes care activities in the state, conducts clinical research, owns and runs a large medical center, and so on. "You're indeed a superman," I said to Dr. Leonard on one occasion. "The only thing you can't do is to fly a plane like the president of the AMA (American Medical Association)."

"My life was saved by Dr. Leonard!" a patient told me the story. "When I was seriously ill and hospitalized 10 years ago, Dr. Leonard canceled his trip to a conference and stayed in town to take care of me.

He persuaded the surgeon to operate on me. I have survived and can talk with you today." I still wonder if I can do the same for my patients.

"I'm glad to see you coming. Dr. Leonard always comes to see me whenever I end up in the ER," a patient spoke to me when I entered the room in the ER. I have learned to do the same thing as Dr. Leonard does.

"Dr. Leonard was very nice, and he did not get upset when I called him for advice at 3 a.m. You have a superb colleague," a nurse told me when I visited a nursing home. I recall that I had lost my temper many times when I was awakened at midnight by pages from the ER or the nursing homes or the answering service company. Since I heard Dr. Leonard's story, I have become calm and relaxed on night calls.

"I'm 76 years old and still alive because Dr. Leonard has been taking care of me all these years," a patient with type 1 diabetes said to me when I admitted her to the hospital. Dr. Leonard attends numerous CME (continuing medical education) conferences every year and 8-am CME teleconferences every Tuesday. I admire his excellent medical knowledge and skills. His dedication to lifelong learning has inspired me to live and learn.

"Dr. Leonard is the best doctor I've ever seen," a patient said to me when I saw her on a weekend. I wish some of my patients would think about me this way.

Another patient said, "I don't want to see other doctors except Dr. Leonard." I am pleased that some of my loyal patients drive 50 miles to see me in my new clinic even though I am only a primary care doctor, not a specialist.

When my patients were discharged and came back to see me in the clinic, they would tell me their experiences in the hospital.

"Dr. Woods doesn't know how to talk with a patient," a patient said to me. "I don't want to be admitted by him in the future." After hearing this, I knew I needed to polish my communication skills as well.

Another patient said, "Dr. Thornton looked nice, but he entered my room for just seconds. So, I didn't have a chance to ask questions." Since then, I have been trying to remember to say, "Do you have any more questions?" before finishing a visit in the hospital or in the clinic.

"Dr..."

They are all good doctors and are my mentors in many ways. I've heard a lot of great things about them during my weekend rounds or during night calls. The practice of medicine is an art, which cannot be learned just from books. I have achieved considerable progress in learning the art of medicine by interacting with patients, doctors, nurses, and other healthcare workers. Nobody is perfect; I have made numerous mistakes myself. I have attempted to emulate my colleagues' good bedside manners and tried not to make the same mistakes in my own practice.

Hopefully, my colleagues would appreciate that I have become a better physician through this learning process. I wish physicians like Dr. Hertz and Dr. Leonard would practice the art of medicine as long as they can. Thus, patients will continue to enjoy their grace and excellence.

The Test Day

When Mr. Thatcher came to see me as a new patient, I asked, "How can I help you today?"

"I need a preoperative form to fill out before my foot surgery," he replied. "I'm seeing a podiatrist for my bunion. The podiatrist recommends surgery for the bunion."

I reviewed the previous record with him. He was 62 years old and basically healthy without complaints, and he did not take any medication.

"You have undergone a lot of tests at another clinic. Do you have chest pain or shortness of breath and any other problems?" I noticed he had numerous office tests, including heart stress testing at that clinic.

"Not at all," Mr. Thatcher replied. "I moved here from New York a year ago. When I saw Dr. Bunch as a new patient, I did not complain about anything. She scheduled me to do all the tests in her clinic on a separate day. I had no idea what's going on, but everybody knows those tests would last a whole day. My neighbor even reminded me, '**Don't forget to bring some snacks or lunch with you on the test day.**'"

"Did your previous doctor tell you why you needed all the tests?"

"No. It seems that all of the patients like this doctor since her clinic waiting room is always full of patients. I need to wait two or three hours to see her each time. That's the reason I came to see you."

It is well known that patients routinely go through all the diagnostic devices in some clinics. Typically, it takes the whole day to complete all of the tests (so called "**the test day**"). After finishing his physical examination, I filled out the preoperative evaluation form for Mr. Thatcher. He never came back to see me again. It is likely that he was satisfied with all the tests he received and he returned back to his previous doctor.

One time, a patient of mine asked me why her doctor scheduled an MRI for her at an imaging facility 30 miles away instead of the local hospital in town. It is not apparent to patients that doctors own these testing machines and have stakes in some imaging facilities.

On a Monday morning, Mrs. Glenn's daughter called, "Mama doesn't look right."

"Please bring her to see me," I said.

"How are you doing?" I asked Mrs. Glenn when she came in.

"I'm not feeling good," Mrs. Glenn replied. "I am drowsy, dizzy and nauseated." She was an 80-year-old lady with diabetes, hypertension, coronary heart disease and depression.

"How long have you been feeling sick?"

"A couple of days."

"Have you started any new medications?"

"They wrote me a prescription for tramadol (a pain drug) a few days ago when I visited an urgent care clinic in the evening because of neck and shoulder pain."

"You should stop taking tramadol, which may be the cause of all your problems."

"I won't take it anymore. They performed an x-ray that day and scheduled me to have an MRI of the neck in their clinic tomorrow. Do I need to go?"

"How are your neck and shoulder doing? Did you have any recent falls or other injuries?"

"I don't have much neck and shoulder pain now and haven't had any falls." She raised and rotated her shoulder without difficulty.

"I don't think you need an MRI. You've been getting better with your neck and shoulder. Furthermore, you had an x-ray. They should have notified you if there is anything wrong with your shoulder on the x-ray. I have expressed my opinion. It's up to you to decide whether you want to have an MRI or not."

"I'll think about it."

Mrs. Glenn came back two weeks later for a follow-up. All her symptoms were gone. She did not go for the MRI and did not complain of neck and shoulder pain during the visit.

Another patient of mine in her 40s went to one of these clinics for abdominal pain when I was on vacation. She told me that she went through six diagnostic tests: ultrasound of the thyroid, carotid study, chest x-ray, abdominal ultrasound, bone mineral density testing and a cardiac stress test.

"Did they find anything wrong?" I asked.

"No. My pain has gone, anyway," she replied happily.

"Just so you know, we have most of those machines in our clinic as well."

"Why didn't you do those tests for me?"

I replied, "We don't perform them unless there is an indication."

She said, "I feel good that I completed those tests, it gave me peace of mind."

"Well, if you feel good, then I have nothing to say."

Occasionally, even patients themselves doubted that some of the office tests were unnecessary. Mr. Stewart asked me during an office visit, "Why does my heart doctor perform a nuclear stress test on me every year for the past five years? She scheduled another one for me in a couple of weeks."

"What's the reason you went to see her in the first place?" I asked.

"I had palpitations a few years ago," he replied. "I haven't had it since she put me on metoprolol (a drug used to treat hypertension, angina, and cardiac arrhythmias)."

"Do you have any chest pain, shortness of breath or other related symptoms?"

"Not a bit," Mr. Stewart responded. He was 66 years old without previously diagnosed coronary heart disease or stroke. The only medication he took was metoprolol.

"According to the current guidelines," I informed him, "you don't need a stress test as you don't have any new or worsening symptoms such as chest pain, shortness of breath, etc.[1, 2] Additionally, you don't have a diagnosis of coronary artery disease. I may not know all the information about your heart. You'd better ask your heart doctor why she scheduled the test."

"Can you refer me to see another heart doctor for a second opinion?"

"Sure," I said without hesitation.

Of course, some of my patients requested CT or MRI scans or other tests without any indication.

"Why do you want all these tests?" I asked. "They aren't routine screening tests, and you don't have any symptoms and signs that indicate these tests."

"I want to make sure there is nothing wrong with me," a patient said. "I don't want anything bad happen to me in the future. Better safe than sorry, right? "

"I've paid for Medicare for more than thirty years," another patient said. "It should pay for all the tests I want."

Not only do unnecessary tests or procedures deplete natural and social resources, but they may produce unfavorable outcomes. As more diagnostic tests are used, some of the patients will have incidental abnormal findings, which may never cause diseases. These patients may suffer from so-called "incidentaloma".

Incidentaloma usually refers to a tumor or growth that is found by imaging studies for other purposes. The most common incidentalomas include adrenal, renal, pituitary, thyroid and pulmonary lesions. Whenever receiving imaging reports revealing any kidney cysts, liver cysts, thyroid nodules, adrenal nodules, lung nodules, etc., doctors have to follow up or refer to appropriate specialists for further evaluation in order to prove those lesions are indeed harmless. The majority of the incidentalomas turn out to be benign and rarely incidental findings can save lives. However, these follow-ups and referrals will result in more tests and procedures, which may lead to more radiation exposure and procedural complications. This is an endless vicious cycle.

Once in a while, even a seemingly harmless nerve conduction study can be harmful to patients.

"My foot hurts." Mrs. Nelson said painfully, limping into the examination room while her 88-year-old husband was holding her arm.

"What's wrong with your foot?" I asked Mrs. Nelson.

"I twisted my ankle when I was having the nerve conduction test this morning," Mrs. Nelson said. "Now my pain is so awful that I can barely walk."

Mrs. Nelson was an 87-year-old woman with well-controlled diabetes. She went to another clinic to have a nerve conduction test earlier that morning.

Nerve conduction studies, which are noninvasive, are used to test how well and how fast the nerves in your body send electrical signals. This test can help diagnose various disorders affecting the peripheral nervous system, such as diabetic neuropathy and carpal tunnel syndrome. Surface electrodes (small patches used to detect or supply electricity) are attached to the skin of arms or legs, nerves underneath the skin are stimulated by electrical pulses, and these responses are measured and recorded. The electrical pulse can cause some discomfort in patients, and most of the patients tolerate the test without long-term side effects.

"Why did you have a nerve test?" I asked.

"Because I have numbness in my feet, and some back pain occasionally," Mrs. Nelson said. "Dr. Poole scheduled the nerve test for me in her clinic. I'm 87 years old and can still walk around without a cane. Those symptoms don't bother me at all. I told Dr. Poole that I don't want to have any procedure or surgery regardless of what the test will find. However, the doctor was persistent and told me to do it anyway."

Mrs. Nelson had diabetes for a long time and developed numbness of her feet (one of the common symptoms for a diabetic patient). Thankfully, this did not affect her activities of daily living. When looking back at my clinical experience, it makes me wonder: Who doesn't have some sort of back or knee pain at her age?

Standards of Medical Care in Diabetes-2015 states, *"Electrophysiological testing or referral to a neurologist is rarely needed, except in situations where the clinical features are atypical or the diagnosis is unclear."*[3]

North American Spine Society states, *"As spinal nerve injury is not a cause of neck, mid back or low back pain, EMG/NCS has not been found to be helpful in diagnosing the underlying causes of axial lumbar, thoracic and cervical spine pain."* [4]

Mrs. Nelson suffered from a moderate ankle sprain, which could be treated with rest and compression. With this conservative treatment, it

233

would take three to six weeks for her ankle to heal. Luckily, she did not sustain an ankle fracture. Her quality of life would have been significantly affected if that were the case. Even though the nerve conduction test itself does not do any harm to patients directly, elderly people can get injured during the test or during the trip to the clinic. Patients have to come for the test on a separate day. Seeing a doctor is a big event for elderly people. If they cannot drive, they need to include other family members.

I attended a conference where a neurologist spoke about a nerve conduction device and explained how to use it.

"Can I perform the nerve test on patients every year and get reimbursements from insurance companies?" One of the audience members asked.

"Yes, you can," the neurologist responded immediately and without hesitation. "But you need to know how to code the procedure. You can't choose the same diagnosis code, such as neuropathy, year after year. If you report symptoms such as numbness, pain, weakness, or tingling, then the insurance will reimburse you for the test." During the entire presentation, the neurologist did not mention anything about why an annual test was indicated or how the test would benefit patients.

It was disappointing to see a doctor like this neurologist teach how to cheat publicly without any embarrassment. No wonder more than 50 percent of the medical recommendations Dr. Oz (a physician and medical TV show host) gave to the public are unproven or incorrect.[5] Unnecessary medical tests hurt patients, poison the society (leading to more cheating and frauds) and damage the earth (polluting the environment by testing machines and waste materials).

Similarly, the longer a patient stays in the hospital, the more the insurance will reimburse doctors. On the flip side, the hospital will lose money if a patient stays in the hospital too long because of DRG (Diagnostic Related Grouping) rule.

DRG is a system to classify hospital cases into different disease groups, which are defined by disease severity, patient characteristics, procedures, etc. Medicare and other health insurance companies

234

determine how much they would pay for each disease group, which is updated and adjusted accordingly. Then hospitals will be reimbursed according to the disease groups no matter how long a patient stays in a hospital or how much the hospitals spend on this patient. DRG system has been implemented by Medicare since the 1980s. DRG system is designed to reward efficiency and improve fairness by the same reimbursement for similar care. (For more details on this topic, see Wikipedia: Diagnosis-related group)

An early discharge will save money for the hospital. However, the DRG system does not affect the practice of private doctors. I remember that the CEO of the hospital pleaded with the doctors at a hospital conference, "Please, please discharge your patients as soon as they are ready." Hospitals specifically hire one case manager (usually a registered nurse) for each ward to check on what a patient is diagnosed with, how long a patient has stayed, why the patient is not discharged yet, etc. Case managers need to deal with insurance personals, physicians and hospital administrators; that is a tough job. Sometimes, physicians get very frustrated by these bureaucratic systems, causing them to lose faith in the system.

Obviously, Medicare patients need to meet the Medicare admission criteria to be admitted. Nevertheless, some of the criteria, such as electrolyte values, hemoglobin levels, oxygen saturation, IV infusion rate, are very unrealistic. Occasionally, a case manager would call me, "Can you put the patient on an IV antibiotic?" or "Can you increase the IV rate to 100-125 milliliter per hour? Otherwise, the patient does not meet the admission criteria." I was frequently asked to talk with insurance medical directors and explain why patients were admitted to or why they were still in the hospital. From time to time, some billing experts would speak at the hospital conferences to help physicians code for the right DRGs. Physicians needed to learn how to properly word the diagnosis in order to obtain a higher reimbursement for the hospital.

Medical care is run like a business in other countries too. According to an article in *The Economist*,[6] people in Japan see doctors more frequently, stay in the hospital longer and take more medications than in other developed countries. Japanese doctors tend to work long hours and some of the doctors see as many as 100 patients a day. They often have their own pharmacies and over-prescribe drugs and tests.

In China, patients are encouraged to be admitted to and stay in the hospital longer if they have good medical insurance. Mrs. Wang (my mother-in-law) was hospitalized for possible stroke a few years ago. She had recovered fully within one week and had resumed normal eating for three days. The doctor wanted her to stay in the hospital for 21 days in order to finish the course of IV herbal therapy. There is no evidence that IV herbal therapy is more "effective" than oral therapy if a patient can eat without difficulty. However, her doctor did not approve an earlier discharge requested by the family.

Undoubtedly, patients should be discharged from the hospital as soon as they are ready, so that they can enjoy their life at home with their family. Particularly, time is limited for elderly people. Extended hospital stays will cause them to lose precious days in life, waste resources, and result in a multitude of complications such as infections, blood clots, even deaths.

The Institute of Medicine (IOM) in a 2012 report estimates that about 30 percent of all health care delivered in the United States is duplicative or unnecessary.[7] Thus, approximately 750 billion dollars were spent in unnecessary health care in 2009. A lot of unnecessary medical care and bad clinical outcomes will be avoided if a doctor always remembers:

"You are in this profession as a calling, not a business." (William Osler)

"What you do not wish for yourself, do not do to others." (Confucius)
Humanity is above business, always.

Medicare Pays

Perhaps you remember the TV ad by the Scooter Store a couple of years ago. In the advertisement, a smiling woman was driving a scooter inside the house and raising both arms high with power. You can judge from the TV ad that this woman with strong arms and hands is not qualified for a scooter prescription. "Just call this number, and we'll do the rest," the ad said. Many patients walked to the clinic with their envelopes from the Scooter Store and requested a scooter or motorized wheelchair.

"You walked into the clinic even without a cane. How can I prescribe a scooter and fill out all these forms for you?" I said to one patient of mine. "The qualification is that you have mobility difficulty and are too weak or painful to push a manual wheelchair. You don't even use a manual wheelchair."

"My neighbor got one from his doctor," he replied unhappily. "He is stronger than me. He drives it to the corner store to buy things."

"The Medicare rule for getting a motorized wheelchair or scooter is that you have to need it to move around inside your house or apartment."

"Why did my neighbor get one from his doctor?"

"I am sorry that I can't help you because you don't meet the Medicare criteria. You may go to see your neighbor's doctor to find out if you can get one from him."

"I'll surely go," he said angrily. He walked out of the room and had never come back to the clinic.

Agents for scooter or motorized wheelchair are so aggressive that they not only go to churches, senior centers and even knock on seniors' doors, but they make telephone solicitation calls to their homes. Another patient told me that a scooter agent knocked on her door and entered her home to talk about a scooter, of which she did not need. She said that the agent did not leave until she agreed to take the paper.

Mrs. Scott walked into the clinic with a big envelope and handed it to me, "The scooter agent told me to give it to my doctor."

"These are the forms for scooter or motorized wheelchair. Do you really need one? You are walking well." I opened the envelope and found the scooter paper enclosed.

"Actually, I don't need one. One agent called my home and talked me into it. She just kept talking and did not want to hang up the phone until I agreed to accept the paper."

"How did she get your phone number?"

"I don't know."

"That sounds strange. We can shred the paper for you since you don't need it."

"That's fine."

I have even witnessed an agent accompany a patient to the clinic for evaluation of a scooter.

"Can I ask who you are?" I asked the man sitting in the room with a paralyzed patient of mine, thinking that he might be a care provider or a case manager. I usually like to talk with others in the room in order to get to know more about how patients live in their home and who helps them.

"I'm a scooter representative," the man replied with some embarrassment.

"Then you can't stay here with my patient while we are talking about his medical issues."

"It's okay. I'm leaving," he said to me. Then he turned to my patient, "I'm waiting for you outside."

"What's going on? Why did a scooter agent come with you here today?" I asked my paralyzed patient. He certainly met the criteria for a scooter and was using one now.

"He called and informed me that I'm qualified to get a new scooter since I have used the old one for many years. He made the appointment for me to see you and have the form filled out. He went to my home, picked me up and drove me here today."

"That's great customer service," I smiled.

"Yes, it surely is," he laughed.

I used to fill out these scooter forms after office hours a few years ago. Now Medicare pays for physician visits specific for the scooter evaluation and filling out the forms thanks to the powerful lobbyists in Washington, DC. According to the government investigation, up to 80 percent of the scooters and power chairs are prescribed to people who don't meet the requirements.[1] In reality, a lot of patients do not use their scooters most of the time after they get them. Nevertheless, they are satisfied that they've got one at home. Patients who use scooters on a daily basis tend to become more sedentary and gain more weight; this results in even more mobility impairment.

Medicare covers hospice care, including medications, medical equipment, 24-hour access to care and even support after death. Hospice has become a booming business with revenue of 14 billion dollars per year.[2] Agents from hospice companies go to churches, assisted living facilities, nursing homes, senior centers, clinics to recruit patients. They talk the family members into accepting hospice for their loved ones. However, many of those patients do not meet the criteria for hospice service.

Hospice is a program of care that is delivered to seriously ill or terminally ill patients and focuses on comfort, not on curing an illness. Hospice services care helps patients live and pass through the dying process more comfortably by alleviating pain and other symptoms. This creates a comfortable environment, providing care for their physical, emotional, social, and spiritual needs. Hospice care is generally provided in the patient's home. Besides, it can be given in hospitals, nursing homes, and assisted living facilities. According to the Medicare policy, a patient's regular doctor and the hospice medical director need to certify that the patient is terminally ill and has six months or less to live.

Occasionally, family members would ask me why I did not approve the hospice service. I explained to them the reasons. Sometimes they are satisfied and other times they will take the patient to see another doctor.

I received a hospice form for Mr. Presley, a 78-year-old man with a history of treated prostate cancer. Mr. Presley did not have symptoms, was eating and walking well, and lived in an assisted facility, for nobody took care of him after his wife died. I noticed that the hospice form listed prostate cancer as the number one reason for hospice.

After Mr. Presley was diagnosed with prostate cancer 15 years ago, he received radiation therapy and did not show signs or symptoms of prostate cancer recurrence. He took only one medication. And he developed bladder infection one to two times per year. When he was found to have a fistula between the bladder and the colon, he refused surgery to fix the fistula, saying the fistula did not bother him. He did not have dementia and was able to perform **basic activities of daily living** (ADLs) – basic self-care tasks – dressing/bathing, eating, ambulating (walking), toileting, and hygiene (grooming) without difficulty. As a matter of fact, he was a cancer survivor, not a terminal cancer patient who needed hospice.

I called the facility manager to ask why this patient needed hospice. The manager stated that the family requested it, and the hospice service would help the assisted facility take care of the patient. I understand the assisted living facility can save money with the addition of hospice service. I also understand that business is business. It's legal and free as long as a doctor signs the paper.

When coming in as a new patient many years ago, Mrs. Hopkins was just recovering from head trauma (subdural hematoma) due to a fall. Back then, she was an 87-year-old assisted living resident with a cheerful smile all the time. After falling at home three months earlier, she was sent to the local ER, where she was found to have a large subdural hematoma. She was transported to the nearby medical center to undergo a brain surgery. After the surgery, she needed to use a walker initially, then she came in with a cane, and finally after a couple months could walk normally without assistance. She had recovered completely without weakness after a few more months of physical therapy.

Now, Mrs. Hopkins was 93 years old and had lived in the same assisted living facility for six to seven years. She was of medium build and looked fit. Whenever she came in for an office visit, she was always dressed up, wore high heel shoes, and made funny jokes.

At the first visit, I noted that Mrs. Hopkins was on two antidepressants and one anti-dementia medication. Mrs. Hopkins did not show any symptoms or signs of depression or dementia.

"Why do you take these psychiatric medications?" I asked. "You look pretty normal."

"I don't know," she giggled. "Nobody has explained it to me. Do I look crazy to you?"

"Absolutely not. You don't seem to have any mental problems."

"I used to be a dancer and teach dancing," she stood up and made a 360-degree turn on tiptoe in front of me, "Do you dance?"

"No, I don't dance at all," I said. "Wow! You can dance so well at this age."

"I don't think I'm old. I can teach you how to dance if you want."

"Maybe in the future. Dance is a great exercise. In addition, you can interact with other people while dancing."

I gradually reduced her psychiatric medications and stopped them completely after six months. Additionally, her hypertension was under good control without medication after her BP medication was discontinued. She was doing quite well without hospital care and without any regular medication. Now and then, she got a cold or bladder infection, but recovered quickly with medications. She continued to be mentally and physically stable without signs of dementia at the age of 93. Still walking in high heels, she showed me some dancing steps from time to time.

"Why do you need hospice service?" I asked Mrs. Hopkins at an office visit while looking at the hospice form she brought in. "You do most of the things yourself and eat well. You can even dance!"

"Someone came to the facility to talk with me," she smiled. "I don't know what hospice can do for me. My major problem is I feel dizzy sometimes. I'm not dying, am I?"

"No, you're not dying. You're going to live long and healthily."

"I can still dance. Do you remember I used to be a dance teacher?"

"Yes. I remember. I recall you told me that your boyfriend died a few months ago. He was 14 years younger than you. Is that right?"

"Yeah, you're right about it," she giggled. "Now I have a new boyfriend, who is 78 years old, 15 years younger than me."

"Why are your boyfriends always much younger than you?" I joked.

"You know, all the old men are dead!"

"Please bring him here next visit to let me have a look," I laughed. "I need to judge if you can marry him or not."

"Sure," she laughed.

"You don't need hospice at this time. I'm going to dispose of your hospice paper. Is that okay?"

"Okay. I think I need a marriage paper first," she busted into laughter.

"You are absolutely right."

Laughter is the best medicine. Mrs. Hopkins' laughter, sense of humor and optimism always remains in my memory.

When I visited the nursing home, I frequently noticed the hospice forms inserted to some patient charts waiting for my signature. Occasionally, I asked the nursing home nurse, "What more care will the hospice company provide for this patient?"

"I don't know. The hospice representatives came in and looked at the patients and the charts. Then they talked to patients' family and left the forms in the charts." Both managers of nursing homes and family members are happy with hospice service as the hospice personnel help with ADL's. Although, in my opinion, those services should be routines provided by the facilities. If they are not qualified for hospice, I did not sign the forms even under the pressure from patients' family and managers. I received calls from time to time that families had changed doctors.

Medicare Part B pays for almost all the medical items you can use at home including canes, walkers, chairs, beds, sugar meters, oxygen, nebulizers, etc. as long as doctors prescribe them. At times, I receive forms for knee braces, lumbar supports, heating pads, etc. on behalf of my patients. I do not initiate the majority of the requests. Apparently, many of these forms were mailed from other states, especially from Florida. Occasionally, I asked them why they needed these supplies. They told me that the supply store staff talked to or called them that they could get the items for free. Most of them said that they really didn't need those items after I discussed the issue with them.

Several patients complained to me the medical supply stores refused to take back oxygen tanks or hospital beds when they did not need them anymore. The supply stores can continue to charge Medicare for the rental fees as long as patients use the equipment. It is common that patients are discharged home with home oxygen if they are hypoxic at discharge. They may not need home oxygen anymore after a few months when they have recovered completely.

"I've called the supply store to take the oxygen tank back several times. However, they refused to pick up the equipment. They said they needed a doctor's order," a patient told me.

"No problem," I said. "I write an order on the prescription paper for you."

"I gave the order to them, but they still didn't do it," the patient said during the following visit.

"You'd better tell them that you'll report it to Medicare if they don't take the stuff back," I said.

"They finally took the stuff back when I said I would call the Medicare office," she smiled at the next visit.

According to a study, the most satisfied patients (based on highest patient satisfaction quartile relative to the lowest quartile) were more likely to be hospitalized, and they caused higher healthcare cost and spent more on prescription medications.[3] It was surprising that these patients had a 26% higher risk of dying. Patients and family members tend to be satisfied when they get what they want, but they do not realize that they may not achieve the best care and outcomes.

There is no free lunch; somebody will pay for it. This is seen in the free lunches brought in by drug representatives. Medicare provides free glucose testing strips and yearly diabetic shoes for diabetic patients, some of my patients have numerous unopened boxes of sugar testing strips and many pairs of diabetic shoes at home. To me, this is a great waste of resources. Additionally, I have noticed that free diet education classes tend to make patients gain more weight instead of losing weight. With a family history of diabetes, I diet most of the time and exercise daily in order to prevent myself from getting diabetes. However, I have to admit that I often eat excessively, sometimes three to four plates of food when dining at a buffet. Through my experiences, I have realized that we share the same human weakness and express it in many different ways.

10. Overdone

The first duty of the physician is to educate the masses not to take medicine.

The young physician starts life with 20 drugs for each disease, and the old physician ends life with one drug for 20 diseases

—William Osler (1849-1919, Canadian Physician and Professor of Medicine)

Nevertheless, moderation is still relevant to the sick. Some problems are better managed than solved. Less data can hasten recovery. Inaction can allow healing. And the old standby may be better than the next big thing.

—Welch, H. Gilbert (Professor of Medicine at the Dartmouth Institute for Health Policy and Clinical Research, USA) [1]

LIFE AND MEDICINE

Statins (Cholesterol-Lowering Drugs)

During an office visit, Mrs. Carter told me an interesting story. **"It looks like you're taking atorvastatin** (a cholesterol-lowering pill, the brand name is Lipitor). Are you taking it?" her sister asked Mrs. Carter when they were walking in the yard. Her sister traveled to visit Mrs. Carter from Boston two months earlier. They had not seen each other for many years.

Mrs. Carter, a 74-year-old woman with diabetes, hypertension, hyperlipidemia, and stroke, had taken atorvastatin for 10 years. She had suffered weakness and body pain for the past few years. Since her symptoms developed gradually, she did not mention them to me, thinking that she was just getting old. Mrs. Carter did not realize that her problems might be due to adverse effects of atorvastatin until her sister inquired about the medication.

"Yes, I am. How did you know that?" Mrs. Carter asked her sister.

"I just guessed when I saw you walk. Ha! I'm right," her sister said.

"You're absolutely right!"

Her sister told her own story that she had the same symptoms, walking slowly like a patient with Parkinson's disease when she was on atorvastatin. All the weakness and pain disappeared after her sister quit taking atorvastatin. Mrs. Carter stopped her atorvastatin as soon as she heard her sister's story, and she had felt stronger and less painful just within two to three weeks.

"I haven't felt so well for years," Mrs. Carter said to me happily. "Doc, I've realized I'm not that old."

A statin medication was still indicated for Mrs. Carter's medical conditions. Thus, she was put on pravastatin (another cholesterol-lowering drug), and she had been doing well for a few years without adverse effects.

Amazingly, by watching the way someone walks, even a layperson can tell the person is taking a statin. In real life, statin medications cause adverse effects on muscular and other body systems much more frequently than reported in the literature. You may miss it if you don't think about it.

The paper on effects of high-dose atorvastatin published in the New England Journal of Medicine in 2005 was still cited in the 2013 lipid treatment guideline.[1, 2] Back then, atorvastatin was a brand-name drug, which cost $100-200 per month and was actively promoted by the drug company. One day, a drug representative came in and handed me a copy of the above paper. It is common practice for drug representatives to bring in copies of newly published papers that favor their products.

"I've already read the article. Do you know that more people died when taking 80 mg of atorvastatin?" I said to him in the hallway while signing for drug samples.

"Are you sure?" he was puzzled. "This paper says 80 mg of atorvastatin daily reduces the incidence of cardiovascular events."

"Did you look at that table in the paper, which shows the mortality is higher in 80 mg group than in 10 mg group?" I pointed out the values in the table to prove my point. The death from any cause in 10 mg group is 5.6 % while the death is 5.7 % in the 80 mg group.[1]

Of course, there is no difference in the death rate between the two groups from a statistical standpoint. At least, we can say that the treatment with a higher dose of atorvastatin did not save more lives even though it led to fewer heart attacks or strokes. Then what's the point of taking a higher dose of atorvastatin?

Higher doses of atorvastatin may even make patients, especially elderly patients, sicker. Mrs. Stone was an 89-year-old woman with coronary heart disease and diabetes. She had two stents placed in her heart. Two months earlier, she was active and could drive her car to see me at the office. One day her daughter called me, "Mom isn't acting right recently. She doesn't want to eat and looks confused and depressed. Now, she is too weak to walk on her own and stays at home all the time."

"Just bring her to see me," I said. My patients usually can see me on the same day or next day whenever they need.

When Mrs. Stone came in for the office visit, she walked unsteadily and looked confused. Her daughter needed to hold her while she was walking. Mrs. Stone was sluggish and gloomy. Her vital signs were normal, and the physical exam was otherwise unremarkable. She just didn't look like herself on that day.

"Have you taken any new medication lately?" I asked Mrs. Stone. She appeared to have difficulty finding her words. Even though she opened her mouth, she could not say a word.

"No new medication," her daughter replied for her. "Well, Mom's cardiologist has increased the dose of atorvastatin from 40 mg daily to 80 mg daily."

"Did your mother start to get sick after that?" I turned to her daughter who was sitting beside her.

"Yes, Mom started to feel bad after the dose change. I called her cardiologist about it. The cardiologist did not think that it was the problem with atorvastatin and told her to see her primary care doctor."

"Your mother is probably suffering from adverse effects caused by atorvastatin. It has been reported that atorvastatin can cause mental status change. Cholesterol is important for maintenance of a normal brain function. Your mother should stop taking atorvastatin right now."

"We'll do that," her daughter replied while Mrs. Stone was sitting silently without her usual smile.

"I'll see you back in one week. Call me or come in if anything happens."

Mrs. Stone was staring at something emotionlessly. Her daughter had to wake her up, "Mom, we're going home now."

"O...o...okay," Mrs. Stone arose slowly from the chair with her daughter's assistance.

Mrs. Stone could talk more fluently on the next visit, "I've felt much better." She could say full sentences and walk without assistance. Her symptoms had resolved completely within one month after atorvastatin was discontinued. Mrs. Stone still needed a statin cholesterol drug for her diabetes and heart disease. After she had recovered completely, she was started on another statin medication. She had since tolerated the new cholesterol medication, and her cholesterol level met the recommended treatment target. Her daughter told me that they had changed to see another heart doctor.

Some patients will suffer more and longer if the cause of mental status change cannot be found promptly. Mr. Compton used to be my patient for more than 10 years at my previous clinic. He is a 79-year-old man with diabetes, hypertension, and hyperlipidemia. After I had moved to another town for a few months, he and his wife came to my new clinic for an office visit. Mrs. Compton told me that she called the Medicare office to find out the address of my new office.

I noticed that Mr. Compton had very slow speech and did not want to talk. He could answer questions passively and asked me the same questions three to four times during the visit. He had also lost 15 lbs. (6.8 kilograms) over the past six months.

"How is your appetite?" I asked.

"Good. I'm eating well," he replied slowly.

"No, he doesn't eat much these months," Mrs. Compton interposed anxiously.

"I just don't want to eat," Mr. Compton said.

"He sits at home and doesn't want to talk and go out," Mrs. Compton added. In fact, family members tend to provide more precise information about elderly's mental status than the actual patient.

"Is he taking any new medications?" I asked because I had not received his previous medical record at that time, and they did not bring their pill bottles with them.

"He was referred to see a neurologist a few months ago as he had become more forgetful for five to six months," Mrs. Compton continued. "He was diagnosed with dementia and put on donepezil (the brand name is Aricept, a drug used for dementia)."

"I think that donepezil probably has caused Mr. Compton to lose weight as one of the adverse effects of donepezil is suppression of appetite." I noted that Mr. Compton had a normal colonoscopy five years ago and had a normal blood count, normal kidney/liver function and thyroid function in the recent blood test.

"What can we do then?" Mrs. Compton asked.

"Just stop taking donepezil."

"Is that okay?"

"I don't think quitting donepezil will cause any problems," I said. "Losing weight is bad for elderly people."

"You're the doctor," Mrs. Compton said. "We believe in you, and will follow your advice. That's the reason we drove 50 miles to see you today."

"I really appreciate it," I said. "I'll see you back in a month."

Mr. Compton had gained six pounds when he came back one month later.

"He is eating better now," Mrs. Compton said. "But still doesn't want to talk."

"Are you depressed?" I asked Mr. Compton.

"No. I feel better since I saw you," he smiled.

His previous medical record arrived a few days earlier. After reviewing the record, I found that he was taking 40 mg of atorvastatin daily instead of 10 mg daily, and his recent cholesterol level was 145 mg/dL (3.7 mmol/L) with LDL cholesterol level of 42 mg/dL (1.1 mmol/L).

"You are taking a higher dose of atorvastatin, 40 mg daily now. I remember that you used only to take 10 mg."

"The new doctor increased the dosage of atorvastatin, saying that my cholesterol was too high," Mr. Compton said.

"You don't have a history of coronary heart disease or stroke," I said. "I don't think you need to take 40 mg daily. You should go back to 10 mg daily. I believe your mental problem may improve if we lower your dose of atorvastatin."

"We can try," Mrs. Compton said.

"You can cut the 40 mg tablets to four pieces and take one piece a day."

"We'll do that."

Mrs. Compton called back, "My husband is so stubborn that he just wants to take the whole tablet of atorvastatin, not the small pieces."

"No problem," I told her. "We can send in a new prescription for 10 mg atorvastatin pills to your pharmacy electronically."

"He talks to me again now," Mrs. Compton said, excitedly, when they came back for a follow-up visit one month later. I was also surprised that Mr. Compton was talking faster and even initiated conversation. He told me that they went to SHONEY'S to have a good breakfast before coming to the clinic. Mr. Compton probably would have been diagnosed with mild cognitive impairment, which might not benefit from acetylcholinesterase inhibitor treatment (donepezil). The high dose of atorvastatin had aggravated his cognitive impairment. Subsequently, he ended up at the neurologist's office and came home with one more medication (donepezil), which made him even sicker.

It is not uncommon that a patient is started on a new drug, which is used to correct the adverse effect of other medications. The new medication may cause more adverse effects, and the patient may get more medications. If the root cause of Mr. Compton's mental problem had not been discovered, Mr. Compton might have been put on more medications, potentially another anti-dementia pill or perhaps an appetite stimulant.

Often, I receive letters from insurance companies, recently even from pharmacies, stating that a patient should be put on cholesterol medications. I always document in the chart why the patient is not on a statin or why the guideline targets are not meet. A patient may not be a good candidate for the statin treatment as a result of comorbid conditions, not tolerating medications, or noncompliance. It is a kind of defensive medicine, which at least does not cost money, but makes me spend more time generating longer office notes in patients' charts.

There is no evidence that patients on hemodialysis benefit from statin therapy.[3, 4] However, when I made rounds in the hospital, I noticed that many dialysis patients with malnutrition were still on statins. By looking at their total cholesterol levels, which were commonly lower than 120-150 mg/dL (3.1-3.9 mmol/L), I could imagine that the adverse effects of statins contributed to the poor quality of life for these patients, who often experience symptoms such as chronic fatigue, weakness, pain, and confusion.

I saw Mrs. Dennis as a new patient at the clinic. She, in her 70s, was very emaciated as a result of malnutrition with numerous comorbid disorders. Weighing only 80-90 pounds, she was too weak to stand up and was confined to a wheelchair. I noticed that she was still on 40 mg of atorvastatin per day. When reviewing her hospital record, I was astonished to find that her total cholesterol level was 46 mg/dL (1.2

mmol/L) with LDL cholesterol level of 26 mg/dL (0.7 mmol/L). I have seen teenagers or people in their 20s put on statins although most of the guidelines do not recommend starting statin therapy in people younger than 40 years of age.[2, 5, 6] Surprisingly, I found that a 101-year-old woman without diabetes or cardiovascular diseases was still on 20 mg of simvastatin while she had generalized weakness and needed to use a walker to move around. Furthermore, she also had memory impairment.

After I had stopped statins or adjusted statin dose or changed drug type, some of my patients' testimonials are as follows:

"I can get out of the car now."

"I can feel the difference within one week, and I have become another person two weeks later."

"I don't need painkillers anymore."

"My shoulder pain at night had gone away after having stopped simvastatin for two days."

"I can walk without a cane now."

"I can think better."

"Not only my body pain is gone, but also my anxiety has got better," a woman said after her simvastatin was reduced from 40 mg to 20 mg daily.

"I haven't had any memory problem since you stopped my atorvastatin a couple of months ago," Mr. Manning said. "Guess what? My arm pain and joint pain have also disappeared."

Mr. Manning had lost his memory suddenly and transiently while he was walking to his car in a parking lot. He told me during the first visit, "My eyes were open, and I could see things, but my mind went blank." He was 80 years old and took only two medications, atorvastatin 20 mg daily and Lisinopril (anti-hypertensive) 20 mg daily. He continued, "I didn't know where I was. Then, I saw the sign of Dollar General and drove to the store. All of a sudden, my brain started to work again like somebody turned on the switch. I could think again and knew where I was. The whole episode lasted about 20 minutes. I recovered completely and drove home."

This type of memory loss is called transient global amnesia (TGA), a temporary short-term memory loss followed by full recovery. On one hand, FDA (Food and Drug Administration) modified safety information about statin drugs in 2012, warning that statins may cause reversible memory loss and confusion, and increase the risk of developing type 2 diabetes.[7] On the other hand, two recent reviews of "published" studies suggest that statins do not pose a risk to memory or cognition.[8,9] However, statin-induced mental dysfunction is so common in the real world that even patients' family members can sense statins are bad for brainpower and take action themselves as Mrs. Wells.

Mrs. Wells brought her husband, 82 years old, to see me for the first time a few years ago. Mrs. Wells told me excitedly, "My husband did not want to eat, and he sat quietly at home most of the time. Now, he is gaining weight and goes out to see his friends after I stopped his pravastatin (a statin drug) just one month ago."

"Good job!" I said. "How did you know the cholesterol pills caused your husband's problems?"

"Truly, I have no idea. I just guessed those pills might have made him lose his mind." Once again, patients and their family members are my teachers.

Surprisingly, two of my patients had suffered from "**off-statin injury**", which is coined by me. "Off-statin injury" is defined as an injury associated with discontinuation of statin treatment. Namely, patients feel so good that they try to do more than their conditions allow, resulting in injuries, including falls. Both these patients had obesity and severe degenerative joint diseases including back, hip and knee pain. They used to walk slowly with a walker. Within three weeks after quitting statins, they felt so much stronger that they walked more but less carefully. One fell in the living room with a large laceration on her left arm while another slipped over the doorstep and suffered a fractured ankle.

Since then I would say to my patients, "Please make sure to remain careful when you feel better and move around more after you stop taking your cholesterol medication."

The new guideline on lipid management was published on November 2, 2013, in the Journal of the American College of Cardiology and Circulation.[2] There are no more recommendations for treating target ranges for LDL- and non-HDL–cholesterol levels. Four groups of primary- and secondary-prevention patients are identified, and the appropriate intensity of statin treatment is recommended to reach the relative reduction goals in LDL cholesterol. Theoretically, a new guideline is supposed to provide a better tool to guide care providers to target the **fewer** patients who truly benefit from a specific treatment. On the contrary, many more people need to be put on statin treatment according to the new lipid therapy guideline.

As a matter of fact, lifestyle change is more effective than medication treatment. Mr. Mill was a 66-year-old man who weighed 250 pounds (113 kilograms) five years ago. He used to inject 200 units of insulin per day and take metformin with A1C level of 9-10 %. After he had lost 60 pounds (27 kilograms) through dieting and exercises, his diabetes came under good control with just metformin. His total cholesterol dropped from 265 mg/dL (6.9 mmol/L) to 170 mg/dL (4.4 mmol/L) without medication.

One time, my cholesterol rose up to 312 mg/dL (8.1 mmol/L) after I had a great time and ate a lot of junk food in China. I resumed my healthy diet and routine exercise after returning to the U.S. My total cholesterol level was decreased to 182 mg/dL (4.7 mmol/L) within two months. That further proves the efficacy of diet and exercise.

Additionally, people on statins were found to consume more calories and have a higher risk of having diabetes. The problem is how to maintain a healthy lifestyle and resist the temptation for delicious food. I tell my patients that almost all the food you eat outside your home is junk food. A recent study shows that restaurant food is as unhealthy as fast food.[10]

"I only eat healthy food such as salad when eating at a restaurant," some patients said.

"When I enter a restaurant," I said to them, "I eat any delicious food that I don't eat at home. Sometimes, I don't care if it is junk food or healthy food. The most important thing is not to overindulge and not to eat out too often. Moderation is always the key."

I like to watch cooking shows on TV. After watching many of them, I now know how all those well-known chefs cook their food. Their food is delicious but unhealthy. The way they cook is not sanitary either. Restaurants or other eating places provide pleasant environments for people to socialize and relax while enjoying tasty food, which usually is detrimental to health. Eating out is mentally beneficial, but physically harmful. Life is contradictory once more. Potentially, being in a good mood may neutralize the harmful effects of delicious food.

How long one lives depends on many things. My father died young of cancer while my Mom has diabetes and hypertension. That means I may not bear genes for long life. However, I have done what I'm supposed to do to keep healthy: regular exercise, healthy diet, enough sleep, and try to laugh every day. When the time comes, God will decide. Since I've tried and done my best, there is no need to regret anything. I'll leave for a better place.

Gout

When I saw him at the first office visit, Mr. Williams said to me. "I'm not feeling well." Mr. Williams, in his late 70s, walked with a cane slowly and looked tired and depressed. While talking in a soft voice, he complained of 3-4 months of upper abdominal pain, fullness, loss of appetite, fatigue, palpitation with rapid heartbeats and elevated blood pressure. He also developed episodic shortness of breath and had lost more than 10 pounds.

I reviewed his medical chart quickly and learned that Mr. Williams had many medical problems including peripheral arterial disease (PAD) with bypass surgery and stents, hypertension, hypercholesterolemia, chronic kidney disease, and gout. His blood pressure had been under good control until a few months ago with lisinopril (an antihypertensive medication). Amlodipine (another antihypertensive) was added one month ago.

Since Mr. Williams started to feel bad a few months earlier, a lot of workups had been done by other doctors. His routine blood tests were normal or stable, x-ray barium swallowing study showed no significant abnormalities or dysfunction and a chest x-ray revealed COPD (chronic obstructive pulmonary disease) changes. He quit smoking 10 years ago. Then, he was referred to GI (gastroenterology) service and had an EGD (esophagogastroduodenoscopy) done, which turned out to be normal. He also had a normal colonoscopy study within five years.

His blood pressure was 162/78 mm Hg, and his heart rate was 106 beats per minute on that day. The remainder of the examination was unremarkable.

"Have you started any new medications?" I asked.

When an old patient complains of not feeling good, the first thing you should do is to review his or her medications instead of prescribing more pills, ordering more tests or scheduling more referrals. Nowadays, many people are on so many medications that we use 'Polypharmacy' to define allegedly excessive or unnecessary prescriptions. Polypharmacy is most common in the elderly. Elderly people are exposed to adverse drug reactions, drug-drug interactions, prescribing cascade, and higher costs. People on many medications tend to have reduced quality of life, decreased mobility, impaired cognition, more ER visits, and hospitalizations.

"No new medication," Mr. Williams replied. "Anyhow, my arthritis doctor increased the dose of my gout medication, febuxostat (the brand name is Uloric), from 40 mg to 80 mg per day three months ago."

"Did the doctor tell you why he increased the dose?" I asked.

"No."

"Did all your symptoms occur after the dose change?"

"I think so."

Then I went to the website, drug.com, which lists all the common side effects of febuxostat. We watched the computer screen together. Surprisingly, all of his symptoms and signs were included there.

"Since your symptoms match the adverse effects of febuxostat, and the timing is also right, I suggest you stop febuxostat right now."

"Do I need to tell the specialist first?" Mr. Williams was concerned.

"You don't have to. It might make things more complicated."

"Is it okay to stop it right away?" he hesitated.

"Please relax. Febuxostat is used to treat your gout only. It's not a life-saving medication. You won't die of a gout attack, will you?"

"I see."

"Actually, patients taking febuxostat face an increased risk of heart attack, stroke, and liver failure.[1] "

"Okay, I'm not going to take it anymore."

"Good. I'll see you in two weeks. Please call me if anything happens."

Mr. Williams appeared like another person when he returned two weeks later. He looked happy and smiled, walking more steadily and faster. His wife said all the symptoms had gone after he stopped taking febuxostat. Now, Mr. Williams was eating well, had no pain and felt well again. His heart rate and blood pressure returned to normal. He also regained his normal weight within two months.

"Do I still need to take some medicine for gout?" Mr. Williams asked.

"It depends on how often you have gout attacks. Why did the doctor start you on febuxostat in the first place?"

"I had foot pain about seven months ago, and I was told I had gout and was referred to the specialist," He said. "That was the first time I had gout pain. She put me on febuxostat 40 mg daily. I was fine with 40 mg of febuxostat and became sick after she increased the dose to 80 mg a day."

"I don't think you need long-term prevention treatment because you don't have frequent and severe gout attacks according to the current guidelines.[2] The elevated level of your uric acid may be due to your age, hypertension, chronic kidney disease and your diuretic medication. There is no need to treat the elevated level of uric acid."

His uric acid had even returned to a normal level after his diuretic was discontinued as a result of dizziness. He has not had any gout attack since then.

Gout is usually characterized by recurrent attacks of joint pain, swelling, redness, and warmth. It frequently involves the metatarsal-phalangeal joint at the base of the big toe. The elevated blood level of uric acid (hyperuricemia) is the main cause of gout. People with hyperuricemia have a 10 percent chance of suffering gout at some point in their lifetimes. Acute attacks of gout can be treated with nonsteroidal anti-inflammatory drugs (NSAIDs), steroids, or colchicine. Gout was described thousands of years ago and used to be regarded as a "rich man's disease". However, it has become more commonly seen in recent decades, which is related to obesity, an aging population, dietary alteration, and medications.

The current guidelines recommend gout prevention therapy in patients with frequent and disabling attacks of gouty arthritis (two or more attacks per year), clinical or radiographic signs of chronic gouty joint disease, tophi, and recurrent nephrolithiasis.[2] The most commonly used medications for preventing further gout attacks are xanthine oxidase inhibitors: allopurinol and febuxostat.

In the United States and Europe, the guidelines do not recommend treating asymptomatic hyperuricemia with drugs. On the contrary, a recent Japanese guideline states that asymptomatic hyperuricemia should be treated if lifestyle modification fails.[3] However, there is no convincing evidence to show the beneficial effect of early intervention in asymptomatic hyperuricemia. Since Japanese doctors usually own their pharmacies, people tend to consume more unnecessary medications in Japan.[4]

My father-in-law is 87 years old and lives in a nursing home in China. He does not have gouty arthritis, hypertension or kidney problems. He called me, "My doctor wanted to start me on allopurinol. Should I take it?"

"Did your doctor tell you why you need to take the drug?" I asked.

"He said that my uric acid level is high," he replied.

"Did he explain to you the benefit of the treatment and side effects of the medicine?"

"No."

"Then, I suggest that you should not take it."

Allopurinol is not a benign drug. It can cause liver and kidney damage. Additionally, it can induce serious skin reactions like Stevens-Johnson syndrome (SJS) or toxic epidermal necrolysis (TEN), which are rare but can be life-threatening. Patients should be warned of this serious reaction. A recent article (2014) reported that some patients suffered from severe adverse effects of allopurinol after being treated for asymptomatic hyperuricemia.[5] One of the patients even died from it.

Indeed, unnecessary medications tend to make elderly patients sick. Mr. Wilson, who was 87 years old, came to see me for a routine checkup. Even with diabetes, hypertension, and coronary heart disease, he was still very active and could drive. Occasional joint pain did not prevent him from walking without assistance. During the office visit, he complained of fatigue and weight loss. After reviewing his medication list, I noticed that he was started on allopurinol recently by another doctor. On physical examination, I could not find anything wrong with him.

"Why are you taking allopurinol?" I asked him.

"The doctor prescribed it for me when I saw him for gout," he replied.

"I didn't refer you to see him, did I?"

"No. I went to see him myself six months ago."

"You have only one or two gout attacks per year, and your age makes you more susceptible to adverse effects of medications," I said. "That's the reason I did not start the preventive treatment of your gout. I am not sure if allopurinol is the cause of your problems at this time. Let's do some blood tests."

The blood tests showed significant liver injury and worsening kidney function. I called Mr. Wilson about the test results and advised him to stop taking allopurinol. He recovered completely and gained his weight back when I saw him again two months later. His liver and kidney function returned to normal too.

How much benefit can an 87-year-old patient gain by taking allopurinol if he does not have frequent gout attacks or debilitating gouty arthritis? Patients tend to think they will gain more when they see more doctors regardless if it is necessary or not. The literature shows that patients have worse medical outcomes in the areas where more doctors are practicing.[6] Additionally, their health expenditure is much higher.

Everyone has aches and pains in the body sometimes, but he or she doesn't need to pop one or more pills for each ailment in order to stay happy and healthy. Mr. Taylor, a patient of mine for 15 years, was a 95-old-year man with coronary heart disease and pulmonary embolisms on long-term warfarin (a blood thinner) treatment. He had two to three gout attacks on his wrist or foot every year. I never started him on long-term gout therapy. Occasionally, I treated him symptomatically with colchicine or prednisone. He was still active and was able to drive a car when I left the clinic one year earlier.

"Should I take allopurinol for my gout? My neighbor is on it," he asked me one time.

"I don't think so," I said. "It's not easy for a man like you to live to 90 years old. Gout attacks won't kill you. However, you may die from the severe skin side effect of allopurinol, even though it happens rarely. The risk of taking the pill outweighs the benefit to you, in my opinion. The pill is good for your neighbor, but it may not be good for you."

"I've got your point," Mr. Taylor nodded.

I was glad to see that even this 90-year-old man understood: one size does not fit all. More is not always better, which is further demonstrated by the stories in the next section.

Many Pills

"Do I need to take Adderall (a drug for ADHD, attention deficit hyperactivity disease)?" Mrs. Addison asked me during an office visit. She was a 68-year-old woman with controlled diabetes, and she did not show any signs of mental illness.

"Why do you ask this question?" I was puzzled.

"Now, almost all the people in my family are taking Adderall, including two grandchildren and two daughters," she continued. "They said ADHD runs in the family. They told me to ask you if I need to take it too."

"I don't think you have ADHD. Taking Adderall won't help you live longer. You don't have to take the pill because somebody else takes it."

"I don't think I need it either. I just ask since my children wanted me to."

It was not surprising that Mrs. Addison asked this question since around 6.4 million children ages 4 through 17 (11 percent of this age group) have received an ADHD diagnosis as of 2011.[1] And this southern state has the highest rate of ADHD drug use in the country according to a report released in 2014.[2] As a matter of fact, I have seen some patients taking these pills in their 80s. Quite a few patients walked out of the clinic unhappily, for I did not prescribe Adderall or other stimulants for eliminating tiredness, achieving higher test scores, getting ready for college, or running a business. One patient even told me to get more education about ADHD.

It is common that as long as a patient mentions a symptom, he or she will get a prescription for it when leaving the office. Some patients will go to another clinic down the street if they can't get what they want. I spend much more time explaining to patients why they don't need a medication than just prescribing what they want. In particular, when it comes to antibiotics, psychiatric drugs, and painkillers, I spend a lot of time explaining the harmful effects. It is the duty of doctors to do no harm to patients.

One day, Mr. Tate came in for an office visit after being absent from the clinic for three years. Mr. Tate was a 45-year-old man who had been seen in my clinic for almost eight years until three years ago when his car-part factory moved to Mexico. Some of his coworkers went to Mexico to keep their jobs. He did not follow the factory and found another job in the U.S. At that time his insurance did not include me as a provider, and he stopped coming to see me.

Recently, he got a new job and a new medical insurance plan. My name was on the new plan list. With well-controlled diabetes and mild hypertension, he was active and muscular. I reviewed his long and extensive medication list at the returning visit.

"Hey, you are taking both tadalafil (the brand name is Cialis, a drug for treating erectile dysfunction in men) and testosterone now," I said. "I haven't seen you for only three years. Now, you look like an old guy taking many medications!"

"I have 'low-T' now (abbreviation of low testosterone level), Dr. Li," Mr. Tate laughed. "I was diagnosed with it two years ago, and I have been on testosterone treatment since then. Additionally, I'm using Cialis."

Three years ago, he asked me to prescribe Cialis. I asked him at that time, "Is there anything wrong with your erection?"

"No. Well, I saw the ad for Cialis on TV," he replied. "The ad says I should ask my doctor about it. I just want to try it to see if I can perform better."

"You should reserve the good pills for the future when you really have a problem."

"Okay, okay. You're right," he smiled. I did not prescribe tadalafil for him.

This time, I asked him, "Do you know that testosterone treatment has been shown to increase cardiovascular events such as heart attack and stroke?" Actually, more and more evidence shows that testosterone therapy increases the risk of heart attack, stroke, and even certain cancers.[3]

"No, I didn't know," he said. "Nobody explained that to me when I was put on testosterone."

"You are only 40 something. Are you going to take it three to four more decades until you're 80 years old?"

"I've never thought about it this way."

"You should think about it now," I emphasized.

"Sure. I may not need to take it anyway."

Mr. Tate never asked me to prescribe testosterone or Cialis for him after he came back to our clinic for care. It seems that he was doing fine without them.

"Low T" appears on TV advertisements so often nowadays that it has become a popular phrase and even a young man like Mr. Tate can say the fancy word "**Low-T**." In fact, I have seen some patients in their 30s receiving testosterone treatment because they feel "tired."

Certainly, TV advertisements for medications are powerful. Some patients of mine asked me if they should take pregabalin (the brand name is Lyrica) after watching TV commercials for it.

"The ad says: ask your doctor about Lyrica," a patient said.

"The medication doesn't cure or modify your neuropathy," I said. "Did you hear the ads mumbling adverse effects at the end?"

"Those side effects scare me. I don't want to try this stuff if I don't have to."

"At least, I can tell you there is no scientific evidence that you are going to live longer with the medication. Taking unnecessary pills may create more problems than it solves."

In real life, patients tend to get a prescription of gabapentin or pregabalin when they mention numbness in the feet and hands. I have seen many patients suffer from adverse effects of gabapentin and pregabalin, which are much worse than the numbness and tingling. A lot of patients develop swelling of legs after taking gabapentin or pregabalin, and then they will get diuretics to reduce edema, sometimes they have to take potassium tablets to treat hypokalemia (low potassium level in blood) induced by the use of diuretics. It is a never ending cycle.

I remember a 73-year-old woman who was started on gabapentin after being seen at another clinic. She became so drowsy and weak that she could not get out of her bed for three days. Her children found her and called EMS to transport her to the ER for evaluation. Another patient, who was 87 years old, was put on pregabalin by another doctor. She subsequently developed severe leg and pulmonary edema and had to be hospitalized.

Diabetic peripheral neuropathy commonly manifests as numbness, tingling, burning, and pain in feet, hands or legs. Although the symptoms usually do not affect patients' daily activities, many of the patients are put on unnecessary medications such as gabapentin or pregabalin by their care providers.

Mr. Huggins, 70 years old, brought in an empty bottle of gabapentin and wanted to refill it at the new patient office visit.

"Why do you take this medication?" I asked.

"I don't know," Mr. Huggins replied.

"I guess it is for your numbness and tingling in hands or feet due to diabetes."

"Maybe so."

"Does your numbness in your feet bother you?" I asked.

"No. When I mentioned it to my previous doctor one year ago, I was started on the medication."

"Do you feel better when you are taking gabapentin?"

"No, I don't feel any difference," Mr. Huggins said.

"This medicine alleviates neuropathic symptoms only. It does not get rid of diabetic neuropathy. Did you know that?"

"No, I didn't know that. I thought gabapentin could cure my neuropathy."

"Since you are out of gabapentin for a couple of months and doing fine without it, why do you still need the medication?" I asked.

"So, I don't think I need it anymore," he said.

"The fewer medications you take, the better you feel."

That's true. The elderly are especially vulnerable to the adverse effects of medications. More medicine tends to be bad for them.

"I don't feel good," Mrs. Keith said at an office visit after she had not been in the clinic for almost one year. She had lost about 20 pounds since her last visit.

Mrs. Keith, 82 years old, was one of my favorite patients, and she was the one who yelled at her husband's girlfriend in the hospital room while her husband was hospitalized. She was mildly obese weighing usually around 180-200 pounds, which is the typical and 'normal' weight of a woman in this area. Local people will say to you, "Are you sick?" if you are below 180-200 pounds.

"Please look at my mouth. It doesn't have any saliva." She opened her mouth and pulled her lips to show me her gum and tongue.

Her oral cavity was so dry that her tongue showed several deep cracks. She complained of dry mouth, palpitations, constipation, losing appetite, drowsiness, and depression. She had mild diabetes, which was controlled without medication (her A1C is 6.7%).

"What's going on?" I asked. "How long have you felt like that?"

"At least three months," she said. "But it's getting worse and worse."

"Are you taking any new medications?"

"Please look at it." She handed over her medication bag to me.

I went over her pill bottles and found a bottle of phentermine, which was prescribed by another doctor in town. Phentermine is an appetite suppressant used for losing weight.

"Why are you taking phentermine?" I asked.

"Because I wanted to lose some weight, I went to see the doctor, who prescribed phentermine for me."

"You know you are 82 years old. Losing weight doesn't make you live better or longer.[4, 5] I've never told you to lose weight, right?" I said.

"Right, you never did."

"You are susceptible to adverse drug effects at this age. Actually, weight-loss medications are not indicated for you because you don't have arthritis, uncontrolled diabetes or uncontrolled hypertension."

"I guess I'm wrong then," Mrs. Keith said.

"Did the doctor explain to you why you need phentermine or what side effects it has?"

"No. Anyway, I'm not going to take it anymore."

"I can't say that phentermine contributed to all your symptoms, but it causes at least some of them. Additionally, your oxybutynin (a drug for overactive bladder disorder, prescribed by a urologist) may trigger dry mouth, constipation, and drowsiness. Phentermine can induce dry mouth, fast heartbeat, nervousness, and hypertension. No wonder your mouth is so dry, and you can't swallow since both oxybutynin and phentermine cause dry mouth. I think you're going to get better if you stop both medications."

Mrs. Keith recovered fully as expected after discontinuing her oxybutynin and phentermine. A month later, she came back with a smiling face, showing me her smooth, moist tongue.

"I'm glad you got better," I said.

"I'll talk to you first if anyone puts me on a new medication in the future," she smiled.

"That's a good idea."

Indeed, many patients of mine would call the clinic for advice when other care providers prescribe new medications for them. Otherwise, some of them could run into trouble.

Mrs. Allison was a 78-year-old woman with mild dementia. During the previous visit, I told the family that Mrs. Allison had very mild symptoms of Alzheimer's disease and did not need medication treatment at this time. They were not happy with my decision and went to a specialist for evaluation. It is not a bad idea to seek a second opinion if you are not comfortable with a medical diagnosis or treatment plan.

When Mrs. Allison came back for an office visit in two months, she looked tired and depressed. She had lost 15 pounds since her last visit.

"She doesn't want to eat," Mrs. Allison's daughter was concerned.

"What's going on?" I asked. "Mrs. Allison has lost a lot of weight."

"I took her to see a neurologist a month ago," her daughter replied. "The neurologist started her on two medications for dementia: donepezil (the brand name is Aricept) and memantine (the brand name is Namenda). She doesn't want to eat and looks weak and tired, and talks less since starting the medications."

"Besides other side effects, both Aricept and Namenda can trigger poor appetite. Losing weight is bad for elderly people, especially demented patients. I suggest that Mrs. Allison should stop taking the new medications and try to enjoy any food she likes."

Mrs. Allison had gained all her weight back and returned to her baseline when she came back a month later. At present, all the medications for Alzheimer's disease are minimally effective, and early initiation of medication treatment has not been proven to improve outcomes. Mrs. Allison may need some medication treatment for her Alzheimer's disease down the road as her symptoms progress. Still, it is prudent to start one medication at a time.

"I feel woozy," Mr. Warren said when he came in for an office visit. He was 70 years old and looked strange today. I reviewed his new medication list, which showed he was started on three psychiatric drugs.

"You have three new medications," I asked. "Who prescribed these to you?"

"A ... clinic doctor gave them to me."

"Why did he give these drugs?"

"I complained of some depression," he replied.

"He prescribed you three medications at the same time?"

"Yes."

"How are you feeling now after taking these medications?" I asked.

"I don't know. I just feel bad."

Why did Mr. Warren need to be started on three psychiatric medications at one visit? He had no psychiatric emergency. He needed to be admitted to the hospital if it were an emergent situation (e.g. suicide). If patients experience drug side effects after taking three new medications, how can we know which of the medications causes the problem?

Geriatric patients are very sensitive to medications and commonly suffer adverse drug effects. Moreover, they tend to take a lot of medications so that drug interactions occur frequently. Oftentimes, I say to patients, "you're not feeling well because you're taking too many medications." I have learned to start one drug at a time when starting a new medication in an outpatient setting. Even when starting drugs on older adults one at a time, I always stick to the principle of "start low and go slow."

Back/Knee Pain

Mr. Black was lying on the examination table moaning when I entered the room. He was a 53-year-old intelligent man working as a store manager. Although he was tall and slim, he suffered type 2 diabetes. He had a history of back pain, which flared up every two or three years.

He did not have a fever, muscle weakness or other systemic symptoms. He could manage to walk slowly, but with pain.

"My back is acting up," Mr. Black said painfully.

"How do you rate your back pain on a scale of 0 to 10 (with 10 indicating the most severe pain)?" I asked.

"It's 10," he replied.

"You have a history of back pain for years without recent injury. Your back pain started four days ago. It is not getting worse. I could not find any dangerous signs on the exam like weakness or loss of sensation. I'm going to treat you as before with a muscle relaxant and pain pills. Is that okay?"

"But this time, I have more pain than before. Do I need an MRI now?"

"I don't think you need it at this time according to the current back pain treatment guidelines.[1] You can call me anytime if you have any new symptoms, or your back pain gets worse.

Two days later while I was seeing patients in the clinic, the secretary told me Mr. Black wanted to talk with me over the phone.

"How are you doing, Mr. Black? What can I help you?" I picked up the phone.

"I'm all right," Mr. Black Sr. sounded very upset. "My son went to see you two days ago. How did you treat him so poorly that day?"

"Your son?" I was puzzled and tried to figure out what was going on. Why was Mr. Black calling for his son? I quickly realized that I was talking with Mr. Black Sr. Mr. Black Sr., 89 years old, was the father of Mr. Black, who saw me for back pain two days earlier.

"Oh, yes," I continued. "Your son came in for back pain a couple of days ago. How is he doing now?"

"He is still in lots of pain. Why didn't you order an MRI for him?"

"Your son has a history of chronic back pain, and he had an MRI three years ago," I said. "When I saw him that day, he did not have indications for MRI according to his symptoms and my exam."

"I'm calling you to let you know that he is still having severe pain. You may need to do something about it."

"That's fine. I'll call your son to find out what's going on. Is that okay?"

"Okay, okay..." Mr. Black Sr. said.

"How are you doing?" I called Mr. Black. "Your father called me about your back."

"Really? My father called?" he sounded surprised.

"Yes, he did. He seems very concerned."

"My back is still killing me!" Mr. Black replied.

"Is it getting worse?"

"Not really, but it's not getting better," he responded.

"Your father wanted me to order an MRI for you," I said. "Do you really want an MRI of your spine?"

"I think I should have an MRI."

I have had quite a few of experiences that some people requested MRIs or CT scans for their family members. A nurse stopped me at the hospital to request an MRI for her father after I saw her father for back pain at the clinic a few days earlier. A worried woman has called me for her teenage son or her husband to order imaging studies in the past. This was the first time a senior called me for his adult son at 53 years of age.

I had no choice but to order an MRI of lumbar spine for Mr. Black under the pressure of his family. It was so easy to schedule and get an MRI done in our town. I guess other physicians would have done the same in this situation. Mr. Black's spine MRI was performed next day, showing a disk herniation at the level of L4-5 (the lower lumbar spine).

Studies have shown that 27 percent of healthy people over 40 have a herniated disc. And 36 percent of people over 60 were found to have herniated discs, and about 80-90 percent of them had significant disc degenerative changes such as stenosis or bulging by MRI imaging.[2] However, these people did not have bothersome back pain.

Because of his severe back pain and abnormal MRI findings, Mr. Black was referred to a spine clinic in the nearby city. One month later, he returned to the clinic for a follow-up visit. He was walking steadily and fast.

"How is your back?" I asked. "You look really good today."

"It has improved by 70-80 percent," he smiled.

"Did you undergo back surgery?"

"No. The neurosurgeon did recommend surgery treatment," he laughed. "But I chickened out the last minute. I went into physical therapy and took your medicine. So, I've got better without surgery."

"Your early MRI had almost placed you on the operation table," I smiled and said. I heard another story like this a few months later. A patient of mine presented to an urgent care with neck and shoulder pain and had an MRI done within one week after the onset of his symptoms. He was referred by the urgent care doctor to a neurosurgeon in a nearby city, who recommended surgery. This patient was so scared that he declined the surgery. He told me that his neck and shoulder pain had improved by 70-80 percent after two days of physical therapy. He was pain-free with full function of his shoulder when he saw me in the clinic one month after his MRI.

Mr. Black came to see me two years later when Mr. Black developed back pain again. This time, I found he had a fever of 101.3 degrees Fahrenheit (38.5 degrees Celsius) and elevated glucose level of 300 mg/dL (16.7 mmol/L). I suspected that Mr. Black must have some infection. Because of his systemic signs and severe back pain, I had to admit him to the hospital.

After Mr. Black had been admitted, I ordered blood culture, urine test, and chest x-ray. Unexpectedly, his chest x-ray showed an infiltrate in the right lung, which was consistent with pneumonia. He was started on antibiotics for pneumonia. His fever subsided after two days of antibiotic treatment. His glucose level was well controlled with insulin treatment. Despite this, his back pain was so severe that he required IV pain medication and could only walk two to three steps. Because of his severe pain, fever and pneumonia, an MRI of the spine was ordered and revealed small fluid collection along the lumbar spine with chronic degenerative changes.

A spine surgeon was consulted, and he ordered aspiration of the fluid. Approximately 2 milliliters of clear fluid was aspirated from the spine by a radiologist. The fluid contained only scant cells without evidence of significant inflammation or infection. The culture of aspirated fluid was negative for bacteria or fungi. The spine surgeon recommended continuing conservative treatment with antibiotic, pain control and physical therapy. With the assistance of a physical therapist, Mr. Black could sit for two to three hours and performed some physical therapy. The repeated chest x-ray showed resolution of the lung infiltrate. Mr. Black was discharged on the 7th day of hospitalization and continued outpatient physical therapy.

His insurance refused to pay for his hospital stay, for they did not consider back pain as the reason for admission. I had to write a letter to his insurance to explain the necessity of the hospitalization. My letter stated that Mr. Black was hospitalized for pneumonia complicated by severe back pain and uncontrolled diabetes. It is true that one of the three disorders alone might not be indicated for admission. Mr. Black told me three months later that his insurance finally paid his hospital bill.

Unfortunately, Mr. Black suffered a heart attack two years later and underwent CABG (coronary artery bypass graft) heart surgery. He had just started to work at a new store about 10 months prior to his heart attack. Once again, his new insurance company refused to pay for his heart surgery for the reason that his heart problem was considered as a pre-existing condition. Mr. Black was never diagnosed with coronary heart disease before his heart attack. How could the insurance company determine how long the blockage of Mr. Black's coronary arteries had been existing?!

Both of Mr. Black's parents, over 90 years old, were still living. Mr. Black's father was diagnosed with diabetes at the age of 82, and his diabetes was well controlled with one oral medication. Mr. Black was diagnosed with diabetes at the age of 40, suffering many diabetic complications including diabetic neuropathy leading to chronic foot ulcers. This was attended by a podiatrist years before Mr. Black became my patient.

"You are receiving the standard treatment of diabetes and taking all the medications you are supposed to take," I said to him one time. "Your A1C, cholesterol, and blood pressure values have been meeting the recommended targets all the time. I still don't understand why you have so many diabetic complications since you got diagnosed with diabetes less than 10 years ago?"

"I might have had diabetes years before I was diagnosed with it," he replied.

"It may be true, your parents are still alive and doing fine in their 90s. It seems that your good genes did not protect you from getting diseases."

"It's most likely due to too much stress in my life."

Mr. Black's story reaffirmed my belief that your son is always your son no matter how old he is. I wonder if I would have done the same to call a doctor for my son to have an MRI scan. We often blame a disease upon our family history, saying 'it runs in the family.' Having good genes is a blessing, yet it does not guarantee good health. It is important to relax, eat healthy and stay active, though it is easier said than done.

Mr. Spencer was a-60-year old accountant. One time he asked me, "I saw a neurosurgeon recently. He said I need another spine surgery. What do you think?"

"I did not know the details of your MRI results," I said. "Anyway, the first question you need to ask your neurosurgeon is: What happens if I don't have the surgery?"

"That's a good question," Mr. Spencer said.

"To my knowledge, few patients with chronic back pain become paralyzed unless they have recent injuries, cancers or infections. Next, you should ask yourself: What do you expect to achieve through the surgery? Do you want to reduce your pain or increase your mobility or both? What improvements will make you satisfied?"

"Those are good questions. After one of the back surgeries, I suffered severe infection and stayed in the ICU for days. I almost died from it. Since I have undergone two back surgeries in the past, I need to think twice about surgery."

"Are you willing to take the risk again since you developed serious complications before?" I asked.

"I'm not sure," he responded.

"You are 60 years old and can walk without a cane at least one circle at Wal-Mart. There is no medical emergency here. Please do not rush; take your time before you make important decisions."

"I agree with you."

"Have you finished the book, How Doctors Think,[2] which I recommended you to read a month ago?"

"I've finished about a half of it."

"There is one chapter talking about back pain. I think you can get some ideas from it."

So many patients told me that they started to take pain pills regularly after back surgery. Frequently, they regret that they had undergone their surgeries.

"However, it's telling that when I've asked many surgeons in individual conversations and during my lectures over the years whether they would undergo a spine fusion for their own LBP (low back pain), the answer is uniformly 'no.'..." stated Dr. David Hansom in his book, *Back in Control: A Spine Surgeon's Roadmap out of Chronic Pain.*[3]

Hopefully, Mr. Spencer will make a right decision and achieve a satisfactory outcome.

"Bone-on-bone" refers to complete joint space narrowing resulting from loss of cartilage, which is shown on x-ray and is one of the findings in osteoarthritis. Osteoarthritis is most commonly seen among people over 65, but people of any age can develop this disorder. Typical symptoms and signs of osteoarthritis include joint pain, stiffness, tenderness, reduced mobility, crackling sound, swelling, warmth, enlargement, and deformity. Osteoarthritis is caused by the damage of cartilage, which acts as a cushion between the ends of bones that form the joint. The bones can glide over one another smoothly with intact cartilage. Wearing out of cartilage may cause the bones to rub each other and induce symptoms. However, a patient may have few or no symptoms while the x-ray reveals bone-on-bone abnormalities indicative of severe osteoarthritis.

Mrs. Stanley underwent a left knee replacement surgery and still had a lot of pain. Her orthopedist recommended a right knee surgery. She asked my opinion.

"Do you feel better after your left knee surgery?" I asked.

"The left knee actually hurts more after the surgery," she replied.

"Which knee bothers you more now?"

"That's the left knee with the replacement surgery."

"Why would you consider a right knee surgery if your right knee is better than the left?" I asked.

"My orthopedist said my right knee looks like 'bone-on-bone' on the x-ray," she said.

"How you feel is more important than the picture of your knee. I think you can make your own decision."

She did not have the surgery and continued to walk well five years later. I do not know how she is doing now since I left the clinic.

Nevertheless, Mr. Lee chose to have the knee replacement. He saw me at the clinic before the surgery.

"You can walk well, drive around and play golf at the age of 83. Why do you want to have the knee surgery?" I asked.

"All my buddies walk better than me after their knee replacement," he replied. "I just want to do the same after knee surgery."

"You have coronary heart disease. I guess your orthopedist has talked with you about the risk of surgical complications."

"I understand the risk. My heart doctor said I'm okay with the surgery after I underwent the heart stress test two weeks ago. I think I'll be fine with the surgery."

Unfortunately, Mr. Lee was not fine after the surgery. I saw him at noon on the second day after surgery. At that time, Mr. Lee was doing well without any complaint and looking comfortable with self-controlled morphine pump for pain relief. Then, I received a call from the surgical ward around 4:30 pm.

"Mr. Lee is not doing well," the nurse said. "He is in labored breathing and the oxygen saturation is dropping."

"Please call the respiratory therapist to do a blood gas test, breathing treatment, and put him on an oxygen mask," I said over the phone. "And transfer him to the ICU now. I'm on my way to the hospital."

When I arrived at the ICU, I found that Mr. Lee was anxious and had difficulty speaking. He was breathing through a nonrebreathing mask with 100% oxygen. The oxygen saturation still maintained above 90%. Nevertheless, the blood gas test showed pending respiratory failure. He was put on BiPaP treatment. His cardiologist happened to be in the ICU, and I consulted him immediately.

Mr. Lee had rapid heartbeat without a fever. His complete blood count and comprehensive metabolic panel were normal. Cardiac enzymes (a heart attack indicator) were negative, and B-type natriuretic peptide (a heart failure indicator) levels were not elevated. The chest x-ray revealed diffuse bilateral opacities with a normal-size heart. Mr. Lee did not have dilated neck veins, peripheral edema, and other signs of heart failure on the exam. The electrocardiogram did not show manifestations of acute heart attack.

Mr. Lee was endotracheally intubated and put on the ventilator as his conditions worsened. His cardiologist performed a bedside echocardiography, which revealed no signs of left or right heart failure. It was likely that Mr. Lee developed ARDS (acute respiratory distress syndrome), which was presumably caused by morphine or/and aspiration. Mr. Lee presented with most features of ARDS: acute onset, severe hypoxemia (lack of oxygen in the blood), bilateral lung opacities, and no evidence of heart failure or fluid overload. He did not show evidence of pneumonia (usually with fever) or pulmonary embolism (usually with clear lungs, right heart failure, and positive D-Dimer).

Mr. Lee was stable initially after being placed on the ventilator. However, his respiratory function started to deteriorate. He developed cardiac arrest and was pronounced dead after 30-minute CPR (cardiopulmonary resuscitation). It was just about five hours from the onset of dyspnea to his death.

In contrast, Mrs. Nolan was lucky enough to overcome a serious complication of knee surgery. She, 78 years old then, developed sudden shortness of breath with severe hypoxemia on the third day after knee replacement surgery. I transferred her from the surgical floor to the ICU to receive supportive treatments. Mrs. Nolan was confirmed to have pulmonary embolism through a series of diagnostic tests. She was treated with injections of blood thinner and BiPaP therapy. Fortunately, she survived after two weeks of staying in the ICU.

The orthopedist recommended a replacement surgery for another knee two years later, but Mrs. Nolan declined to have it. She said to me: "I don't want to get into trouble again, and I want to live longer." When I left for another town, she was 87 years old. She was doing well without pain pills and walked steadily, carrying a cane with her, just in case she needed sometimes.

There are about 600,000-700,000 knee replacements in the U.S. each year. According to a study published in 2014, only 44 percent of knee replacement surgeries were classified as appropriate.[4] One-third of cases was considered to be inappropriate, namely with expected risks outweighing the benefits. It is true that some patients have achieved their goal: reducing pain and improving function. Apparently, according to my experiences, some of my patients have sacrificed too much for the improvement of the quality of life by undergoing knee replacement.

******

It is disappointing to see that an 87-year-old man was put on allopurinol (a drug for gout prevention), an 82-year-old woman on phentermine (a drug for appetite suppression), and an emaciated patient on a statin with a total cholesterol level of 46 mg/dL (1.2 mmol/L). I always say to my patients, "Please make sure that you understand why you need to take a particular medication and what major side effects it has. Avoid any medication or surgery if it is not considered as a lifesaving measure, or if the harms may outweigh the benefit. Try not to start more than one long-term medication at the same time. If you don't understand why new medications are prescribed, or why a surgery, procedure or imaging study is scheduled by other care providers, please come see me first and let me explain to you."

I have learned not to overdo anything in medicine and life from patients' stories. Enough is enough. Simplicity and moderation are the keys.

11. Unsatisfactory Health Care

America has the best doctors, the best nurses, the best hospitals, the best medical technology, and the best medical breakthrough medicines in the world. There is absolutely no reason we should not have in this country the best health care in the world.

—Dr. Bill Frist (Cardiologist, the Former United States Senator) [1]

Consider this: I can go to Antarctica and get cash from an ATM without a glitch, but should I fall ill during my travels, a hospital there could not access my medical records or know what medications I am on.

—John Nathan Deal (the Governor of Georgia) [2]

Too many Americans who are uninsured or under-insured do not receive regular checkups because they can't afford coverage or their insurance doesn't cover enough of the costs. The lack of preventive care results in countless emergency room visits and health care disasters for families.

—Jeff Merkley (the United States Senator) [3]

Painkillers

The United States has less than 5 percent of the world population, but it consumes more than 80 percent of all prescription opioid painkillers used in the world.[1] American people take about 99 percent of the world's hydrocodone (an opioid pain medication). The latest CDC (Center for Disease Control and Prevention) Vital Signs states, *"Each day, 46 people die from an overdose of prescription painkillers in the US. Health care providers wrote 259 million prescriptions for painkillers in 2012, enough for every American adult to have a bottle of pills.* "[2] Thus, around 16,000 people die from opioid painkiller overdose in the U.S. each year.

However, almost 100 million people in the U.S suffer from chronic pain, and the cost of pain management is about $300 billion per year according to the recent report by IOM (Institute of Medicine)[3] Do Americans enjoy excellent non-cancer chronic pain managements, which are available and applicable in the U.S.? It's unlikely they do. As stated above, millions of narcotic painkillers are used, and thousands of people die from opioid overdose each year.

It is estimated that nine million epidural steroid injections are performed per year in the U.S. Each treatment costs a few hundred to over two thousand dollars.[4] Many patients of mine with chronic back pain received multiple spinal steroid injections. However, most of them told me that the injections relieve their back pain for only a couple of days or weeks, which is confirmed by many studies.[5]

Quite a few of my patients had spinal cord stimulators placed in their bodies. Regrettably, none of them was happy with their stimulators. As a result of ineffectiveness, some of the stimulators were not turned on, some were taken out, and some stayed in the body forever. Several patients said the stimulator had paralyzed their legs. Only one patient told me the stimulator helped control his pain (this patient had a deep brain stimulator for his postherpetic neuralgia).

Additionally, a lot of patients stated that they started to take strong painkillers on a regular basis after back surgery. Many of them regretted

283

that they had undergone their back surgeries. It is uncommon that patients on long-term pain management come in for office visits with a happy smiling face. There are so many pain pills on the street that some of them will get into the wrong hands.

Mrs. Vincent, in her 80s, came in for a follow-up visit after recent discharge from the hospital. She was in a wheelchair with numerous medical disorders including COPD (chronic obstructive pulmonary disease), heart disease, diabetes and chronic back/joint pain.

"Mama needs pain pills to help her knee and back," the daughter of Mrs. Vincent said at the end of the office visit.

"Do you need to take these strong pain pills?" I asked Mrs. Vincent, noting that she got hydrocodone pain pills occasionally for knee and back pain in the past.

"Ah, yeah," she replied hesitantly.

"Yes! Yes! She needs them. Mama complains a lot of pain at home," her daughter interrupted loudly.

"Yes, I need some pain pills in case of severe pain," Mrs. Vincent said reluctantly.

"I know you have chronic knee and back pain," I said. "You'd better take Tylenol for your pain. You have a bad lung. Taking strong pain pills can make it difficult for you to breathe."

"I take them only when I have unbearable pain," she said. "And I did well with pain pills in the past."

"I can prescribe 30 pain tablets per month to help you relieve your severe pain. Is that okay?" How could I refuse to give some pain pills to an elderly patient in her wheelchair?

"That's okay."

"Here is the prescription. Please not to give your pills to other people." I wrote a prescription for 30 tablets of hydrocodone and handed it to Mrs. Vincent.

"I won't," she replied.

Mrs. Vincent left with her daughter, who pushed the wheelchair, holding the prescription in her hand.

"Dr. Li, I am Mrs. Vincent's daughter," a woman called the office one week later. "Mama needs more pain pills for her back pain. Please call in some for her."

"I gave her the prescription for pain pills one week ago when you came in with your mother," I replied.

"I didn't come that day. It's my sister who accompanied Mama to the clinic. She has got all the pain pills and left for Florida."

"You got me confused. If you want pain pills for your mother, you need to come to the clinic with your mother again. I can't call in controlled medications to the pharmacy in this situation."

They had never shown up in the clinic since then. I guessed that her daughter or daughters had taken Mrs. Vincent to see other doctors.

Mrs. Curry requested a refill of her opioid painkillers when she came in for an office visit. I reviewed the record and said to her, "You just filled the prescription two weeks ago. It is too early to refill."

"Dr. Li, let me tell you the story," she said with a smile. "I traveled to Tennessee and visited my old friend one week ago and stayed at her home for one night. Next morning, I could not find my pain pills in the bathroom. I asked my friend where my pain pills were. My friend said that perhaps her grandkids got them."

"That's a funny and sad story," I said.

"Believe me, Dr. Li. I'm not a drug addict. I'm 77 years old and have been seeing you for 13 years. You know me well."

It is likely that her story was true. Another patient told me that he had to hide his pain pills in four separate secret places in order to prevent his grandchildren from stealing them.

Following are a few excuses some of my patients provided when they wanted more pain pills:

"A visitor stole my pain pills in my home!"

"My pain pills were stolen in the Greyhound on my way home from New York," quite a few patients said.

"Somebody broke into my house and stole the pain pills. I have a police report to prove it."

"The ambulance people held my pain pills when I was being transported to the hospital. They did not return the pills to me in the ER."

"My husband (or my demented mother) flushed my pain pills in the toilet by accident."

There are some more stories regarding pain drug issues.

A patient of mine told me that she needed to buy a safe to store her pain pills because her son was put in jail as a result of stealing pain pills.

A patient's daughter changed her mother's pain pill prescription in order to get more pills.

A patient stole a prescription pad from the clinic and wrote prescriptions for narcotic pills himself.

Another patient pretended to be a clinic nurse to call in hydrocodone painkillers to the pharmacy for her. This problem will not arise anymore since hydrocodone pills cannot be called in after October 6, 2014, according to the new DEA (Drug Enforcement Administration) regulation.

"Why do American people use 99 percent of the world's hydrocodone?" I asked some of my patients who are on long-term narcotic pills.

"Lots of people abuse pain pills, but not me. I have real pain," all replied like that. However, all these hydrocodone pills are prescribed by doctors, who tend to say the same thing, "The patients I treat have real pain. Other doctors over-prescribe painkillers."

News spreads fast and widely if a doctor is known to give narcotic pills easily. People will drive hundreds of miles to seek pain drugs, even from other states. The prescribing laws have been strengthened and enforced promptly in Florida since 2010. Many "pill mills" have been shut down, and some doctors were arrested. The death rate of oxycodone overdose in Florida had dropped by more than 50 percent from 2010 to 2012.[6] In our area, several local doctors were also put in jail or disciplined for wrongly prescribing controlled drugs or taking patients' pain pills themselves.

A few years ago, I saw a new patient with chronic back pain, who requested to refill his painkillers. I was astonished to find out that this patient was taking four opioid pain medications (morphine, hydromorphone, oxycodone and fentanyl skin patch) daily for more than a year, which was confirmed by the drug monitor record. The same doctor prescribed his pain medications. That means he did not shop around for pain pills. Did he really need all these opioid pain medications to control his back pain?

There is not enough evidence to show that long-term opioid treatment is effective in ameliorating chronic pain.[7] Available data indicate that it increases the risk for harmful outcomes such as abuse, addiction, overdose, heart attacks, fractures, erectile dysfunction and motor vehicle accidents.[7] The high dose of opioid causes more harms. And no studies on opioid therapy lasted longer than one year. It is true that some patients require strong pain pills to control their unbearable pain, maintain their daily activities and improve their quality of life. Nonetheless, I can sense that many of the patients on long-term opioid therapy may not need so many pills a day for their conditions.

"Are you going to die if you take three oxycodone pills per day instead of four?" I asked my patients jokingly when I intended to reduce their opioid dose.

"No. I don't think so," most of them smiled, and some even laughed.

I remember seeing one new patient, a young man in his 30s, who was on 120 tables of opioid pain pills per month. I reviewed his record and found that he had been on long-term opioid treatment, and on disability for more than 10 years as a result of back/neck pain after a car accident.

"How are you doing these days?"

"I think I'm better. I play golf almost every day. Recently, I can even finish 18 holes."

"I see that. You look like a healthy young man now. Why are you still taking so many pain pills a day?" It is true that pain can be a subjective feeling. However, objectively, you can have a good idea if a patient is in real pain, when observing the way the patient walks, sits, and arises from the chair or the exam table, watching his or her facial expressions, and doing some simple physical exams.

"The doctor has been giving those pills to me all these years. I get them, and I take them."

287

"I'm going to reduce 5 or 10 tablets per month to help you get rid of the painkillers. Then you will be a new healthy man again. Is that okay?"

"That's okay; please cut it down to 90 tablets per month. Otherwise, I'll take all the pills when I see the bottle."

"Wonderful! You are one of the few patients, who volunteer to reduce more pain pills than I suggest," I was surprised and excited. "You have a good motivation to do things. You're going to succeed." All the patients on long-term opioid treatment tend to get upset or angry initially when I suggest a reduction of painkillers.

"Nobody has talked to me like that except you!" he smiled.

"You should go back to school and work again," I continued.

"Yes, I'm thinking of attending the technical college here. I have not figured out what to study."

"I recommended that people went to pharmacy school many years ago," I said. "But now there are too many pharmacists, and they have difficulty getting a job. You should choose anything within the healthcare field since health expenditure will increase every year no matter what happens. You can look into MRI or CT technology if you are good at science and math."

"I am good at math, and I think I can study MRI or CT courses. Thanks for your advice."

I was overwhelmed by the feeling that this young man was going to have a new life. It takes less than one minute to write or print a prescription for opioid pain pills. However, one needs to spend much more time evaluating why a patient needs pain pills, whether the patient continues to need them, whether it is safe for the patient to take them, whether there is another way for pain relief, how the pain medications can be tapered, and so on. I was gratified that the society or the world might be a little bit better, for the young man had become healthy again, happier and more productive. (This patient needed only 30 opioid pills per 30 days several months later.)

Patients will teach you if you are willing to spend time asking questions and listening to them. A patient told me his story proudly, "I underwent two spine surgeries in the past due to back pain. My previous doctor had been given me 180 tablets of hydrocodone pills per month for many years, but my back was still killing me all the time. So, I weaned myself off a regimen of six pills per day. Now I am down to 30 tablets per month."

"Wow, that's incredible," I said. "You've done a great job on your own."

"Guess what? I don't even take pain pills every day. When the pain hits me hard, I pop a pill, and the pill works. Now I feel less pain and much happier." Truly, this patient taught me a great lesson. I have been using his story to encourage other patients to reduce or get rid of opioids.

Another patient surely suffered from chronic pain as she had two back surgeries and several foot surgeries, walking with an unsteady gait. After reviewing her record, I noticed that she was taking 120 tablets of oxycodone and 120 tablets of hydrocodone monthly for a few years.

"Why do you need to take both oxycodone and hydrocodone?" I asked.

"I used to take just hydrocodone alone many years ago," she said. "Later, I was referred to see a pain doctor, who gave me oxycodone. It did work better. When I came back to see my previous doctor, he had been giving me both since then."

"In my opinion, hydrocodone should have been discontinued after you were started on oxycodone," I told her.

"I have been taking both for many years. You know, I only take what my doctor gives me. You can just refill the oxycodone pills if you don't think I need both. I am fine with it. Anyway, I don't think I need both."

However, there are always some difficult patients or drug addicts. They frequent the ER to get pain shots and shop around for doctors to seek controlled drugs. Occasionally, I received letters from pain specialists, saying that my patients had caused trouble in their pain clinics, and they had to call the police for help.

Drug addiction was unknown, at least to me, in China 30 years ago. While walking down the streets of Guangzhou during my recent visits, I occasionally encountered government advertising signs: Please check into a drug rehabilitation program if you have a drug problem. You can imagine how serious the drug abuse problem is in China nowadays.

However, in China, people abuse mainly illicit drugs because prescription opioids are difficult to obtain.

I often think why the improved economy always goes hand in hand with the drug problem. Is it the price we have to pay for gaining prosperity? Do people have to take marijuana or other illicit drugs to enjoy their life? Why does freedom always bring in drug abuse problems all over the world? I don't have a satisfactory answer to these questions. It is likely that this is one of the human weaknesses, which is embedded in our genes and will never go away. At least, we doctors should follow the Platinum Rule of Medicine *"Treat every patient like you'd want a member of your family treated"* and prescribe opioid pain medications responsibly in order to make America a little bit safer.

Electronic Health Record (EHR) and Nursing Homes

On one Sunday, I went to a nursing home to round on my patients. When I entered the nursing station, I noticed one of the nurses was reading the local newspaper. The newspaper published annual incomes of some local doctors involved in a federal lawsuit related to the hospital. The nurse spoke to me, "Look, you doctors are making so much money!"

"Anyway, I don't think my name is in the newspaper," I smiled.

"I haven't found your name yet," she laughed. "You need to come here to see patients on Sunday. I don't think you make that kind of money."

The local newspaper carried articles about local doctors and the hospital on the Sunday front page for two to three months during that time. Several of my patients and some nurses at the hospital spoke to me in the same way during that period when the doctor's income was a hot topic in town.

"I didn't know the income of doctors was that high until I read the newspaper," a nurse at the hospital said to me.

"It is not a secret," I replied. "You can obtain this kind of information on the internet easily. Just type 'physician salary' in Google, you'll get it."

Physicians earn the highest salaries of all the professionals in the U.S.[1] No wonder their incomes surprised the local people in town. It was amazing that the federal government drew the conclusion: doctors cannot afford electronic health records (EHR) and need subsidies from the government. The government has been awarding each physician $40,000-$60,000 to update or start an EHR during the recent years.[2] As a result, there are more than 100 EHR companies in the United States, each of which generates more than one million dollar revenue per year.[3] The top ones have their revenues more than one billion per year. However, those EHRs do not talk to each other. Therefore, using EHR

291

does not reduce fragmentation of health care. And the majority of doctors do not like and complain about their EHRs.

I'm going to talk about some of the trivial EHR problems I had encountered before the end of 2014. Hopefully, EHRs will get better sooner or later. The ONC (the Office of the National Coordinator for Health Information Technology) released its roadmap in June 2014, *Connecting Health and Care for the Nation: A **10-Year** Vision to Achieve an Interoperable Health IT Infrastructure.*[4] A 10-year wait! Anyhow, I understand I need to be patient.

Indeed, not only do most of the EHRs not talk to each other, but they are not user-friendly. The EHR I used in the previous clinic did not allow me to write the text explanation for a consult. Nevertheless, the EHR company refused to address this simple problem after many calls by the clinic manager. EHR companies decline to do any improvements or corrections after they have sold their products to customers, who have to be put up with the annoying defects because few people afford to change to another company.

The EHR in the clinic frequently broke down, and a computer engineer had to be called in to fix it. Defects of the EHR also secured the maintenance business. One of our clinic physicians had to use his money to hire a scribe to help him out. One day, another physician at my clinic got so frustrated with the slow response of the electronic record that he threw his stethoscope to the floor in the hallway and groaned, "I can't take it anymore!" Unfortunately, several of his patients were still waiting for him in the exam rooms.

Now, I am working at a new clinic. LabCorp (an American S&P 500 company, one of the largest clinical laboratory networks in the world) sends test results to our clinic by fax. Afterward, printed lab reports need to be scanned to our clinic EHR manually. It takes time to look for where the scanned reports are located. When you find out the scanned reports you want, you need to open and enlarge them before you can review them as they are saved as images.

A cheap smartphone can take and store thousands of photos. I have no idea that one of the top five EHRs, which I am using, cannot take patients' photos and store them in the system to facilitate patient care. If the system can save the scanned reports as images that can be retrieved, why cannot the system save a patient's photo? The lab tests performed at the hospital are in one section while tests done within the clinic are stored in another section of the EHR.

Why does LabCorp not export the results to the hospital EHRs directly? Ironically, the LabCorp lab is located just one block from the clinic. As a matter of fact, Labcorp can connect to the facility where I used to work. These faxes waste both paper and ink, scanning paper documents requires a lot of labor and may make errors, and searching for those scanned reports forces a doctor to talk to the computer screen instead of talking to patients.

Since all these EHRs cannot talk to each other, EHR companies are starting new big projects to tackle so-called inter-operator connections. Why do we need so many EHRs? It seems that the more problems occur, the more people are employed to deal with them. Where there is a problem, there is a new business. Why can't we just use a couple of good ones and make them communicate with each other in the first place?

As far as I know, most of the chart auditors are not physicians. How do they know the physical examination findings in the chart, which are recorded by physicians, are real? I still can encounter PMI (point of maximum impulse) in some office notes. I just received another consult note that contained PMI while revising my memoir. It can be a surprise that someone will perform this examination at each office visit: palpate the left anterior chest wall to look for the apex beat (the point of maximum impulse (PMI). This time-consuming exam requires taking off patient's clothes, counting the number of ribs, and measuring the distance between PMI and the midclavicular line. The normal apex beat can be palpated in the precordium left 5th intercostal space, at the point of intersection with the left midclavicular line. It is not easy to feel the intercostal space in an obese patient or a female patient. I wonder if these doctors have a ruler in their pockets to measure the PMI. Furthermore, I do not think PMI provides useful information for routine office visits in the era of modern medical technology.

I have seen some office notes that contain items such as PERRLA (pupils are equal, round, reactive to light and accommodation) in patients with one eye and "bilateral pedal pulses present" in patients with leg amputations. Occasionally I notice some routine office notes including a detailed review of systems with 50-100 questions and a complete physical examination, which takes more than 20-40 minutes to finish. Thus, many electronic chart notes comprise so many pages filled with irrelevant information that quite often pertinent impressions and plans are nowhere to be found.

Mr. Carson had been seeing a new doctor after I left for another town. He drove 50 miles to see me at the new clinic a few months later.

"What's wrong?" I said. "You are 79 years old and drive 50 miles to see me. I am quite moved."

"I went to your previous clinic to see a new doctor after you left," Mr. Carson said. "This doctor is very nice. But, when he walks into the room, he just starts typing and rarely asks questions, and doesn't even look at me and touch me. He doesn't do things like you."

Patients feel comfortable and relieved when you touch them, look into their eyes, explain things nicely and answer their questions without haste. They will sense that they are in good hands, and they will act on your advice. I am pleased to state that 90 percent of my smoker patients quit smoking after having seen me for one to two years. Most of them need no assistance such as nicotine products, medications, or electronic cigarettes. One of the patients said to me, "I quit smoking just for you. Since you're nice to me, I should be nice to you, Doc." My secret weapon is just a candid talk with a smile at each office visit.

It is certainly a challenge to preserve this kind of doctor-patient interaction in the era of internet and in the digital wireless world. Presently, more than 80-90 percent of physicians are using electronic medical records, and the majority of them are unhappy with their EHRs.[6] I have come to realize that *"EHRs were not designed with physicians in mind."* Since I am not a superman, I have to adapt myself to this system in order to survive. Smiling while taking things as they are is much more fun than grumbling.

LIFE AND MEDICINE

During office visits, I have been trying to interact less with the computer and to make more eye contact while talking with patients. But still, my eyes have to be glued to the computer screen in order to click on requisite boxes, type in diagnosis codes, print controlled drug prescriptions, send out other prescriptions electronically, order tests, explain education materials, arrange follow-up visits, make referrals, etc. (I usually complete the full visit notes after office hours.)

I always ask my patients to sit at the table with me and look at the computer screen together. Thus, they can see what diagnoses I put in their records, what medications I am going to send to their pharmacies, what lab tests I order, and so on. Occasionally, they even help me look for a diagnosis code or medication on the screen when I have difficulty finding one. Whenever I make a new diagnosis of any medical condition, I will show and explain to my patient the medical disorder on Google Image, Wikipedia, Mayo Clinic, etc. Hopefully, my patients and I can adapt to the digital world by this kind of **doctor-patient-computer** interaction for the time being instead of waiting for the arrival of better EHRs.

Furthermore, the old fashioned bodily and eye to eye contact is being more and more replaced by telemedicine (by phone), e-mail, and even virtual visits by video in reality. No one can stop the advance of technology and science. The question is how we take the advantage of them to improve medical outcomes. At the same time, it is important to make this new way of medical practice more human and be satisfied by patients.

Even though the federal government remembers that doctors need money for their EHRs, it forgets to help nursing homes establish computer or EHR systems. The nursing homes in town lagged behind in terms of technology and didn't even have a decent computer system; at least before the end of 2013 (I stopped nursing home service at the time). When I asked about a new admission, nurses needed to call all the stations to find out if there was a new patient or where the patient was. At the nursing stations, there were some antique computers with 9-inch monitors, which could be found only in a museum. I had not seen anybody using them when I made rounds there. During the last two years,

I saw some newer computers in one of the local nursing homes. I did not know what the nurses could do with these new computers since they could not even search the names of nursing home residents.

I had to spend a lot of time obtaining clinical information by leafing through many logbooks in the nursing homes, which had no computer systems. Strangely, in one of the local nursing homes, a logbook held vital signs, and another one contained weight readings while glucose testing readings were recorded in medication logbooks. The vital signs and body weight values used to be recorded in the same logbook. The new company acquired this nursing home a few years ago and operated it in a new way, placing these numbers in different logbooks for an unknown reason. I frequently could not find the weight logbook and had to ask a nurse to help me. However, she could not find it either on several occasions. Body weight is a very important parameter to evaluate an elderly nursing home patient. Occasionally, I got the book, but could not see the weight values. I needed to ask a nurse to weigh patients while making rounds on other patients.

Tracking down the laboratory test results was also a nightmare. There were some logbooks for storing laboratory reports and some logbooks for test orders. If a test report could not be found, a nurse had to check if the order was written in the chart and then check if the order had been carried out by going through the order logbook. Frequently, nurses had to call the laboratory to fax the reports to the station while I was rounding on patients.

If I called the nursing home about lab results or medication issues from the clinic, a long wait was expected, for a nurse had to look through many logbooks, medication books, and paper charts as a result of no computer systems and no electronic medical records. Whenever I entered a nursing home, I noticed that all the nurses and other staffs were busy taking care of patients, and looked stressed out. The nursing homes in town accepted discharged patients only before 2 p.m. The patients had to wait in the hospital for one more day if the paperwork had not been completed by 2 p.m. One time a patient was already sent to the nursing home by ambulance. To my surprise, the patient was transported back to the hospital because it was one hour late for the nursing home admission.

It was common for me to wait for 5-20 minutes to get an answer from the nursing home. I needed to get through the operator, who transferred me to the nursing station. Sometimes the operator was too busy to pick up the phone while the calling nurse might not be at the nursing station or be talking on another line. I could become frustrated with lengthy phone waiting when I was busy seeing patients in the clinic or the hospital. One physician (a nursing home director) told me that on one occasion, he was so annoyed with long waiting that he yelled, "Please pick up the damn phone now!"

Only a couple of excellent software like Google, Facebook, YouTube, etc. have been working so well and improved people's daily activities. EHR is related to the human health, the most valuable thing in life. Doctors, nurses, and other medical personnel need the similar features of EHR. There is no reason that we cannot create a few good EHRs that are easy to use and can talk to each other.

All of us will get old and become debilitated someday, and some of us may end up in nursing homes. I hope congresspersons and senators can add a tiny item like computerization or EHR for nursing homes when they draft bills for pork-barrel projects or earmarks. If the National Security Agency (NSA) can use a huge data bank to collect and store the phone records of all Americans, then we should be able to provide our nursing homes with decent computer systems to save patients' names, and hopefully their clinical data as well.

Health Insurance

Everyone knows that the United States is the only developed country that does not provide universal health care, and 15 percent of the US population (about 45 million people) did not have medical insurance before Obamacare started in 2013.[1] I was surprised to find out that many private clinics did not provide their medical staff with health insurance at least in the area. Of course, all the doctors including me have good medical insurance. The private clinic where I used to work had been buying health insurance for all our 35-40 employees for more than 25 years. It cost $5,000 -$10,000 to purchase health insurance for one employee. Although our clinic physicians' income was affected, we were proud of providing health insurance for our clinic employees.

It is estimated that approximately 45,000 people die from lack of health insurance in the U.S. yearly, according to a study published in 2009.[2] Mrs. Fleming is one of the victims who suffer from medical catastrophes as a consequence of no insurance coverage. She, 40 years old then, was obese and diagnosed with diabetes at 30. She had missed many appointments and did not comply with her treatment regimen. I tried to help her with insulin and other medication samples whenever she came in for office visits. But this time she had not been to the clinic for more than one year.

Mrs. Fleming ended up in the ER because of suffering from a large area of MRSA (Methicillin Resistant Staphylococcus Aureus) induced necrotizing fasciitis across her abdominal wall. Necrotizing fasciitis is a severe destructive infection involving the deep skin and underlying tissues and is associated with a high incidence of morbidity and mortality. Her diabetes was out of control with a glucose level of 660 mg/dL (36.6 mmol/L). After being admitted to the ICU, she received IV antibiotic treatment and underwent two debridement surgeries. Fortunately, she survived and was discharged home after three weeks of hospitalization. It took six months for her wound to heal completely.

"You must have been sick for one to two weeks, I guess," I asked her after she was stabilized. "Why did you wait so long before coming to the ER?"

"You know I don't have insurance," she replied. "I just can't afford to see doctors."

"You have been working at a doctor's office for several years," I said.

"I still have no medical insurance. The doctor said to me that he **can't afford** to buy insurance for me. Anyhow, he is a good doctor, and I like him very much."

"What can I say? You may try to apply for Medicaid in the future." There was no Obamacare back then.

"I had Medicaid before. However, I lost it after I got my present job."

As far as I knew, she worked at a top high-paid specialist's clinic. It is just unbelievable that medical personnel don't have health insurance while inmates have the best insurance plans in the U.S. as described in the previous Chapter-Diabetes.

Elderly people usually have Medicare coverage. The government Medicare has transferred its service to private insurance companies. As a result of that, there are sixteen Medicare programs in this state. Sometimes, patients ask me which Medicare program they should choose. I just cannot give any advice because of so many programs. How can ordinary elderly people decide which plan fit their needs, for instance, how can they figure out which plan can cover their medications better? Occasionally, I tell them, "Ask your children or grandchildren to help you, or just pick the one most people use. Anyway, you need to make sure my name is on the provider list."

Some patients with health insurance still have difficulty seeing doctors in town. They cannot afford to pay $150 in front to have a procedure or pay $100-$200 in front to see some specialists. Some clinics don't accept patients with both Medicare and Medicaid because these patients don't need to pay the 20 percent Medicare copay according to the state rules. Patients with Medicaid have even more difficulty seeing specialists and have to travel long distances to the big cities to receive medical care.

In spite of being hospitalized with recurrent seizures, a patient of mine was irritated by a doctor's bill. A consultant doctor entered the patient's room and said to her, "I can't see you since you haven't paid your bills..." Then the doctor went back to the nursing station and wrote in the chart, "I cannot do a consultation for this case because this patient has not paid me for the previous consultations and office visits. The patient should go to the university medical center for care..." This patient got so furious that she called the hospital office about the event. That doctor's note was shown to other doctors by the administration at a medical staff conference as an example of inappropriate hospital notes.

Before Obamacare was implemented, quite a few patients complained about it.

One patient on Medicare and Medicaid said to me, "I don't like Obamacare."

"How much do you know Obamacare?" I asked. "Can you tell me which items of Obamacare bother you?"

"I don't know," she replied.

"Does Obamacare change your plan? You are on both Medicare and Medicaid."

"No. But I need to pay a higher premium for Medicare every year."

"The yearly increase in Medicare premium had happened long before Obama took office," I said. "That's nothing to do with Obamacare."

"That's true."

"Then why are you complaining?"

"Ah..." she smiled.

"Be honest, I don't know well about Obamacare as its regulations are made up of thousands of pages."

After Obamacare had been implemented, another patient said during an office visit, "I hate Obamacare."

"What's wrong?" I asked.

"My father got sick and was admitted to the hospital. He fell and developed bedsores in the hospital."

"Does he have Obamacare insurance?"

"No. He has good commercial insurance."

"Then there is nothing to do with Obamacare," I said.

301

"Okay. But he was taken care of by hospitalists, not by his regular doctor."

"Hospitalist system has existed more than ten to twenty years, and it will be more and more common in the future. Still, it's not related to Obamacare."

"Okay, you're right. How about the wars in Syria and Iraq?" he smiled.

"Do Iraqi people have Obamacare?" I giggled.

"Okay, you've won," he laughed. "Let's stop from here and talk about my medical problems."

Obamacare is complicated, imperfect, and possibly expensive. At least, it has allowed more people to afford medical insurance since Obamacare enrollment started in October 2013. The uninsured rate for the adults 18 to 64 years of age had dropped from 20 percent to 13 percent by March 4, 2015.[1, 3] I have seen several new patients with Obamacare insurance. They told me that they could not afford health insurance until Obamacare started. But still, some people have difficulty buying Obamacare insurance.

"Why don't you apply for Obamacare?" I asked one of the self-pay patients.

"Obamacare suc…!" he complained. "I just don't have $400-$500 monthly for that stuff."

"Do you have a job?"

"Yes, I do."

"You're earning a good income, aren't you?" I asked.

"No way! You know what kind of job I'm doing. I may pay a much lower premium for Obamacare if I work less or stay at home. But I like to work."

"Then you have to make sure not to get sick," I said helplessly.

"I'll try."

Modern medicine can treat numerous diseases, save lives, and make people live longer. Nevertheless, the most important thing is that all the people can afford to access medical care, buy their medications and pay for procedures, surgeries, and imaging studies.

"It's time to recognize the Internet as a basic human right," said recently Berners-Lee, who is considered as the inventor of the World Wide Web.[4] *"Human rights are international norms that help to protect all people everywhere from severe political, legal, and social abuses."*[5] If internet access can be considered as a basic human right, then universal health care is definitely a basic human right. I wish the people of the world, including all Americans, could enjoy this basic human right, the right to access health care equally.

I often hear people saying: we do not worry about pain and sickness in heaven. Hopefully, we all do not have to wait until we arrive in Heaven to live a fear-free life.

Epilogue

The United States of America is a democratic country with an abundance of natural and human resources, a stable political system, and the most advanced science and technology. This country has the best medical education, medical research and technology, and medical facilities in the world. Nurses, physicians, and pharmacists are the top three most trustworthy professions according to the 2014 survey from Gallup.[1]

We have made great achievements in medicine, and numerous patients come from all over the world to the U.S. to seek medical care. If you ask the typical patient where he or she wants to go to receive medical care, I am sure that this patient would say: America. However, our healthcare system is facing enormous challenges. And we doctors as human beings are far from perfect. Still, I believe that we all have a responsibility to make our health care the best it can possibly be.

A warm smile or a hearty laugh may be one of the best and costless remedies for many things in life and medicine. Where there is a smile, there is a chance, peace, and happiness. Smile. Tomorrow will be better.

Acknowledgements

I am very grateful to the following people who helped make this book a reality.

First of all, Zhou (Jo), my wife, has read my book many times, comes up with numerous bright ideas, and occasionally makes caustic remarks. At present, she is translating it into Chinese. Hopefully, the Chinese version of the book will be published later this year. Her support and love have made my life meaningful.

Erin Castellano, APRN, my colleague, proofread the whole book, provided critical comments, and corrected my English grammar errors.

Jason, my son, read the majority of the book, corrected grammar mistakes, and improved my English writing.

Huanran Huang (cousin), Wu Wang (brother-in-law), Wei Wang (sister-in-law), Fangming Chen (friend), and Shijian Mo (medical school classmate) read a few chapters and gave constructive feedback.

Matthew Colhoff (medical student), proofread two chapters of the book and critiqued my writing.

Brian Di Giacinto (medical student), proofread two chapters of the book, polished my writing, and provided thoughtful commentary.

Robert Holloman (friend), read several chapters and gave invaluable suggestions.

Vicki Olsen (friend), read one chapter and improved my English writing.

Some of my patients including Joseph DeCarlo, Alvin Lunsford, Rosa McCray, Marguerite Smith, and Tony Wong, have read their own stories before the book is published.

All my patients, whom I have seen over the years, have entrusted me with their health issues and shared their life stories with me. They teach me every day and have made me a better person.

I would like to thank my mentors who helped me grow professionally and personally.

My medicine mentors: Barbara L. Schuster, MD; Timothy B. Sorg, MD; Hassan Mehbod, MD; Partha Banerjee, MD; … They had confidence in me and trained me to become a qualified and dedicated physician.

My pathology mentors: Mary A. Sens, MD, PhD; Winfield S. Morgan, MD; William Chang, MD; Roger S. Riley, MD, PhD; … They gave me the opportunity to study the origin, nature, and course of diseases so that I can see and treat patients from both internal and external perspectives.

My science mentors: Gabor Szabo, PhD; Angela S. Otero, PhD; Chujie Li, MD; … They taught me how to think critically and solve problems scientifically, and supported me in every aspect.

My practice mentors: Usah Lilavivat, MD and Pusadee Suchinda, MD. Because they offered me the job, I could work in such a wonderful town that I could learn, grow, and collect these stories described in the book. They are always ready to help me. Their working ethics has inspired me to keep learning and serving.

All the teachers at Guangzhou Medical College. They are dedicated and devoted teachers who guided me through the hard times in medical education.

While working on the final draft of my book, I was deeply saddened to learn that Aunty Qianru had just passed away. Aunty Qianru, a paragon of virtue, was as beautiful and kind as her name means. She always cared for me and showed me how to love.

I had a happy childhood, for she always took me with her when going on outings or attending parties. She sewed, repaired and altered my clothes. She cooked delicious food for my wife, Jo, and me. When conflicts occurred within our extended family, she acted as a counselor or negotiator. She worked very hard and took care of everybody known or unknown to her. Being amiable, optimistic, and open, she never got angry, smiled at all times, loved and cared for everyone…Aunty will live on in my hearts forever.

About the Author

Dr. Yongxin Li graduated from Guangzhou Medical College (Guangzhou Medical University) in China in the 1980s. He came to the U.S. in 1986 and received his Ph.D. degree in physiology from the University of Texas Medical Branch at Galveston in 1991. He finished two-year residency training in pathology at West Virginia University School of Medicine. He completed his internal medicine residency at Wright State University School of Medicine in Dayton, Ohio in the 1990s. Since then, he has been practicing internal medicine in a southern state. The time period of this book is the first fifteen years of his medical practice.

Reference

Introduction

[1] Rosenow III EC. The Art of Living and the Art of Medicine. Trafford Publishing, 2003.

[2] Avila J, Murray M. Prescription Painkiller Use at Record High for Americans. ABC News. April 20, 2011
(http://abcnews.go.com/US/prescription-painkillers-record-number-americans-pain-medication/

[3] Opioid Painkiller Prescribing. CDC VitalSigns. July 2014.
(http://www.cdc.gov/vitalsigns/opioid-prescribing/)

[4] Wilson TD. Redirect: Changing the Stories We Live By. Little, Brown and Company, 2011

Father

Dad's Illness

[1] Fan JH, Wang JB, Jiang Y, et al. Attributable Causes of Liver Cancer Mortality and Incidence in China. Asian Pac J Cancer Prev 2013; 14 (12), 7251-7256.
(http://www.apjcpcontrol.org/paper_file/issue_abs/Volume14_No12/7251-7256%2010.9%20Jin-Hu%20Fan.pdf)

[2] Chen JG, Zhang SW. Liver cancer epidemic in China: past, present and future. Semin Cancer Biol. 2011 Feb; 21(1):59-69.
(http://www.ncbi.nlm.nih.gov/pubmed/21144900)

Beginning

Learning

[1] Saad ER, Diamond HS. Polymyalgia Rheumatica. Medscape.com (http://emedicine.medscape.com/article/330815-overview#a0156)

[2] Carroll AE. To Be Sued Less, Doctors Should Consider Talking to Patients More. The New York Times. June 1, 2015. Accessed on June 20, 2015.
(http://www.nytimes.com/2015/06/02/upshot/to-be-sued-less-doctors-should-talk-to-patients-more.html?_r=0&abt=0002&abg=1)

"Good Stuff"

[1] Opioid Painkiller Prescribing. CDC VitalSigns. July 2014. (http://www.cdc.gov/vitalsigns/opioid-prescribing/)

[2] Chang YH, Windish DM. Cannabinoid hyperemesis relieved by compulsive bathing. Mayo Clin Proc 2009; 84(1):76–78.

[3] Simonetto DA, Oxentenko AS, Herman, Margot L, Szostek, JH. Cannabinoid Hyperemesis: A Case Series of 98 Patients. Mayo Clinic Proceedings 2012; 87 (2):114–9.

[4] Legality of cannabis by U.S. jurisdiction. From Wikipedia, accessed on March 28, 2015.
(https://en.wikipedia.org/wiki/Legality_of_cannabis_by_U.S._jurisdiction)

[5] Groopman J. How Doctors Think. Mariner Books, 2007.

[6] Allen JH, de Moore GM, Heddle R, Twartz JC. Cannabinoid hyperemesis: cyclical hyperemesis in association with chronic cannabis abuse. Gut 2004; 53(11):1566–1570.
(http://www.ncbi.nlm.nih.gov/pmc/articles/PMC1774264/)

Faith

Blood Transfusion

[1] American College of Physicians Ethics Manual: Sixth Edition. Ann Intern Med. 2012; 156.

[2] Carson JL, Noveck H, Berlin JA, Gould SA. Mortality and morbidity in patients with very low postoperative hemoglobin levels who decline blood transfusion. Transfusion. 2002; 42(7):812. (http://www.ncbi.nlm.nih.gov/pubmed/12375651)

Tithe

[1] Moeller P. Religion Makes People Happier—But Why? U.S. News & World Report. April 12, 2012 (http://money.usnews.com/money/personal-finance/articles/2012/04/12/religion-makes-people-happierbut-why)

Afterlife

[1] Lipska KJ, Ross JS, Wang Y, et al. National Trends in US Hospital Admissions for Hyperglycemia and Hypoglycemia among Medicare Beneficiaries, 1999 to 2011. JAMA Intern Med. 2014; 174(7):1116-1124. (http://archinte.jamanetwork.com/article.aspx?articleid=1871566&JamaNetworkReader=True)

[2] Bible (NLT) Matthew 25:41. "Then the King will turn to those on the left and say, 'Away with you, you cursed ones, into the eternal fire prepared for the devil and his demons."

Wife

[1] Adjuvant Therapy for Breast Cancer. NIH Consensus Statement Online 2000 November 1-3; 17(4): 1-23. (http://consensus.nih.gov/2000/2000AdjuvantTherapyBreastCancer114html.htm)

[2] Global Cancer Facts & Figures. 2nd Edition. Atlanta: American Cancer Society; 2011. (http://www.cancer.org/acs/groups/content/@epidemiologysurveilance/documents/document/acspc-027766.pdf)

[3] Rosenow III EC. The Art of Living and the Art of Medicine. Trafford Publishing, 2003.

Diabetes

[1] Xu Y, Wang L, He J, et al. Prevalence and Control of Diabetes in Chinese Adults. JAMA. 2013; 310(9):948-958.

[2] Statistics About Diabetes. Data from the National Diabetes Statistics Report, 2014 (released June 10, 2014) (http://www.diabetes.org/diabetes-basics/statistics/)

[3] Standards of Medical Care in Diabetes—2015. Diabetes Care. 2015; 38(Suppl. 1) (http://care.diabetesjournals.org/content/38/Supplement_1)

Lifelong Struggle

[1] Schwirtz M and Winerip M. Gross Incompetence Cited in Rikers Island Death. New York Times. JAN. 22, 2015 (http://www.nytimes.com/2015/01/23/nyregion/gross-incompetence-cited-in-rikers-island-death.html?_r=0)

[2] Selk A. Irving jail staff knew diabetic inmate had no insulin before death. The Dallas Morning News. December 09, 2013 (http://www.dallasnews.com/news/community-news/irving/headlines/20131209-irving-jail-staff-knew-diabetic-inmate-had-no-insulin-before-death.ece)

[3] Santora M. City's Annual Cost Per Inmate Is $168,000, Study Finds. The New York Times. Aug. 23, 2013 (http://www.nytimes.com/2013/08/24/nyregion/citys-annual-cost-per-inmate-is-nearly-168000-study-says.html?_r=0)

[4] Correctional Health Care: Guidelines for the Management of an Adequate Delivery System. 2001 ed. National Institute of Corrections. Oct. 31, 2006 (http://nicic.gov/library/017521)

[5] Sommers BD, Musco T, Finegold K, Gunja MZ, Burke A, McDowell AM. Health Reform and Changes in Health Insurance Coverage in 2014. N Engl J Med 2014; 371:867-874

[6] Health Insurance Coverage and the Affordable Care Act, May 5, 2015. The Assistant Secretary for Planning and Evaluation (ASPE). The U.S. Department of Health and Human Services. (http://www.aspe.hhs.gov/health/reports/2015/uninsured_change/ib_uninsured_change.pdf)

[7] Stanglin D. Man says he robbed bank of $1 to get access to medical care in jail. USA TODAY. Jun 21, 2011 (http://content.usatoday.com/communities/ondeadline/post/2011/06/man-says-he-robbed-bank-of-1-dollar-so-that-he-can-get-medical-coverage-in-jail/1#.VRNwofnF_cU)

[8] Keyes S. Sick Oregon Man 'Robs' Bank For One Dollar to Get Health Care in Jail. Think Progress/News Report. September 1, 2013 (http://www.nationofchange.org/sick-oregon-man-robs-bank-one-dollar-get-health-care-jail-1378042832)

[9] Bernstein RJ. Dr. Bernstein's Diabetes Solution: The Complete Guide to Achieving Normal Blood Sugars. Little, Brown and Company, 2011

[10] Mohajer ST. Man celebrates 85 years of living with diabetes. Associated Press. May 30, 2011 (http://phys.org/news/2011-05-celebrates-years-diabetes.html)

Foot Exam

[1] Standards of Medical Care in Diabetes—2015. Diabetes Care 2015; 38(Suppl. 1) (http://care.diabetesjournals.org/content/38/Supplement_1)

Metformin as Herbal Medicine

[1] Bailey CJ, Day C. Metformin: its botanical background. Practical Diabetes Int 2004; 21(3): 115–117 (http://onlinelibrary.wiley.com/doi/10.1002/pdi.606/full)

[2] Bailey CJ, Turner RC. Metformin. N Engl J Med 1996; 334:574-579

[3] Standards of Medical Care in Diabetes—2015. Diabetes Care 2015; 38(Suppl. 1) (http://care.diabetesjournals.org/content/38/Supplement_1)

[4] Bannister CA, Holden SE, Jenkins-Jones S, et al. Can People With Type 2 Diabetes Live Longer Than Those Without? A Comparison of Mortality in People Initiated With Metformin or Sulphonylurea Monotherapy and Matched Non-diabetic Controls. Diabetes Obes Metab. 2014; 16:1165-1173 (http://www.ncbi.nlm.nih.gov/pubmed/25041462)

[5] Seth A. Berkowitz SA, Krumme AA, Avorn J, et al. Initial Choice of Oral Glucose-Lowering Medication for Diabetes Mellitus A Patient-Centered Comparative Effectiveness Study. JAMA Intern Med. 2014; 174(12):1955-1962.
(http://archinte.jamanetwork.com/article.aspx?articleid=1918925)

[6] Scirica BM, Bhatt DL, Braunwald E, et al. Saxagliptin and Cardiovascular Outcomes in Patients with Type 2 Diabetes Mellitus. N Engl J Med 2013; 369:1317-1326
(http://www.nejm.org/doi/full/10.1056/NEJMoa1307684#t=article)

[7] Lipscombe LL, Gomes TG, Lévesque LE, Hux JE, Juurlink DN, Alter DA. Thiazolidinediones and Cardiovascular Outcomes in Older Patients With Diabetes JAMA. 2007; 298(22):2634-2643.
(http://jama.jamanetwork.com/article.aspx?articleid=209722)

[8] Yu OHY, Kristian B. Filion KB, Azoulay L, Patenaude V, Majdan A, Suissa S. Incretin-Based Drugs and the Risk of Congestive Heart Failure. Diabetes Care 2015; 38:277–284
(http://care.diabetesjournals.org/content/38/2/277.full.pdf+html)

[9] Inzucchi SE, Zinman B, Wanner C, et al. SGLT-2 inhibitors and cardiovascular risk: Proposed pathways and review of ongoing outcome trials. Diabetes & Vascular Disease Research 2015; 12(2):90–100
(http://dvr.sagepub.com/content/12/2/90.full.pdf+html)

[10] Budnitz DS, Lovegrove MC, Shehab N, Richards CL. Emergency Hospitalizations for Adverse Drug Events in Older Americans. N Engl J Med 2011; 365:2002-2012

[11] Vijan S, Sussman JB, Yudkin JS, Hayward RA. Effect of Patients' Risks and Preferences on Health Gains with Plasma Glucose Level Lowering in Type 2 Diabetes Mellitus. JAMA Intern Med. 2014; 174(8):1227-1234.

Seeing Doctors in China

Take Mom to See Doctors

[1] Ganguli I, Wasfy JH, Ferris TG. What Is the Right Number of Clinic Appointments? Visit Frequency and the Accountable Care Organization. JAMA. 2015; 313(19):1905-1906

[2] Jourdan A. China aims to double doctor numbers as cure for healthcare woes. Reuters. Mar 31, 2015 (http://in.reuters.com/article/2015/03/31/china-healthcare-idINL3N0WX1R120150331)

IV (Intravenous) Tonic

[1] Zeng ZP, Jiang JG. Analysis of the adverse reactions induced by natural product-derived drugs. Br J Pharmacol. 2010; 159(7): 1374–1391. (http://www.ncbi.nlm.nih.gov/pmc/articles/PMC2850395/)

[2] Lie DA. Can Complementary and Alternative Therapies Relieve GERD Symptoms? Medscape Family Medicine > Cases in CAM. July 03, 2014 (http://www.medscape.com/viewarticle/827662)

[3] Zhang CX, Qin YM, Guo BR. Clinical study on the treatment of gastroesophageal reflux by acupuncture. Chin J Integr Med. 2010; 16:298-303. Abstract (http://www.ncbi.nlm.nih.gov/pubmed/20697939)

[4] Zhang C, Guo L, Guo X, Guo X, Li G. Clinical curative effect of electroacupuncture combined with zhizhukuanzhong capsules for treating gastroesophageal reflux disease. J Tradit Chin Med. 2012; 32:364-371. Abstract (http://www.ncbi.nlm.nih.gov/pubmed/23297557)

[5] Hinman RS, McCrory P, Pirotta M, et al. Acupuncture for Chronic Knee Pain A Randomized Clinical Trial JAMA. 2014; 312(13):1313-1322.

[6] Lian BJ, Zhee BG, Yun CR, Huan JB. Ma Huang/Ephedra, Sho Saiko To and Dai Saiko To, Shou Wu Pian. Herbals in the Subclass Chinese and Other Asian Herbal Medicines. LiverTox. References Last Updated: 12 May 2014

(http://livertox.nih.gov/ChineseAndOtherAsianHerbalMedicines.htm #overview)

[7] Hwang SJ, Tsai JC, Chen HC. Epidemiology, impact and preventive care of chronic kidney disease in Taiwan Nephrology 2010; 15:3–9 (http://www.ncbi.nlm.nih.gov/pubmed/20586940)

[8] Yang HY, Chen PC, Wang JD. Chinese Herbs Containing Aristolochic Acid Associated with Renal Failure and Urothelial Carcinoma: A Review from Epidemiologic Observations to Causal Inference. BioMed Research International 2014; Volume 2014, Article ID 569325, 9 pages (http://dx.doi.org/10.1155/2014/569325)

[9] Angell M, Kassirer JP. Alternative Medicine -- The Risks of Untested and Unregulated Remedies-- Editorial NEJM 1998; 339: 839-841

Yi Nao (Medical Disturbance)

[1] Editorial. Violence against doctors: Why China? Why now? What next? The Lancet. Volume 383, No. 9922, p1013, 22 March 2014.

[2] Hesketh T, Dan Wu, Linan Mao, Nan Ma. Violence against doctors in China. BMJ 2012; 345:5730 (http://www.bmj.com/content/345/bmj.e5730)

[3] "Violence against doctors: Heartless attacks". The Economist. Jul 21, 2012. Retrieved May 21, 2013. (http://www.economist.com/node/21559377)

[4] Andrew LB. Physician Suicide. Medscape.com (http://emedicine.medscape.com/article/806779-overview)

[5] Janocha JA, Smith RT. Workplace Safety and Health in the Health Care and Social Assistance Industry, 2003-07. Bureau of Labor Statistics Originally Posted: August 30, 2010 (http://www.bls.gov/opub/mlr/cwc/workplace-safety-and-health-in-the-health-care-and-social-assistance-industry-2003-07.pdf)

[6] Kelen GD, Catlett CL. Violence in the Healthcare Setting. JAMA. 2010; 304(22):2530-2531

[7] Anti-abortion violence. Wikipedia.org. Retrieved May 21, 2013. (http://en.wikipedia.org/wiki/Anti-abortion_violence)

[8] Gunman fatally shoots one person, kills himself at Army medical facility in Texas. Reuters. Tue Jan 6, 2015 10:14pm EST (http://www.reuters.com/article/2015/01/07/us-usa-texas-shooter-idUSKBN0KF25P20150107)

[9] Bidgood, J. Brigham and Women's Surgeon Dies After Hospital Shooting. The New York Times. JAN. 21, 2015 (http://www.nytimes.com/2015/01/22/us/dr-michael-davidson-brigham-womens-dies-after-shooting.html?_r=0)

[10] Jena AB, Seabury S, Lakdawalla D, Chandra A. Malpractice Risk According to Physician Specialty. N Engl J Med 2011; 365:629-36.

[11] Blumenthal D, Hsiao W. Lessons from the East — China's Rapidly Evolving Health Care System. N Engl J Med 2015; 372:1281-1285

[12] Xiaoyan Z. To Drip or Not to Drip. Beijing Review. No. 4, January 27, 2011 (http://www.bjreview.com.cn/health/txt/2011-01/23/content_327938.htm)

[13] Wang G. Health experts warn antibiotics "heavily overused" in China. Xinhua News Agency. October 19, 2011-10-19 (http://www.xinhuanet.com/english/)

[14] Yang F. Abuse of antibiotics drops in Chinese hospitals. Xinhua News Agency. May 8, 2012 (http://www.xinhuanet.com/english/)

[15] Beech H. How Corruption Blights China's Health Care System. Time. Aug. 02, 20131 (http://world.time.com/2013/08/02/corruption-blights-chinas-healthcare-system/)

[16] Ross L, Zhou K. China's New Anti-Corruption Policies in the Health Care Industry. WilmerHale. January 9, 2014 (https://www.wilmerhale.com/pages/publicationsandnewsdetail.aspx?NewsPubId=10737423049)

[17] Schwarz A, the Selling of Attention Deficit Disorder, the New York Times. DECEMBER 14, 2013 (http://www.nytimes.com/2013/12/15/health/the-selling-of-attention-deficit-disorder.html?pagewanted=all&_r=0)

[18] Lowes R. Rogue-Surgeon Case Raises Question of Who Knew What. Medscape Medical News. December 12, 2013

(http://www.medscape.com/viewarticle/817708)

[19] Windrum B. It's Time to Account for Medical Error in "Top Ten Causes of Death" Charts. Journal of Participatory Medicine. Commentary April 24, 2013 (http://www.jopm.org/opinion/commentary/2013/04/24/it%E2%80%99s-time-to-account-for-medical-error-in-%E2%80%9Ctop-ten-causes-of-death-charts/)

[20] Rosenthal E. After Surgery, Surprise $117,000 Medical Bill From Doctor He Didn't Know. The New York Times. SEPT. 20, 2014 (http://www.nytimes.com/2014/09/21/us/drive-by-doctoring-surprise-medical-bills.html?_r=0)

[21] Median and Average Sales Prices of New Homes Sold in United States (https://www.census.gov/construction/nrs/pdf/uspricemon.pdf)

[22] Mangan D. Medical Bills Are the Biggest Cause of US Bankruptcies: Study. CNBC. Jun 25, 2013 (http://www.cnbc.com/id/100840148)

[23] Brawley OW, Goldberg P. How We Do Harm: A Doctor Breaks Ranks about Being Sick in America. St. Martin's Press; Reprint edition. 2012

End of Life

"I don't want to die."

[1] University of Toronto Quality of Life Research Unit (http://sites.utoronto.ca/qol/qol_model.htm)

Fight for Life

Hemodialysis

[1] World Kidney Day, March 12, 2015.
(http://www.worldkidneyday.org/faqs/chronic-kidney-disease/)

[2] Estevez D. Mexico's Carlos Slim Reclaims World's Richest Man Title From Bill Gates. Forbes. 7/15/2014 @ 4:35PM
(http://www.forbes.com/sites/doliaestevez/2014/07/15/mexicos-carlos-slim-reclaims-worlds-richest-man-title-from-bill-gates/)

[3] Frellick M. Physician Donated Kidney to Patient She Hadn't Met. Medscape Medical News. September 08, 2014
(http://www.medscape.com/viewarticle/831366)

Optimism

[1] Washington Manual of Medical Therapeutics. LWW, Thirty-Fourth edition, 2013

Resilience

[1] Murphy LM, Lipman TO. Percutaneous endoscopic gastrostomy does not prolong survival in patients with dementia. Arch. Intern. Med 2003; 163 (11): 1351–3.
(http://www.ncbi.nlm.nih.gov/pubmed/12796072)

[2] Whitcraft T. Malala Yousafzai Calls on World Leaders to Invest in Books, Not Bullets. ABC NEWS. Jul 7, 2015, 12:16 AM ET
(http://abcnews.go.com/International/malala-yousafzai-calls-world-leaders-invest-books-bullets/story?id=32262472)

Medicine as Art and Business

The Art of Medicine

[1] Nagourney A, Rutenberg J, Zeleny J. Near-Flawless Run Is Credited in Victory. The New York Times. Published: November 5, 2008 (http://www.nytimes.com/2008/11/05/us/politics/05recon.html?pag ewanted=all)

[2] Daily News Editorial Board. They said it in 2008: The year in quotes. Tuesday, December 30, 2008, 9:30 PM (http://www.nydailynews.com/opinion/2008-year-quotes-article-1.355758)

[3] Tindle HA, Omalu B, Courcoulas A, Marcus M, Hammers F, Kuller LH. Risk of Suicide after Long-term Follow-up from Bariatric Surgery. The American Journal of Medicine 2010; 123:1036-1042 (http://www.amjmed.com/article/S0002-9343 (10)00574-7/fulltext)

Test Day

[1] Five Things Physicians and Patients Should Question. "Don't perform annual stress cardiac imaging or advanced non-invasive imaging as part of routine follow-up in asymptomatic patients." American College of Cardiology. Released April 4, 2012. (http://www.choosingwisely.org/doctor-patient-lists/american-college-of-cardiology/)

[2] Chou R. the High Value Care Task Force of the American College of Physicians. Cardiac Screening With Electrocardiography, Stress Echocardiography, or Myocardial Perfusion Imaging: Advice for High-Value Care From the American College of Physicians. Ann Intern Med. 2015; 162(6):438-447. (http://annals.org/article.aspx?articleid=2197181&atab=11)

[3] Standards of Medical Care in Diabetes—2015. Diabetes Care 2015; 38(Suppl. 1), S62 (http://care.diabetesjournals.org/content/38/Supplement_1)

[4] Five Things Physicians and Patients Should Question. North American Spine Society. Released October 9, 2013 (http://www.choosingwisely.org/doctor-patient-lists/north-american-spine-society/)

[5] Korownyk C, Kolber MB, McCormack J, et al. Televised medical talk shows—what they recommend and the evidence to support their recommendations: a prospective observational study. BMJ 2014; 349:g7346
(http://www.bmj.com/content/349/bmj.g7346)

[6] Health Care in Japan: Not all smiles. The Economist. Sep 10th 2011
(http://www.economist.com/node/21528660)

[7] Smith M, Saunders R, Stuckhardt L, McGinnis JM. Best Care at Lower Cost: The Path to Continuously Learning Health Care in America (2013), Institute of Medicine (IOM), September 6, 2012.
(http://health-equity.pitt.edu/3972/1/Best_Care_at_Lower_Cost.pdf)

Medicare Pays

[1] Stossel J. Medicare Duped by the SCOOTER Store. Fox Business. March 04, 2013
(http://www.foxbusiness.com/on-air/stossel/blog/2013/03/04/medicare-duped-scooter-store)

[2] Waldman P. Aunt Midge Not Dying in Hospice Reveals $14 Billion U.S. Market. Bloomberg Business. December 6, 2011.
(http://www.bloomberg.com/news/articles/2011-12-06/hospice-care-revealed-as-14-billion-u-s-market)

[3] Fenton JJ, Jerant AF, Bertakis KD, Franks P. The Cost of Satisfaction. A National Study of Patient Satisfaction, Health Care Utilization, Expenditures, and Mortality. Arch Intern Med. 2012; 172(5):405-411.
(http://archinte.jamanetwork.com/article.aspx?articleid=1108766)

Overdone

[1] Welch, H. Gilbert (2015-03-03). Less Medicine, More Health: 7 Assumptions That Drive Too Much Medical Care (p. 194). Beacon Press. Kindle Edition.

Statins

[1] LaRosa JC, Grundy SM, Waters DD, et al. Intensive lipid lowering with atorvastatin in patients with stable coronary disease. N Engl J Med 2005; 352:1425–35.
(http://www.nejm.org/doi/full/10.1056/NEJMoa050461#t=article)

[2] Stone NJ, et al. 2013 ACC/AHA Guideline on the Treatment of Blood Cholesterol to Reduce Atherosclerotic Cardiovascular Risk in Adults. "The high-intensity statins atorvastatin 80 mg and rosuvastatin 20 mg daily reduce LDL-C ≥50% on average and have been shown to reduce ASCVD events in RCTs."
(https://circ.ahajournals.org/content/early/2013/11/11/01.cir.000043 7738.63853.7a)

[3] Wanner C, Krane V, März W, et al. Atorvastatin in patients with type 2 diabetes mellitus undergoing hemodialysis. N Engl J Med 2005; 353:238–48.

[4] Fellström BC, Jardine AG, Schmieder RE, et al. Rosuvastatin and cardiovascular events in patients undergoing hemodialysis. N Engl J Med.2009; 360:1395–407.

[5] Standards of Medical Care in Diabetes—2015 Diabetes Care 2015; 38(Suppl. 1)
(http://care.diabetesjournals.org/content/38/Supplement_1)

[6] National Institute for Health and Care Excellence. Lipid Modification: Cardiovascular Risk Assessment and the Modification of Blood Lipids for the Primary and Secondary Prevention of Cardiovascular Disease. London, England: National Institute for Health and Care Excellence; July 2014.
(http://www.nice.org.uk/guidance/cg181/evidence/cg181-lipid-modification-update-full-guideline3)

[7] FDA Drug Safety Communication: Important safety label changes to cholesterol-lowering statin drugs [2-28-2012] The U.S. Food and Drug Administration (FDA) has approved important safety label changes for the class of cholesterol-lowering drugs known as statins.

(http://www.fda.gov/Drugs/DrugSafety/ucm293101.htm)

[8] Richardson K, Schoen M, French B, et al. Statins and Cognitive Function: A Systematic Review. Ann Intern Med. 2013; 159(10):688-697.
(http://annals.org/article.aspx?articleid=1770674#References)

[9] Martin et al. Statin Medications May Prevent Dementia And Memory Loss With Longer Use, While Not Posing Any Short-Term Cognition Problems. Mayo Clinic Proceedings. 2013; 88 (11):1213–1221
(http://www.mayoclinicproceedings.org/article/S0025-6196 (13)00613-7/pdf)

[10] Lehman S. Restaurant food not much healthier than fast food. Reuters. Health | Wed Jul 15, 2015 5:55pm EDT
(http://www.reuters.com/article/2015/07/15/us-health-nutrition-restaurant-food-idUSKCN0PP2R820150715)

Gout

[1] Gray CL, Walters-Smith NE. Febuxostat for Treatment of Chronic Gout. Am J Health Syst Pharm. 2011; 68(5):389-398.
(http://www.medscape.com/viewarticle/738620_8)

[2] Khanna D, Fitzgerald JD, Khanna P, et al. 2012 American College of Rheumatology guidelines for management of gout. Part 1: Systematic nonpharmacologic and pharmacologic therapeutic approaches to hyperuricemia. Arthritis Care & Research 2012; 64(10):1431–1446.
(http://onlinelibrary.wiley.com/doi/10.1002/acr.21772/full)

[3] Yamanaka H. The Guideline Revising Committee of Japanese Society of Gout and Nucleic Acid Metabolism. Essence of the Revised Guideline for the Management of Hyperuricemia and Gout. JMAJ 2012; 55(4): 324–329.
(https://www.med.or.jp/english/journal/pdf/2012_04/324_329.pdf)

[4] Health Care in Japan: Not all smiles. The Economist. Sep 10, 2011
(http://www.economist.com/node/21528660)

[5] Carnovale C, Venegoni M, Clementi E. Allopurinol Overuse in Asymptomatic Hyperuricemia: A Teachable Moment. JAMA Intern Med. 2014; 174(7):1031-1032.
(http://archinte.jamanetwork.com/article.aspx?articleid=1867180&JamaNetworkReader=True)

[6] Fisher E, Goodman D, Skinner J, Bronner K. Health Care Spending, Quality and Outcomes. The Dartmouth Atlas of Health Care. February 27, 2009
(http://www.dartmouthatlas.org/downloads/reports/Spending_Brief _022709.pdf)

Many Pills

[1] Key Findings: Trends in the Parent-Report of Health Care Provider-Diagnosis and Medication Treatment for ADHD: United States, 2003– 2011, CDC (the Centers for Disease Control and Prevention),
(http://www.cdc.gov/ncbddd/adhd/features/key-findings-ADHD72013.html)

[2] Report: Turning Attention to ADHD. Express Scripts. Mar 12, 2014
(http://lab.express-scripts.com/insights/industry-updates/report-turning-attention-to-adhd)

[3] FDA Drug Safety Communication: FDA cautions about using testosterone products for low testosterone due to aging; requires labeling change to inform of possible increased risk of heart attack and stroke with use.
(http://www.fda.gov/Drugs/DrugSafety/ucm436259.htm)

[4] Murphy RA, Patel KV, Kritchevsky SB, et al. Weight change, body composition, and risk of mobility disability and mortality in older adults: a population-based cohort study. J Am Geriatr Soc. 2014; 62(8):1476-83.
(http://www.ncbi.nlm.nih.gov/pubmed/25039391)

[5] Brown RE, Kuk JL. Consequences of obesity and weight loss: a devil's advocate position. Obesity Reviews. 2015; 16: 77–87
(http://onlinelibrary.wiley.com/doi/10.1111/obr.12232/pdf)

Back/Knee Pain

[1] American Academy of Family Physicians. Search recommendations from the Choosing Wisely campaign
(http://www.aafp.org/afp/recommendations/search.htm?sf22148131= 1)

[2] Groopman J. How Doctors Think. Mariner Books; Reprint edition, 2008

[3] Hanscom D. Back in Control: A Spine Surgeon's Roadmap Out of Chronic Pain. Vertus Press; 1 edition, 2012

[4] Riddle DL, Jiranek WA, Hayes CW. Use of a Validated Algorithm to Judge the Appropriateness of Total Knee Arthroplasty in the United States: A Multicenter Longitudinal Cohort Study. Arthritis & Rheumatology 2014; 66(8):2134–2143 (http://onlinelibrary.wiley.com/doi/10.1002/art.38685/abstract)

Unsatisfactory Health Care

[1] Frist B. (n.d.). BrainyQuote.com. Retrieved March 17, 2015, from BrainyQuote.com (http://www.brainyquote.com/quotes/authors/b/bill_frist.html)

[2] Nathan Deal. (n.d.). BrainyQuote.com. Retrieved May 24, 2015, from BrainyQuote.com (http://www.brainyquote.com/quotes/quotes/n/nathandeal342952.html)

[3] Jeff Merkley. (n.d.). BrainyQuote.com. Retrieved May 24, 2015, from BrainyQuote.com (http://www.brainyquote.com/quotes/quotes/j/jeffmerkle623916.html)

Painkillers

[1] Avila J and Murray M. Prescription Painkiller Use at Record High for Americans. ABC News. April 20, 2011 (http://abcnews.go.com/US/prescription-painkillers-record-number-americans-pain-medication/)

[2] Opioid Painkiller Prescribing. CDC VitalSigns. July 2014. (http://www.cdc.gov/vitalsigns/opioid-prescribing/)

[3] Committee on Advancing Pain Research, Care, and Education. Relieving Pain in America: A Blueprint for Transforming Prevention, Care, Education, and Research. Institute of Medicine of the National Academies. Released: June 29, 2011 (http://www.iom.edu/Reports/2011/Relieving-Pain-in-America-A-Blueprint-for-Transforming-Prevention-Care-Education-Research.aspx)

[4] Anson P. Experts Say Epidural Steroid Injections Overused. Pain News Network. August 19, 2015 (http://www.painnewsnetwork.org/stories/2015/8/19/experts-say-epidural-injections-overused)

[5] Chou R, Hashimoto R, Friedly J, et al. MPH. Epidural Corticosteroid Injections for Radiculopathy and Spinal Stenosis: A Systematic Review and Meta-analysis. Ann Intern Med. Published online 25 August 2015 doi:10.7326/M15-0934 (http://annals.org/article.aspx?articleid=2430207#r97-5460) accessed on August 28, 2015

[6] Johnson H, Paulozzi L, Porucznik C, Mack K, Herter B. Decline in Drug Overdose Deaths After State Policy Changes — Florida, 2010– 2012. Morbidity and Mortality Weekly Report (MMWR). July 4, 2014 / 63(26); 569-574. (http://www.cdc.gov/mmwr/preview/mmwrhtml/mm6326a3.htm)

[7] Chou R, Turner JA, Devine EB, et al. National Institutes of Health Pathways to Prevention Workshop: The Role of Opioids in the Treatment of Chronic Pain. Ann Intern Med. 2015; 162(4):276-286. (http://annals.org/article.aspx?articleid=2089370&resultClick=3)

Electronic Health Record (EHR) and Nursing Homes

[1] Smith J. The Best- And Worst-Paying Jobs In America. Forbes. 5/13/2013 (http://www.forbes.com/sites/jacquelynsmith/2013/05/13/the-best-and-worst-paying-jobs-in-america-2/)

[2] Terry K. The EHR Stimulus: A Complete Primer. Physicians Practice. July 15, 2009 (http://www.physicianspractice.com/ehr/ehr-stimulus-complete-primer)

[3] Verdon DR. Top 100 EHRs: Why understanding a company's financial performance today may influence purchasing decisions tomorrow. Medical Economics. October 25, 2013 (http://medicaleconomics.modernmedicine.com/medical-economics/top-100-EHRs)

[4] Connecting Health and Care for the Nation: A Ten Year Vision to Achieve Interoperable Health IT Infrastructure (http://www.healthit.gov/sites/default/files/ONC10yearInteroperabilityConceptPaper.pdf)

[5] Verdon DR. Medical Economics. Physician outcry on EHR functionality, cost will shake the health information technology sector. February 10, 2014

(http://medicaleconomics.modernmedicine.com/medical-economics/content/tags/ehr/physician-outcry-ehr-functionality-cost-will-shake-health-informa?page=full)

Health Insurance

[1] Sommers BD, Musco T, Finegold K, Gunja MZ, Burke A, McDowell AM. Health Reform and Changes in Health Insurance Coverage in 2014. N Engl J Med 2014; 371:867-874

[2] Wilper AP, Woolhandler S, Lasser KE, McCormick D, Bor DH, Himmelstein DU. Health Insurance and Mortality in US Adults. American Journal of Public Health 2009; 99(12): 2289–2295. (http://ajph.aphapublications.org/doi/abs/10.2105/AJPH.2008.15768 5)

[3] Health Insurance Coverage and the Affordable Care Act, May 5, 2015. The Assistant Secretary for Planning and Evaluation (ASPE). The U.S. Department of Health and Human Services. (http://www.aspe.hhs.gov/health/reports/2015/uninsured_change/ib _uninsured_change.pdf)

[4] Hui S. The Web's Inventor Says Affordable Internet Should Be A 'Human Right'. The Huffington Post. Posted: 12/10/2014 (http://www.huffingtonpost.com/2014/12/11/internet-human-right-web-inventor_n_6305312.html)

[5] Edward N. Human Rights. Stanford Encyclopedia of Philosophy (Fall 2010 Edition), (http://plato.stanford.edu/archives/fall2010/entries/rights-human/)

Epilogue

[1] Riffkin R. Americans Rate Nurses Highest on Honesty, Ethical Standards. The Gallup Poll. Special Issue December 18, 2014 (http://www.gallup.com/poll/180260/americans-rate-nurses-highest-honesty-ethical-standards.aspx)

The End

Made in the USA
San Bernardino, CA
18 November 2017